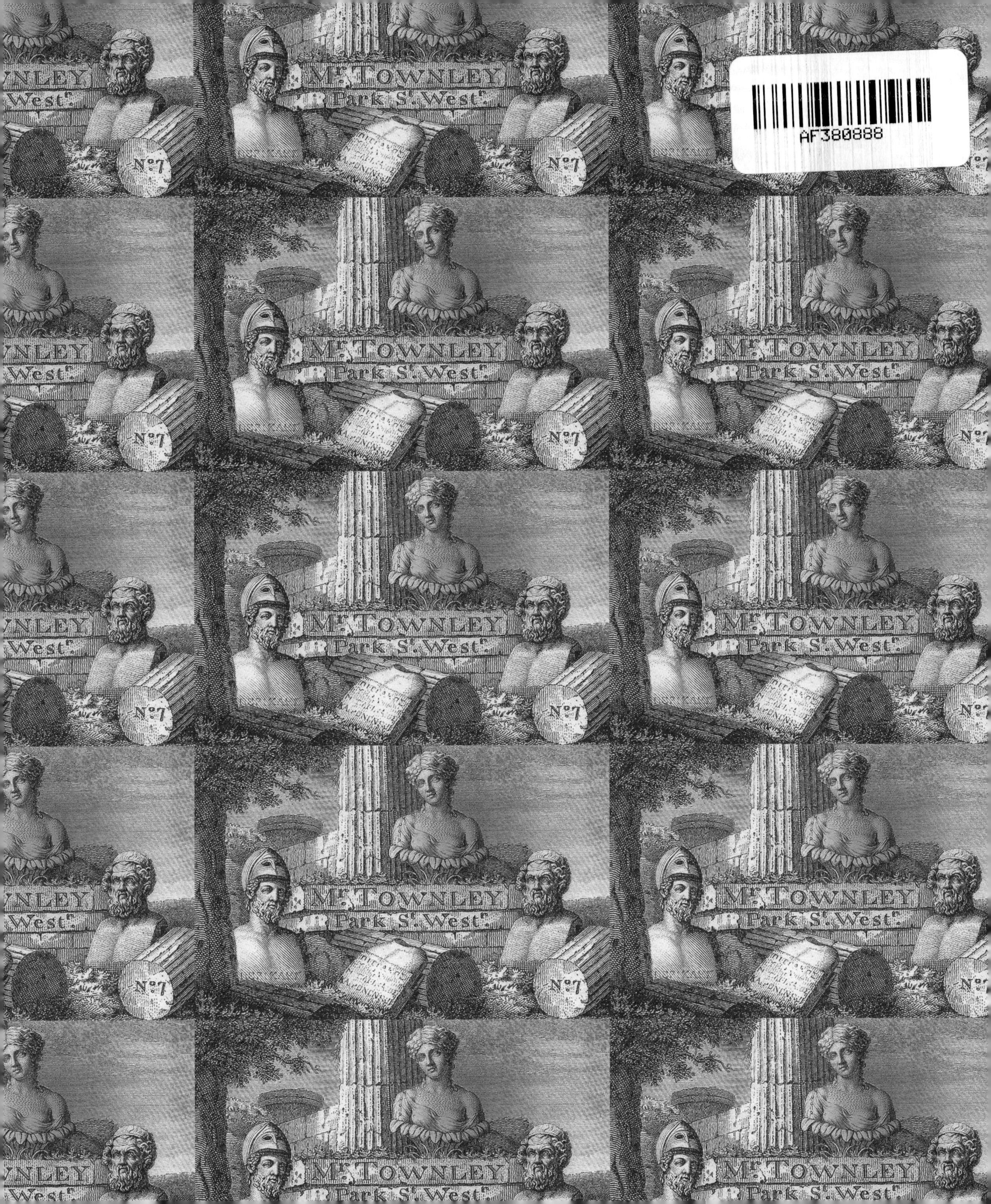

Mr TOWNLEY
Park St West.
No 7

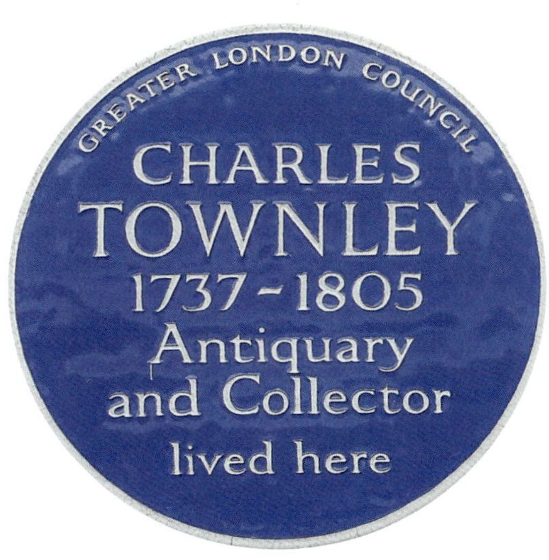
GREATER LONDON COUNCIL
CHARLES
TOWNLEY
1737~1805
Antiquary
and Collector
lived here

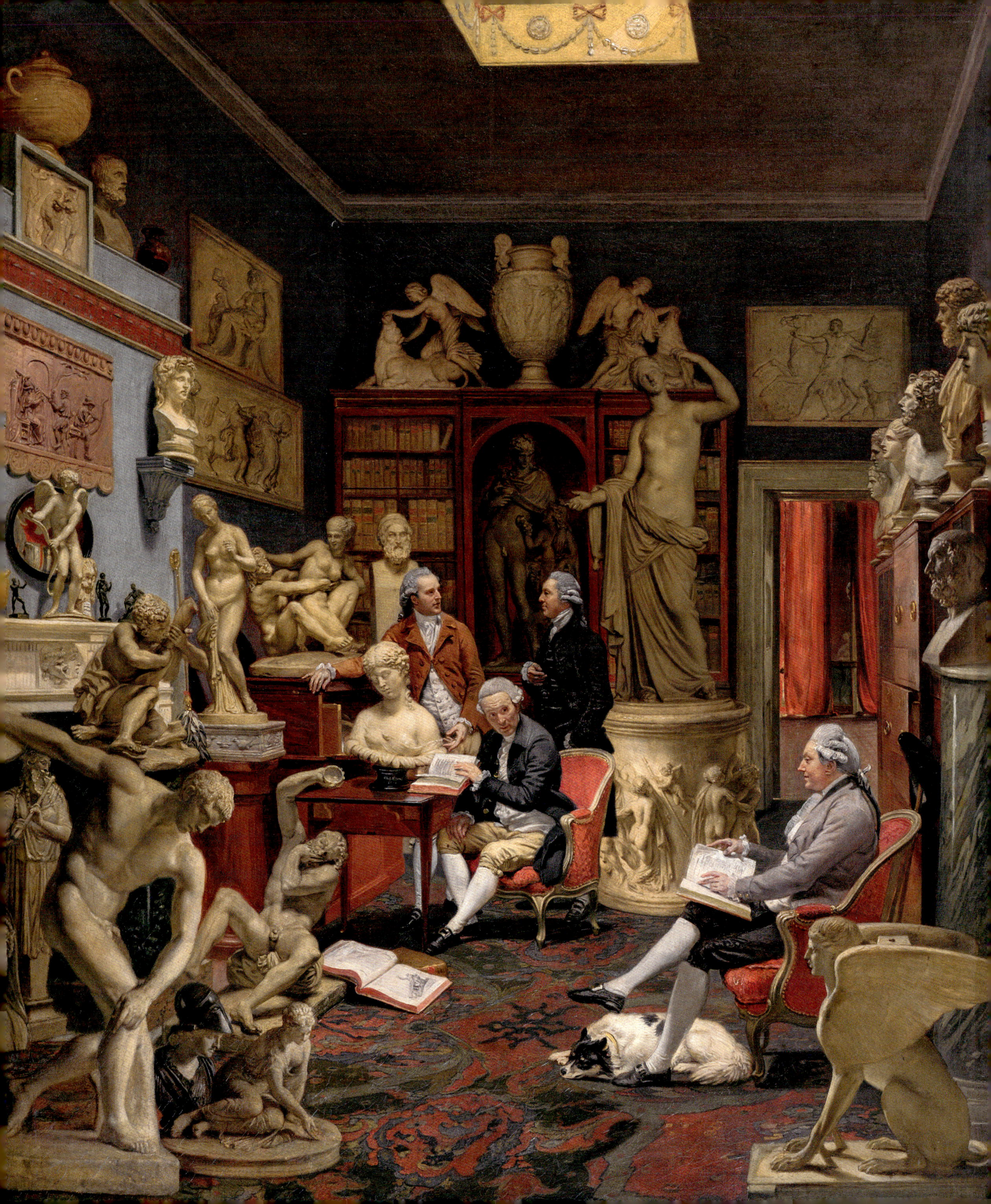

THE MUSEUM BY THE PARK

14 Queen Anne's Gate from Charles Townley to Axel Johnson

Max Bryant

PAUL HOLBERTON PUBLISHING

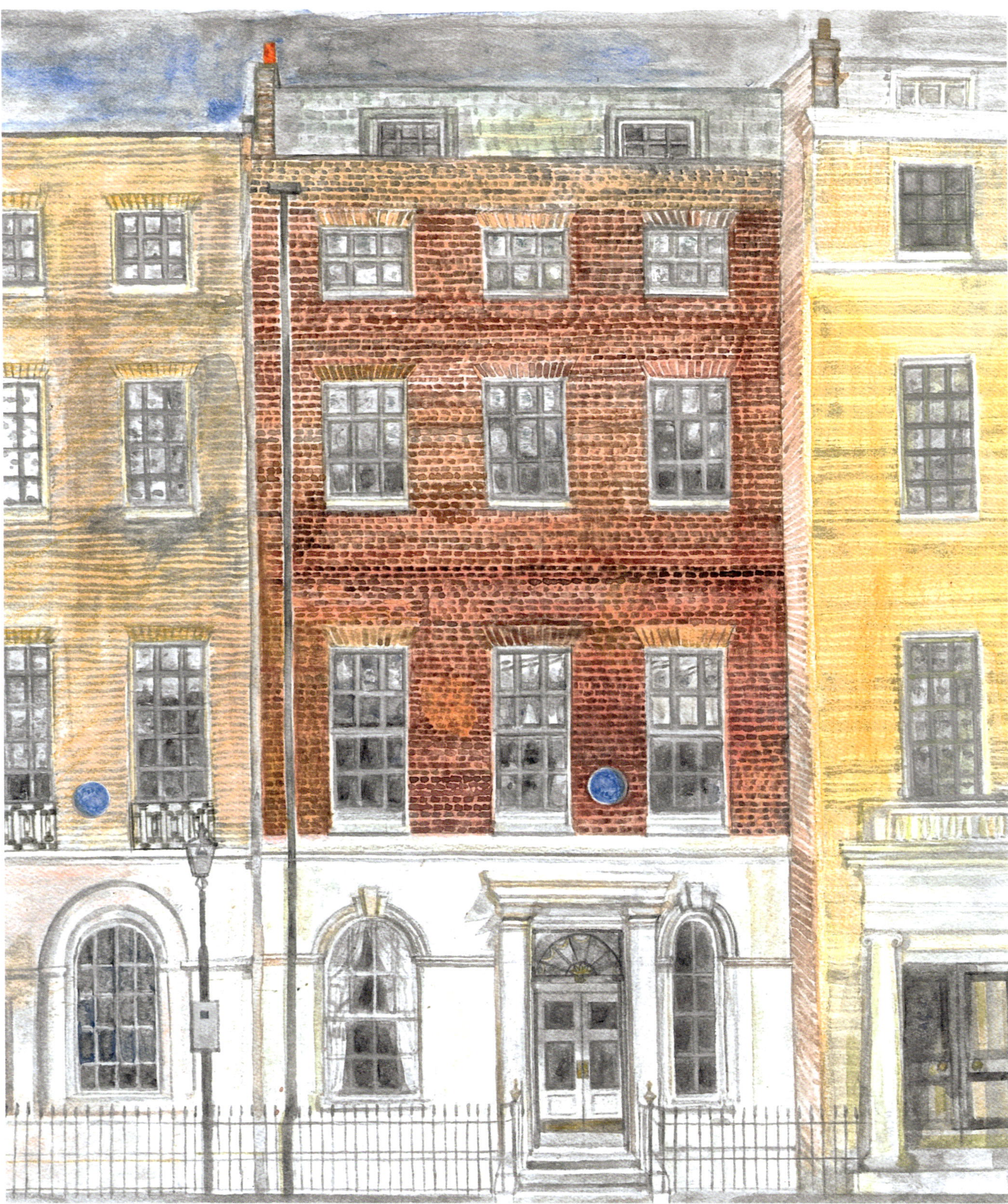

CONTENTS

INTRODUCTION

τ' ἀρχαῖ' ὅτ' οἶσθα καὶ τὰ καίν' εἴσει σαφῶς.
Knowing the old, you will understand the new.

THE DEPTH OF HISTORY AT QUEEN ANNE'S GATE is unusual even in London, and few houses resonate with more memories than No. 14. It was itself designed as a temple to the past, reviving in the modern city the occult practices of the ancient world. Here visitors would have found an assembly of Roman sculpture unrivalled outside Italy, as well as non-Western art, a library, and a collection devoted to understanding a universal 'generative spirit' worshipped by early civilizations. That spirit may be found in the succession of major roles the house has continued to take through generations of dramatic change.

The above motto was inscribed on a bust of Charles Townley. No. 14 Queen Anne's Gate was built for him, a full-time connoisseur and *virtuoso*. The public display of antiquities that he created on the first two floors of the house was described by a German newspaper at the time as the most magnificent private museum in all Europe.[1] Its fame has made the address an iconic part of British culture in the two centuries since his death.

The motto expresses a sentiment familiar from Thucydides, but is a modern composition, probably by Townley himself as an exercise in the metre of classical drama.[2] It was later used as the epigraph to a publication he had been working on before his death.[3] The motto encapsulates Townley's approach to antiquity – the idea that we must look to the past to understand the present, that the esoteric principles of early civilization continue to be relevant. It is an Enlightenment idea, though one more interested in the shadows that light can cast.

The inscription may also serve as a motto for this book, which presents the history of No. 14 Queen Anne's Gate, from its earliest conception, construction and alteration, through to our own time. Across the centuries the area south of St James's Park has transformed from a peripheral one, inhabited by wealthy eccentrics and radicals, to one at the heart of the British establishment. The story of this house features political revolutionaries, occult initiations, clandestine war meetings, and a severed head. Following Townley's motto, we may also find in that story the spirit of the house today.

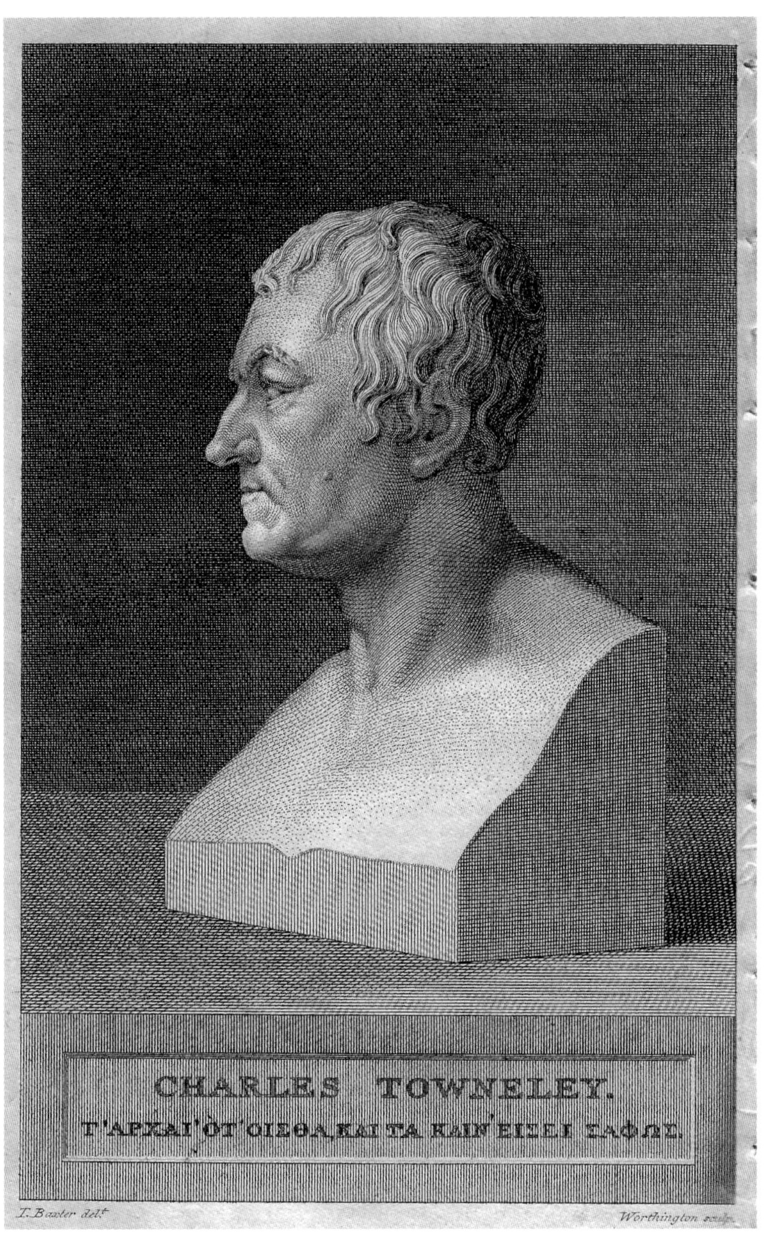

Charles Townley (1737–1805). This engraving, first published in 1812, shows a posthumous portrait bust of Townley by the sculptor Joseph Nollekens. The bust was made in 1807 using a cast taken after Townley's death. It is in the form of a herm, incorporating the Greek inscription on the lower front. The original is at Towneley Hall in Lancashire.

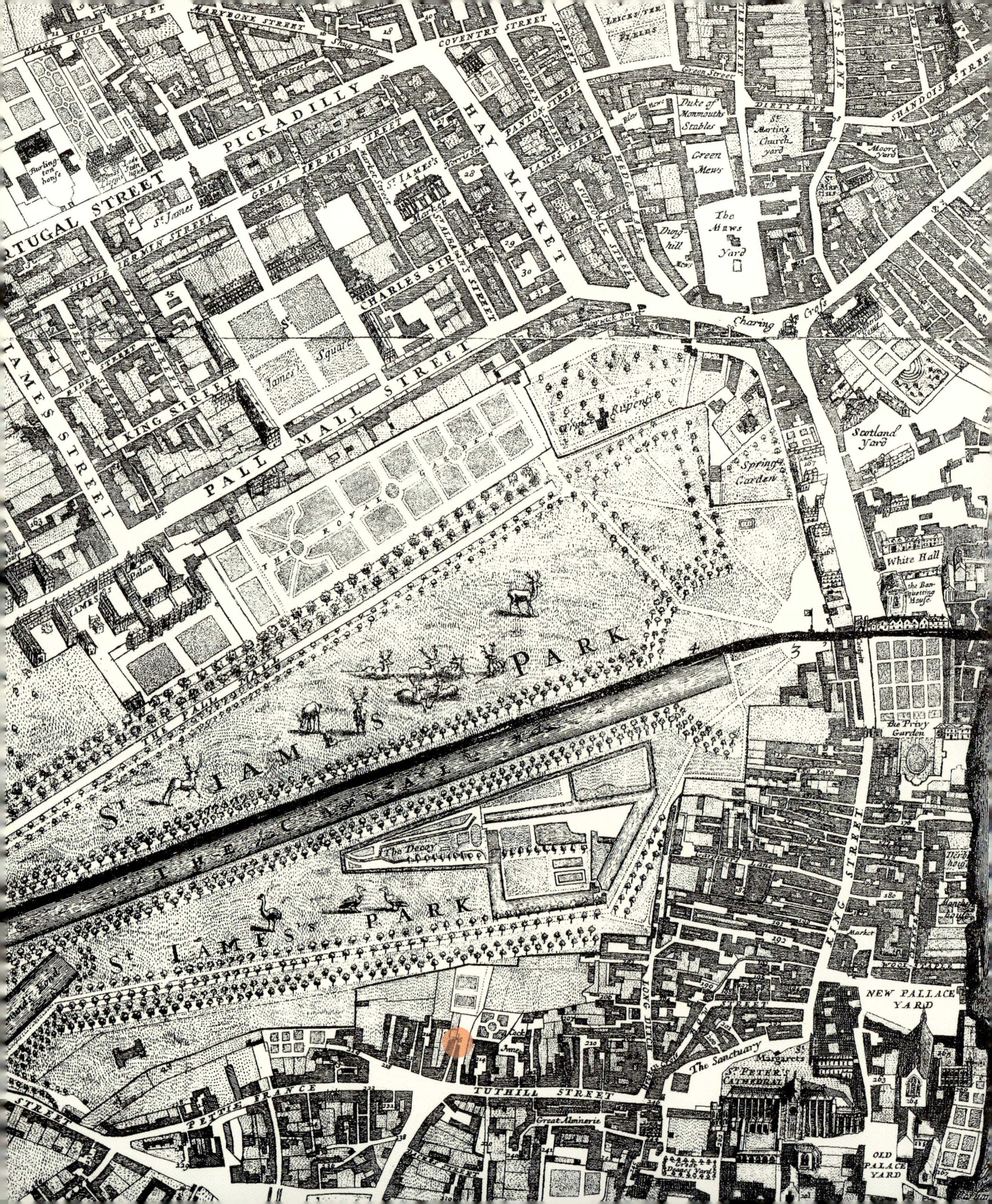
JAMES HOUSE STREET
MARYBONE STREET
COVENTRY STREET
LEICESTER
FIELDS
Green Street
Duke of Monmouth
Stables
St Martin's Churchyard
Green Mews
SHANDOIS STREET
DIRTY LANE
Moors Yard
PICKADILLY
HAY MARKET
PANTON STREET
OXENDEN STREET
Burlington House
St James
PORTUGAL STREET
GREAT TERMIN STREET
LITTLE TERMIN STREET
ST JAMES STREET
St James's Market
CHARLES STREET
St ALBAN'S STREET
Dung hill
The Mews Yard
Charing Cross
JAMES STREET
KING STREET
PALL MALL STREET
James Square
Scotland Yard
Prince Rupert's
Spring Garden
White Hall
the Banquetting House
THE ROYAL
Palace
ST JAMES
ST IAMES PARK
ST JAMES PARK
THE CANAL
ST IAMES PARK
The Decoy
The Privy Garden
KING STREET
Market
NEW PALLACE YARD
Long Ditch
The Sanctuary
St PETER's CATHEDRAL
St Margarets
TUTHILL STREET
PETTY FRANCE
Great Almnerie
OLD PALACE YARD

I. PARK STREET

THERE HAS ALWAYS BEEN AN ELEMENT OF THE exotic about the environs of Queen Anne's Gate [1]. St James's Park was originally used for the menagerie of animals belonging to James I in the early seventeenth century: these included antelopes from the Moghal Emperor and a leopard from the House of Savoy. The area had been laid out by Henry VIII as a deer park for St James's Palace. Sovereigns have not lived in the palace since the nineteenth century, but nevertheless it remains officially one of their residences.

The urban area of Westminster immediately below St James's Park is a particularly challenging part of London to characterize, as it was for most of its history on the south-west limits of the city. There were isolated developments, but no clear urban character to compare to the density of Soho or the squares of Mayfair. Partly this was for practical reasons: the land was extremely marshy and not conducive to building. The reasons were also economic: the Abbey was not a freeholder with great urban vision, and the few major

developments were private enterprises. Two of these building projects now comprise the street known as Queen Anne's Gate; they were originally known as Queen Square and Park Street.

The main artery of the area below the park was the road leading west from the Abbey, comprising Tothill Street and Petty France. The latter had been named for its Huguenot refugee population, fleeing violence against Protestants during the French Wars of Religion (1562–98). John Milton moved to a garden house on Petty France in 1651. The poet was working for the republican government based in Westminster as an official propagandist, but he also sought the salutary benefits of proximity to St James's Park, which became open to the public on the fall of the monarchy. It was during his residence on Petty France that he began composing his great epic poem *Paradise Lost*, and his vision of the Garden of Eden may recall the nearby park, probably the last he had seen before the onset of his blindness.

St James's Park as we know it today is a creation of the nineteenth century, landscaped by the architect John Nash. However, its early grandeur was mostly due to James I's grandson Charles II [2]. After the fall of the republican government and the restoration of the monarchy, the king allowed it to remain public, and renovated it as a grand public space in 1660. The layout was said to be the work

1. William Morgan's map of 1682 was the first to show the city in plan rather than from a bird's-eye view. This detail shows the public space of St James's Park, with 'The Decoy' being a device to capture ducks within Charles II's aviary. To the south is Black and White Court (shown in red), the predecessor to Carteret Street, at the end of which Park Street would be built. St Peter's Cathedral, to the east, is now known as Westminster Abbey.

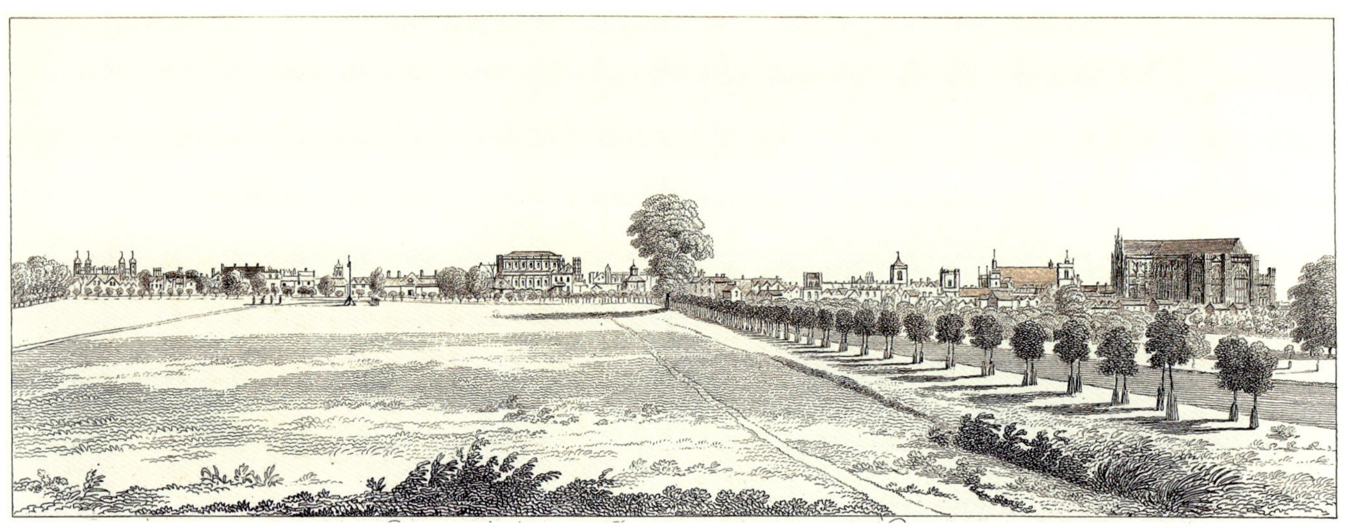

2. A view by an unknown artist of St James's Park with the new canal, during the reign of Charles II (1660–85). In the background, figures are attempting to hit a ball through a ring: they are playing the game of 'pall-mall' that gave its name to the nearby street.

3. A plan of the land owned by Christ's Hospital, made c.1586, showing the area from 'Tuthill Streate' to 'The kinges pke called St James pke'

of André Le Nôtre, and the project was described by Samuel Pepys in his diary and by Edmund Waller in a commemorative poem. Charles also used it for his collection of exotic birds, leading to the names for Birdcage Walk and Duck Island. It became extremely fashionable, and was often referenced in popular theatrical comedies of the time.

Park Street was built on land owned by Christ's Hospital [3], a charitable institution founded in 1553 by Edward VI, son of Henry VIII. In the manner of other European monarchs capitalizing on the weakness of the Papacy during this period, Henry broke ties with the Roman Catholic Church and established an independent Church of England in the early 1530s. A consequence of the break, or rather a cause, was the dissolution of

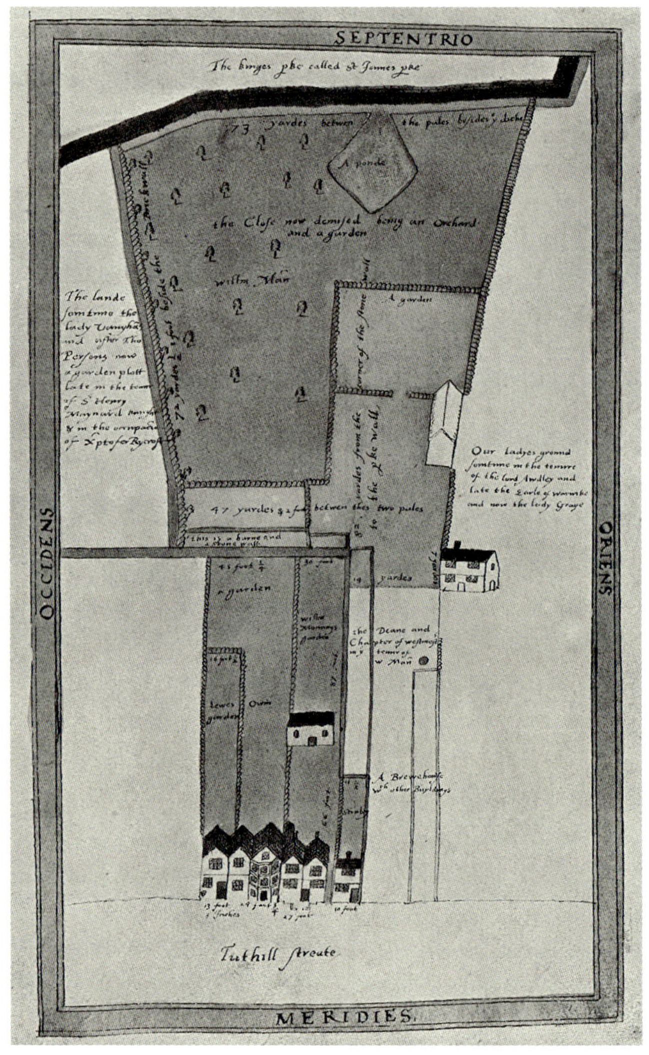

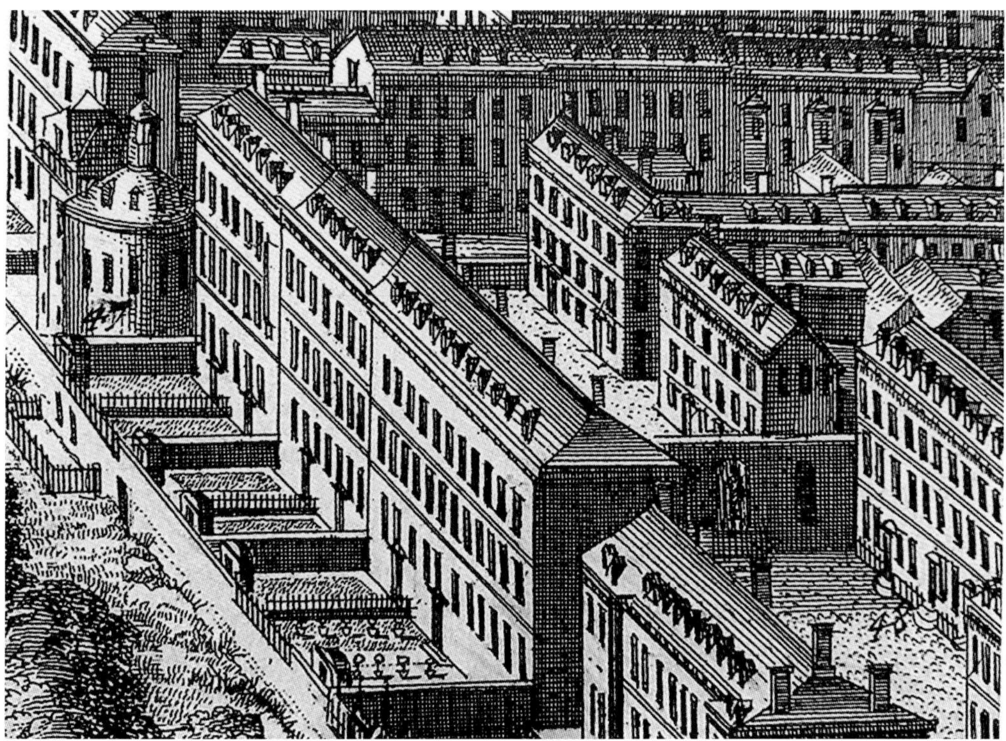

4. *This detail of an engraving by Jan Kip shows the first buildings of Park Street in 1710, the predecessors to the present terrace. At one end can be seen the rotunda of the Royal Cockpit, and at the other the statue of Queen Anne on the wall separating Park Street from Queen Square.*

the monasteries and the transfer of their buildings and assets to the crown. One such monastery was Greyfriars in the City of London, where Edward later established a school for the poor, which moved to its present site in West Sussex in the twentieth century. A bequest to Christ's Hospital by a successful shoemaker, Richard Castell, in his will of 1554 had given the Hospital the land on which Park Street was to be built.

For the next century after the bequest the charity's Governors did not do much with the land other than lease it out. One lessee was Sir Edward Carteret, who took on the land in 1671. The purchase must have been made possible by his elevation, the same year, to the role of 'Black Rod', the usher best known for ceremonially banging on the door of the House of Commons during the State Opening of Parliament.

The laying out of Park Street happened slowly. On a map published in 1682, the land was still completely undeveloped, and Carteret Street was a small dead end called 'Black and White Court' [1]. Sir Edward Carteret's death in 1683 seems to have delayed progress. An unrelated lease of 1686–87 referred to an existing street 'intended to be called Park Street', suggesting that work was under way.[1] Finally, in 1708, the surveyor Edward Hatton's street directory, *New View of London*, referred to Park Street as 'newly built' and 'N[orther]ly from Carteret Street, making it like a T' [4].[2]

During this protracted construction, Queen Square was built next door in c.1704–05. The

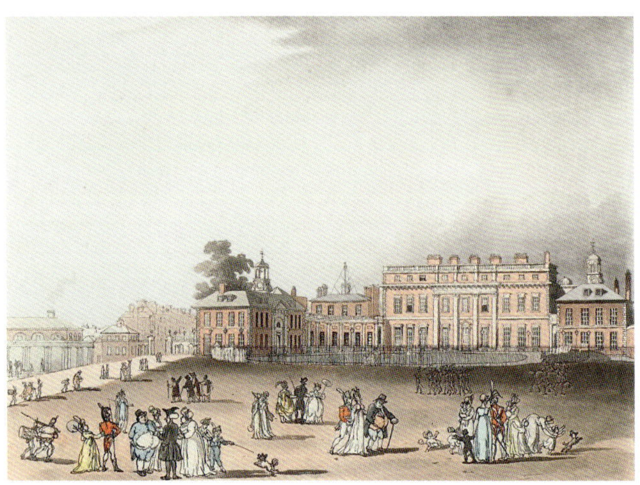

5. Buckingham House was renamed 'The Queen's House' to denote its new use as a home for Queen Charlotte. It was remodelled for her by William Chambers in 1762–73. This view is by Thomas Rowlandson, in the third volume of Ackermann's Microcosm of London *(1810). It shows the palace prior to being rebuilt by the architect John Nash in the form that partly survives today.*

houses represented the finest London architecture of the period, and they survive today, identified by their delicately carved wooden door-hoods. The original buildings of Park Street were wood-framed, with brick chimney-breasts, of much lower status than these. A railed separation between them was included during the construction of Queen Square, including a statue by an unknown sculptor of the reigning monarch, Queen Anne, flanked by two gates.

The statue became a target of vandalism after the end of Anne's reign because, without an inscription, it was mistakenly assumed that a statue of a queen must represent the Catholic Tudor monarch Mary I. Her reign (1553–58) was remembered for the 'Marian persecutions', in which dissenting Protestants were burned at the stake. With Protestantism the overwhelming influence on the Church of England in the late eighteenth century, Mary I became 'Bloody Mary', a figure on whom

the British projected all their anti-Catholic hostility. Local children would righteously vandalize the statue until 1862, when the words 'Anna Regina' were carved on a plinth below [82].

A development during this time was the increased royal presence in the area. Large displays of military pageantry took place at the nearby Horse Guards, the home of the Household Cavalry since 1755. The ceremony, known as 'trooping the colour', still takes place on the monarch's official birthday. Meanwhile the royal family were spending more domestic time in the area. St James's Palace just north of the park had been their London residence, but in 1762 George III bought Buckingham House as a home for his wife Queen Charlotte [5].

The royal presence brought two major local landmarks to the area around Park Street and Queen Square. One was a barracks, on the site now occupied by the Ministry of Justice. The other was the 'Royal Cockpit', facing St James's Park, on the site belonging to Christ's Hospital, and now occupied by the gardens of Nos. 4, 6, 8, 10 and 12 Queen Anne's Gate [6]. Cockfighting was ubiquitous in the eighteenth and early nineteenth centuries, to the point that it was called the 'national sport of England'.[3] There was a venue in most towns, and fights were also staged in country houses. The Royal Cockpit was the highest-status venue for the sport in the capital, having as it did a five-shilling admission charge. It was portrayed by chroniclers of modern life such as William Hogarth and Thomas Rowlandson [7]. The cockpit was remembered as a 'next-door noisy nuisance' for its neighbours on Park Street.[4] It was demolished in 1816, and its audience moved to the cockpit on Tufton Street.[5] Cockfighting was falling out of fashion in Britain: it was made a misdemeanour in 1835, and finally wiped out in 1849 with the passing of the Cruelty to Animals Act.

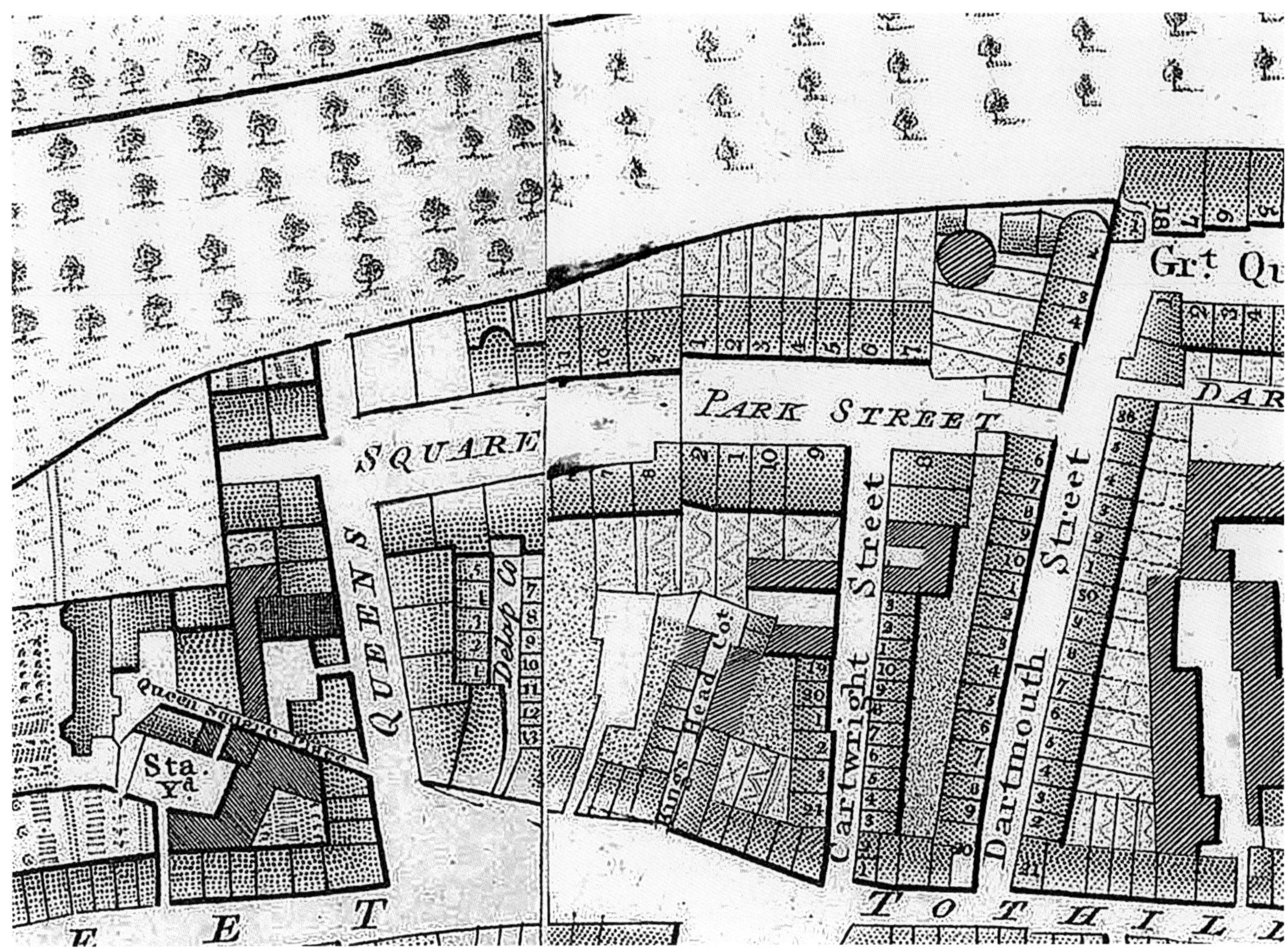

*6. Richard Horwood's great map of London of 1792–99
shows the Royal Cockpit as a large circular building,
entered from the park side via a smaller square structure.*

The Governors of Christ's Hospital responded
to changes in the area with some efforts at
gentrification. An arch was erected at the east
end of Park Street in 1758, creating a continuous
route along the properties facing the park from
Dartmouth Street into Park Street and on through
the gates into Queen Square. In 1770–01 they
developed Nos. 9–13 on the south side of Park
Street with their own surveyor, and this is the
row that can be seen today as Nos. 5, 7, 9, 11 and
13 Queen Anne's Gate. In 1773, the leases of the

properties on the north side were sold to a property
developer, Michael Barrett; the charity retained the
freehold, which is still held by the institution. On
the north side Barrett built 1–7 Park Street, now 14,
16, 18, 20, 22, 22a and 24 Queen Anne's Gate [9].

Work progressed quickly on the houses at 1–7
Park Street. After Barrett had bought the leases,
he cleared out all the residents within a year. In
1774 he drew up a contract with a young Catholic
landowner from Lancashire for the largest of the
houses in the development, No. 7 Park Street,

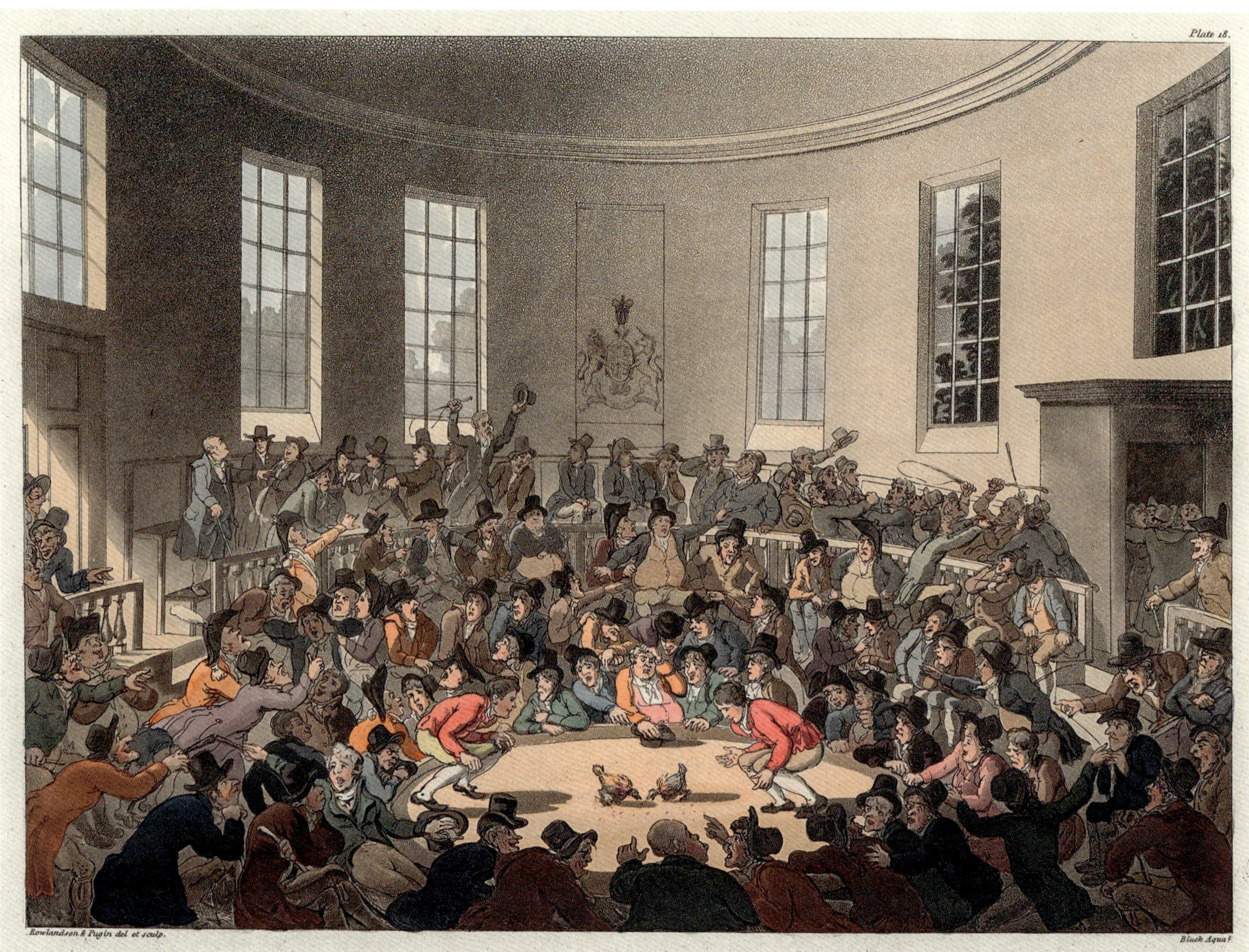

7. *The Royal Cockpit, as illustrated by Thomas Rowlandson
in the first volume of Rudolph Ackermann's* Microcosm of
London *(1808)*

now No. 14 Queen Anne's Gate. Charles Townley
secured a sixty-year lease, for which he was to
pay 45 guineas a year in ground rent. Barrett was
to complete the house's shell by September 1776.[6]
Townley took total control of the interior, in terms
of both plan and decoration, and Barrett was to
build this to his specifications by December
1777 [8].

The shells were finished successfully, and
Barrett was given the chance to build 8 Park
Street on the south-east corner by the arch
(1 and 3 Queen Anne's Gate). However, Townley's
standards were exacting and, when December 1777
arrived, Barrett required a six-month extension.[7]
Looking through Townley's careful room-by-
room analysis of every detail he had got wrong,
the developer may have wondered for whom he
had agreed to build. Here our story must turn to
the biography of the man who made this house
into a landmark of Georgian London.

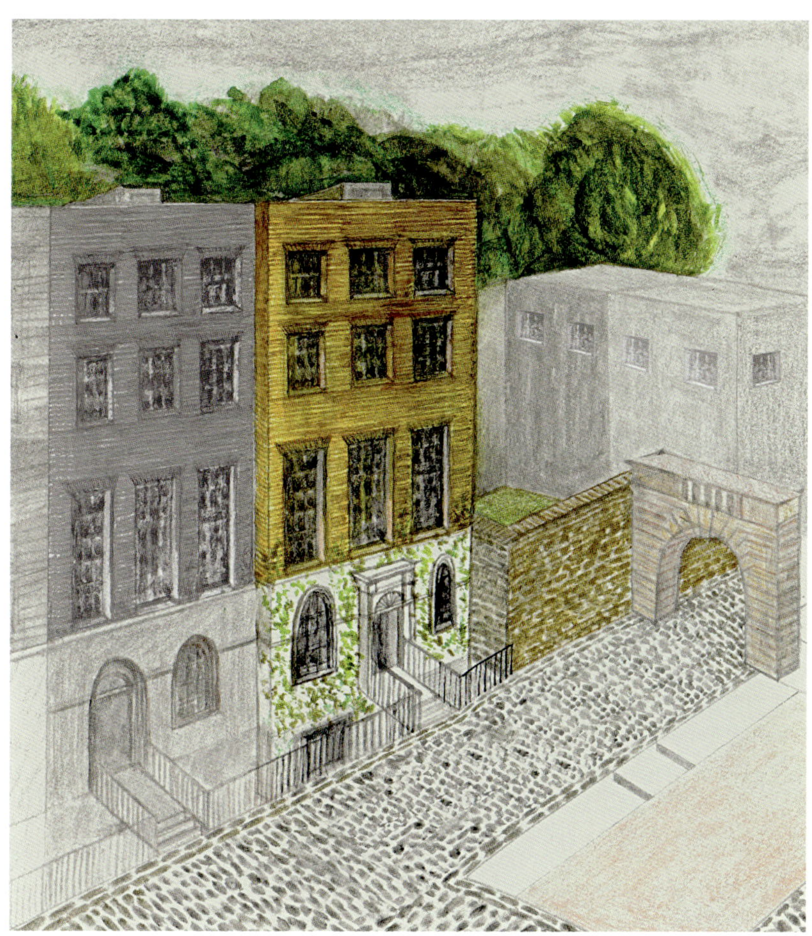

8. *Historical reconstruction, made in 2017, of Park Street after its completion in 1776, before changes to the area in the early nineteenth century. No. 7 is shown with its original facing in yellow Malm brick, to contrast to the others in grey stock*

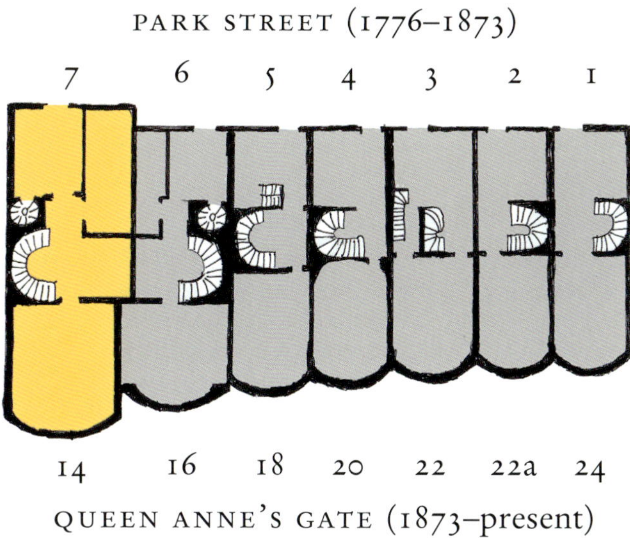

9. *Reconstruction, made in 2017, of the original layout of the street at ground floor level*

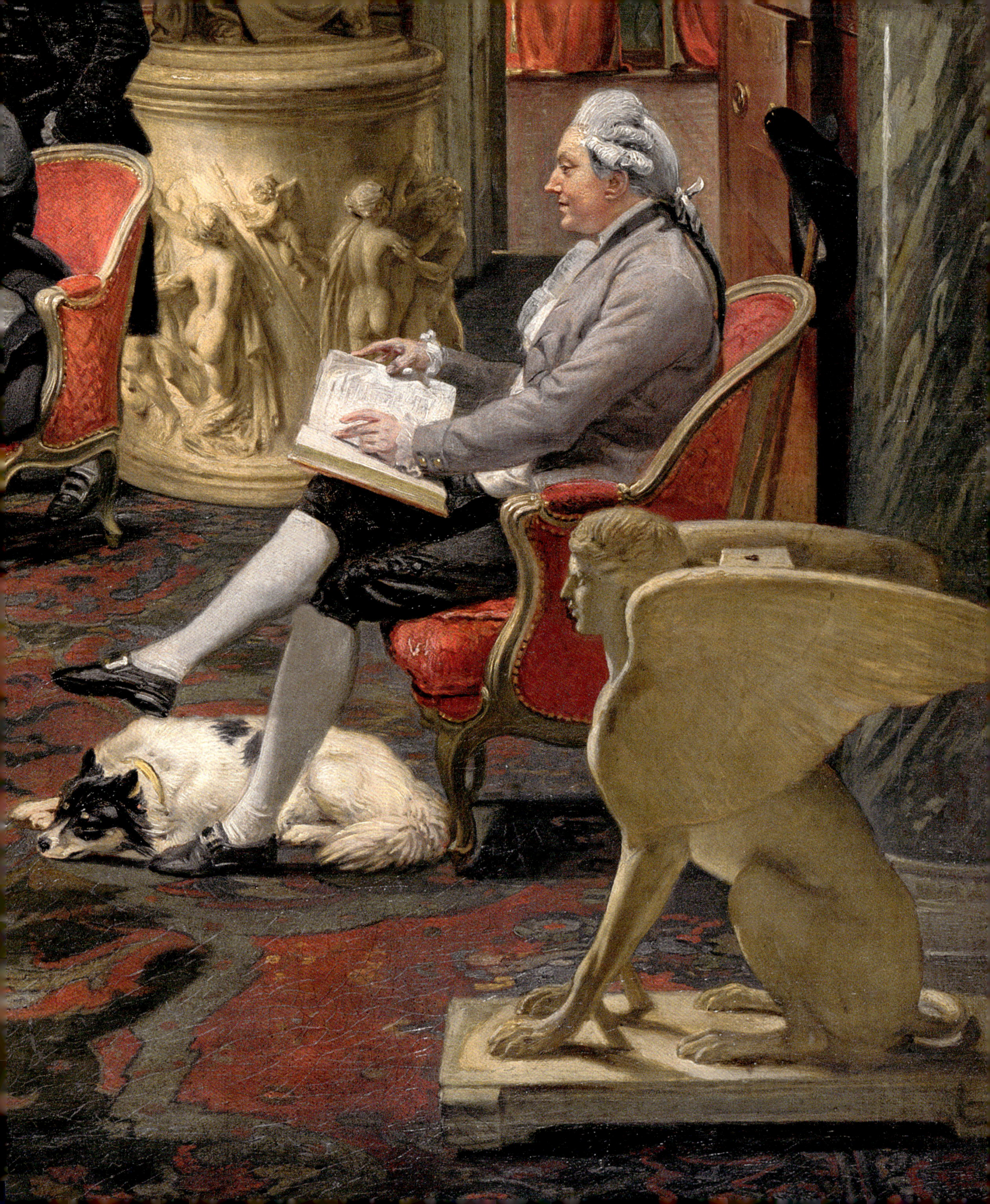

2. CHARLES TOWNLEY

CHARLES TOWNLEY WAS A FIGURE BOTH marginal and emblematic [10]. On the one hand he was Catholic and bisexual, and forged a life literally on the borders of the Protestant British establishment. He did not even speak English well, preferring to converse in Italian or French.[1] But Townley simultaneously embodied the values of the Enlightenment perhaps more completely than any other figure in the art world of eighteenth-century Britain. He remains little understood or appreciated in his homeland. While some of his peers are the centres of small industries of scholarship, Townley has never been the subject of a major exhibition or publication.[2]

The 'emblematic' side of Townley's life was dedicated to *virtù*, the term used for an appreciation of fine art pursued for its own sake. We are now most familiar with the concept in the derived term *virtuoso*. Despite being derided by the Victorians, *virtù* represented the first mass movement in aesthetic taste; it was the basis for any modern subculture that defines itself by the art that it consumes. The 'marginal' side of Townley, by contrast, manifested itself in a fascination with the ancient occult, particularly the Bacchic mysteries. These two sides of his personality are somewhat contradictory, but an account of him that omitted either would be partial. The house he made for himself on Park Street was at once a temple to *virtù* and to Bacchus.

Townley was born in 1737, at the family home in Lanchashire, named Towneley Hall in the traditional spelling of the name. The Towneleys were a family of untitled Catholic gentry from the far north of the country that traced its ancestry to the early fourteenth century. Their land was primarily used for arable farming and timber, but from the 1730s it also included coal mines. When the family estate was finally divided in the late nineteenth century, it was found to cover 40,000 acres. Charles was the eldest son of William Towneley. William did not have a chance to do much more than inherit, marry and father four children before he died in 1742, aged twenty-eight. Charles was four years old, and inherited the entire estate.

Catholicism, or 'recusancy', was common among the landowners of the north of England, although they practised their religion in secret. Catholics had been a target in England since the English Reformation had begun in the 1530s:

10. Detail of Charles Townley in A Nobleman's Collection *by Johan Zoffany [75]. At Townley's feet is his dog Kam, who was supposedly born from one of the huskies that had pulled the sled of a Royal Navy officer in Kamchatka in 1779, during the homeward journey of James Cook's third exploratory voyage. Siberian huskies were not bred in Europe until the 1950s.*

much like today, minority religious communities were often believed to owe their principal loyalty to a foreign power rather than the British state. A foundational event in national history was the Gunpowder Plot of 1605, in which Catholic conspirators including Guy Fawkes attempted to blow up the Houses of Parliament. The British still express their anti-Catholic heritage by burning an effigy of Fawkes on the anniversary of the event, 5 November.

A nadir was the Popery Act of 1698, when monetary reward was offered to anyone who caught Catholics celebrating Mass. The Popery Act was followed by the Act of Settlement in 1701, which prevented anyone who became a Catholic or married one from inheriting the throne. In the Perth Agreement of 2011 many of the restrictions on succession were removed, but the prohibition on a Roman Catholic becoming monarch was retained.

Townley's love of Bacchic mystery cults may be related to the fact that, like Catholicism, they operated outside mainstream religious institutions. The lack of documentary evidence for them is due to the importance they placed on secrecy as a source of power, just as mass had to be held in secret by British Catholics. Furthermore, the classically educated would have known of mystery cults partly by their condemnation: the Senate outlawed them in the famous inscription *Senatus consultum de Bacchanalibus* (186 BC).

Like all Catholic families in Britain the Towneleys suffered taxation and fines for their beliefs. They were also excluded from any kind of public office unless they explicitly renounced the Pope. What set the Towneleys apart, however, was the fact that the heads of the family avoided ever being legally convicted of insurrection. In the Civil War they fought on the Royalist side before the victory of the Parliamentarians and the establishment of the short-lived republican

Commonwealth (1649–60). They had also actively participated in the Jacobite Rising of 1715, led by the son of James II, who had been deposed in favour of the Protestants William III and Mary II in the Glorious Revolution of 1688. The major event of Townley's earliest years was another unsuccessful Jacobite rising, that of 1745–46, led by 'Bonnie Prince Charlie', the grandson of James II. Had he not died two years before, Townley's father would probably have supported the rebellion, and thus bankrupted the family by being convicted of insurrection. Without a patriarch the Towneleys stayed rich.

Townley's father's uncle, Francis Towneley, participated in the uprising of 1745–46, and Charles would have been seven when Francis was publicly hung, drawn and quartered in London. Furthermore his head had been covered in tar and put on a pole at Temple Bar; it remained there for many decades as a warning to Catholics. Townley himself does not seem to have had the slightest interest in seeing a Catholic on the British throne, and a desire to separate themselves from the more radical members of the family is perhaps evident in the decision by Townley and his brother to drop the central 'e' when they signed their surnames.

Townley's earliest years were spent at the family estate at Burnley, Lancashire. Towneley Hall [11] was a fifteenth-century tower house that had been extended in the early seventeenth century. Not long before Townley's birth its provincial design had been partially updated by his grandfather into that of a sophisticated Baroque mansion. In the 1720s, when architectural style was an ideologically charged issue, that would have been a pointed assertion of Catholic allegiance. A spectacular new entrance hall was decorated with plasterwork by craftsmen from continental Europe: the *Dancing Faun* and the Medici *Venus* from the Tribuna of the Uffizi were copied in plaster over the fireplaces. These then

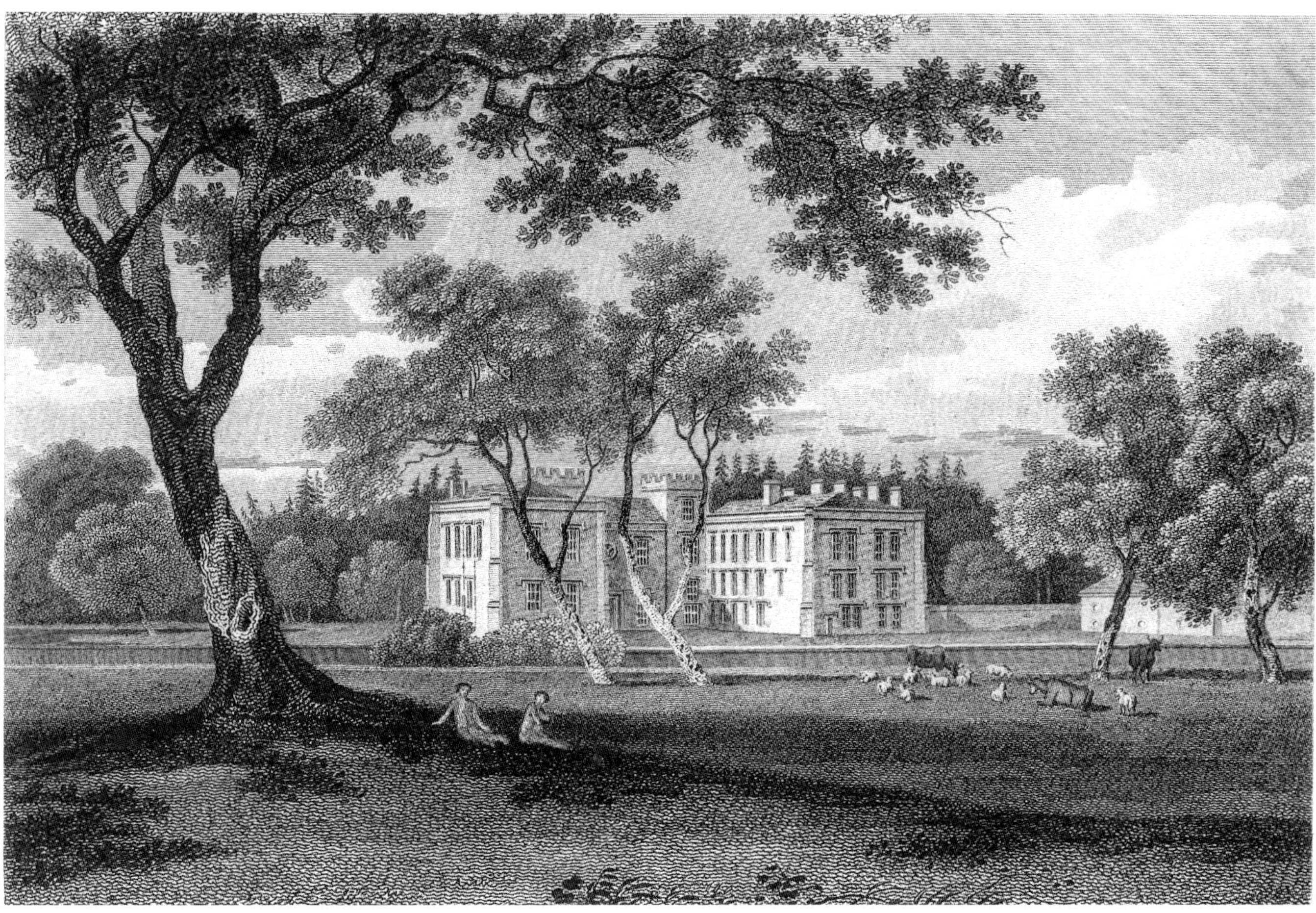

11. *An engraving after a watercolour by J.M.W. Turner, showing Towneley Hall, c.1797*

were the first classical sculptures that Townley would have ever seen. A cast of the *Dancing Faun* was also the first work of classical sculpture that Goethe remembered seeing, and it seems likely that Townley carried the memory through life in the same the way that the German poet described.[3]

Another resonant possession of Towneley Hall was the 'Towneley Mysteries'. This unique manuscript recorded a series of 32 plays based on biblical stories, presented for a popular audience in the medieval and early modern eras.[4] Following the English Reformation, the performance of the plays was outlawed, associating them thereafter with recusancy. The designation of

them as 'mysteries' reflected their presentation of miracles outside the institutions of the Church, and connected them by verbal coincidence to the mystery cults of pagan antiquity.

After his father's death, Townley's early years were dominated by various guardians and by his mother, born Cecilia Standish. She was a member of another wealthy Lancashire family that had retained the old faith. Cecilia's mother was the great-granddaughter of Thomas Howard, Earl of Arundel, who had been the most significant art collector and patron of the early seventeenth century, during the reigns of James I and Charles I. Arundel created the collection known as the

'Arundel Marbles', a group of antiquities taken directly from excavations in Rome and Smyrna. Arundel displayed these sculptures at his house in London at the Temple, and the collection was later split between the great manors of Wilton and Easton Neston. Apart from this major artistic lineage, Cecilia was also extremely wealthy, all her siblings having died, making her the sole heir of the Standish estate. Her son thus had the means to create a collection to rival that of her ancestor.

After the failed Jacobite uprising, the Towneley heir was sent to be educated at the English College at Douai a few years early, aged ten. The institution, founded in 1569, was located in northern France near Lille. Most of his teenage years, however, were spent in Paris, being privately tutored and moving in the social circles of his expatriate uncle John Towneley [12]. John was an important figure throughout his nephew's life, later moving to London, and finally living at 7 Park Street after his nephew's death. In Paris, John Towneley planted the seeds for his nephew's antiquarianism through his personal connections with many significant figures in the study of classical art, such as the comte de Caylus and the traveller James Dawkins.

After the Seven Years' War (1756–63) required him to return to the land of his birth, Charles Townley spent most of his twenties hunting in Lancashire and partying in London. His circle was rakish and libertine in a way that was out of step with the times. The 1760s in Britain were the era of the humanist essayists Samuel Johnson and Oliver Goldsmith, and the doctrine of 'sentiment' was in ascendance. Anticipating literary Romanticism, novels such as Sterne's *A Sentimental Journey* (1768) and Mackenzie's *The Man of Feeling* (1771) presented subjective emotional response, particularly towards the vulnerable and distressed, as a general principle of conduct. The kind of unapologetic hedonism discussed in the letters

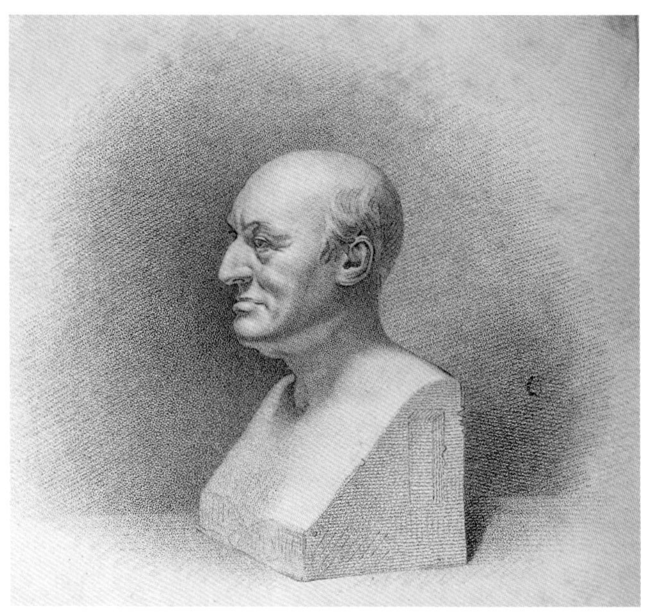

12. *John Towneley (1731–1813). This engraving shows an early example of a modern portrait herm, which was made in 1801 by the sculptor Joseph Nollekens, and is now at Towneley Hall.*

of Townley's friends would have been more subversive than in previous decades.

A likely inspiration for Townley's turn to *virtù* was Mary Howard, the Duchess of Norfolk. Cecilia Towneley was a cousin of Mary's husband Edward, Cecilia's mother having been born into the Howard family. But even without this family connection, their religion would probably have brought them together in London. The Howards were much more combative Catholics than the Towneleys: Edward's father had been imprisoned in the Tower of London, and his mother supported the rebellions financially. Edward himself had been an active participant in the Jacobite Rising of 1715 and only escaped prosecution because no witnesses would come forward to accuse such an eminent nobleman. But Mary was completely unsympathetic towards the Howard family's rebelliousness, and worked hard to establish a rapprochement with the political establishment.

In 1756, the construction of her house in St James's Square was finally finished. The opening of Norfolk House was marked with a grand party that confirmed Howard as one of the greatest patrons and social figures of her era. Today her significance is obscured by the destruction of this house, as well as her other principal creation, Worksop Manor near Sheffield. A year after the grand opening, the Duchess met Townley for the first time on his arrival in London from Paris. Just as she had guided the Howards away from self-destructive acts of political opposition, so she may have found in her hedonistic relative another opportunity for pastoral guidance.

The Duchess was probably the main catalyst for the Grand Tour of continental Europe that Townley embarked on in 1767, a few months before his thirtieth birthday. Letters from her would have established his entrée into Roman high society. As well as the escape it offered from the rounds of rakery in London and Lancashire, there may have been a plan for him to source art and furniture for Worksop Manor. However, the Duchess's heir died, and she abruptly terminated work there at the end of 1767, so any such order would have been cancelled before Townley had a chance to act on it.

Whatever the initial motivation, Townley took an active interest in the ancient world on his tour. He travelled to the newly excavated temple of Paestum with two draughtsmen, Pierre-Jacques Volaire and Vincenzo Brenna, the first to sketch landscapes and local people, the latter to make measured architectural drawings. By the time of his return to London, together with over thirty crates, Townley seems to have been on the path to *virtù*. In their letters, his friends portray him as genuinely passionate about scholarship, even when they are joking about sex. One wrote that 'I should have liked extremely to have rifled the Charms of the Italian Goddesses; those of marble and canvas I should have left to your superior judgement'.[5]

The initial plan had apparently been to return to the family house in Lancashire, but at some point Townley changed his mind. The crates of his marbles were redirected from Liverpool to London, and in December 1769 he purchased a house on Whitehall. He quickly moved in, renovated and furnished it. The principal addition must have been a chimneypiece designed by Giovanni Battista Piranesi, purchased in Rome.[6] Piranesi is best known for the *Carceri*, his engravings of architectural spaces created from collaged Roman structures. Piranesi applied the same principle of collage, or *capriccio*, to his own designs, putting antique elements together to create a fantastical result. The chimneypiece probably incorporated a relief of the masks of comedy and tragedy [13].[7]

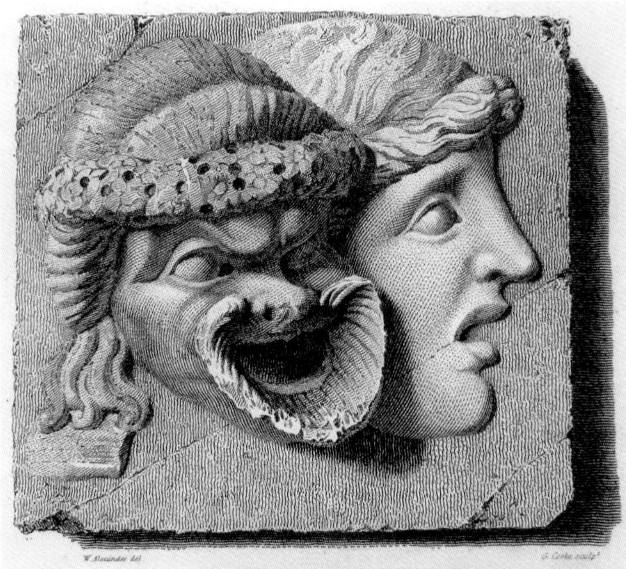

13. *Marble relief with tragic and comic masks. This is probably a work that was incorporated by Piranesi into the chimneypiece that Townley bought from him during his first Grand Tour. Unless otherwise stated, illustrations of the Townley marbles are taken from* A Description of the Collection of the Ancient Marbles in the British Museum with Engravings *(1812–61).*

Townley remained at the Whitehall house for almost two years, during which time he seems to have resumed much of the debauchery that he had been pursuing in the 1760s. When Townley left for a second trip to Italy, Richard Cosway wrote that 'there can be no *life* here [in London] without you'.[8] *Virtù* turned out to be perfectly compatible with the libertine lifestyle: Cosway wrote that in Italy Townley balanced both of his enthusiasms, with barely 'an Hours relaxation from *virtù* and fucking'.[9] This libertine dimension soon became apparent outside the circles of *virtuosi*: in 1792 a 'Society for the Reformation of Principles' was set up to fight 'the corruption which prevails among scholars and persons of the higher orders of life'.[10]

While in Italy on his second tour Townley was already planning to move out of the Whitehall property. He wanted a smaller house, including a large, top-lit room for the display of sculpture. His uncle John was tasked with finding such a property, and the search is recorded in their letters to each other.[11] John suggested properties in St George Street, off Hanover Square, Grosvenor Street, off Grosvenor Square, Whitehall, and Portland Place. For posterity's sake it is fortunate that his nephew did not choose them, as they would have likely been demolished in the nineteenth century or bombed in the twentieth.

The renovations at the Whitehall property were not wasted, however, because Townley sold the house to his antiquarian protégé Richard Payne Knight in March 1775. It must have suited the younger man, because Knight made it his home for the next three decades; he only left when the government forced him to sell the property so that the site could be used for new offices.

The area below St James's Park is now a centre of British Catholicism because of the presence of Westminster Cathedral, constructed in the late nineteenth century. For Townley, Westminster would have represented a balance between the central and peripheral. It was near his natural social circle that lived north of the park, the artistic and aristocratic community that itself sought proximity to the court of George III at St James's Palace. But Westminster was also somewhat marginal, providing a geographic separation from a king who was especially hostile to Catholics.

Townley's new neighbours were wealthy, erudite but somewhat marginal men like himself. Perhaps the most like Townley was Clayton Cracherode, who lived at No. 12 Queen Square (now 32 Queen Anne's Gate). Cracherode had inherited the house from his father's estate, and is recorded as in residence from 1775.[12] Like Townley, Cracherode was a full-time connoisseur, without a family. He was also a trustee of the British Museum and a member of the Society of Antiquaries. His collection was mostly literary, with around 4,500 books, but also included drawings, minerals and gems. He and Townley would divide up deliveries of Roman gems among themselves when they arrived in London.[13] Cracherode lived in Queen Square until his death in 1799, when he was buried in Westminster Abbey, and his collections passed by his bequest to the British Museum.

Townley's most eminent neighbour was Henry Temple, 2nd Viscount Palmerston, who had a house three doors down at No. 4 Park Street (now 20 Queen Anne's Gate). The two would probably have had much to discuss, being both more enamoured of foreign lands than their own British milieu. Temple had gone on a Grand Tour a few years before Townley, and knew his scholarly friends in Naples; he also preceded Townley as a member of the Society of Dilettanti. Although the Park Street house was not Temple's principal residence, his son was born there, who later became one of the greatest Prime Ministers in British history.

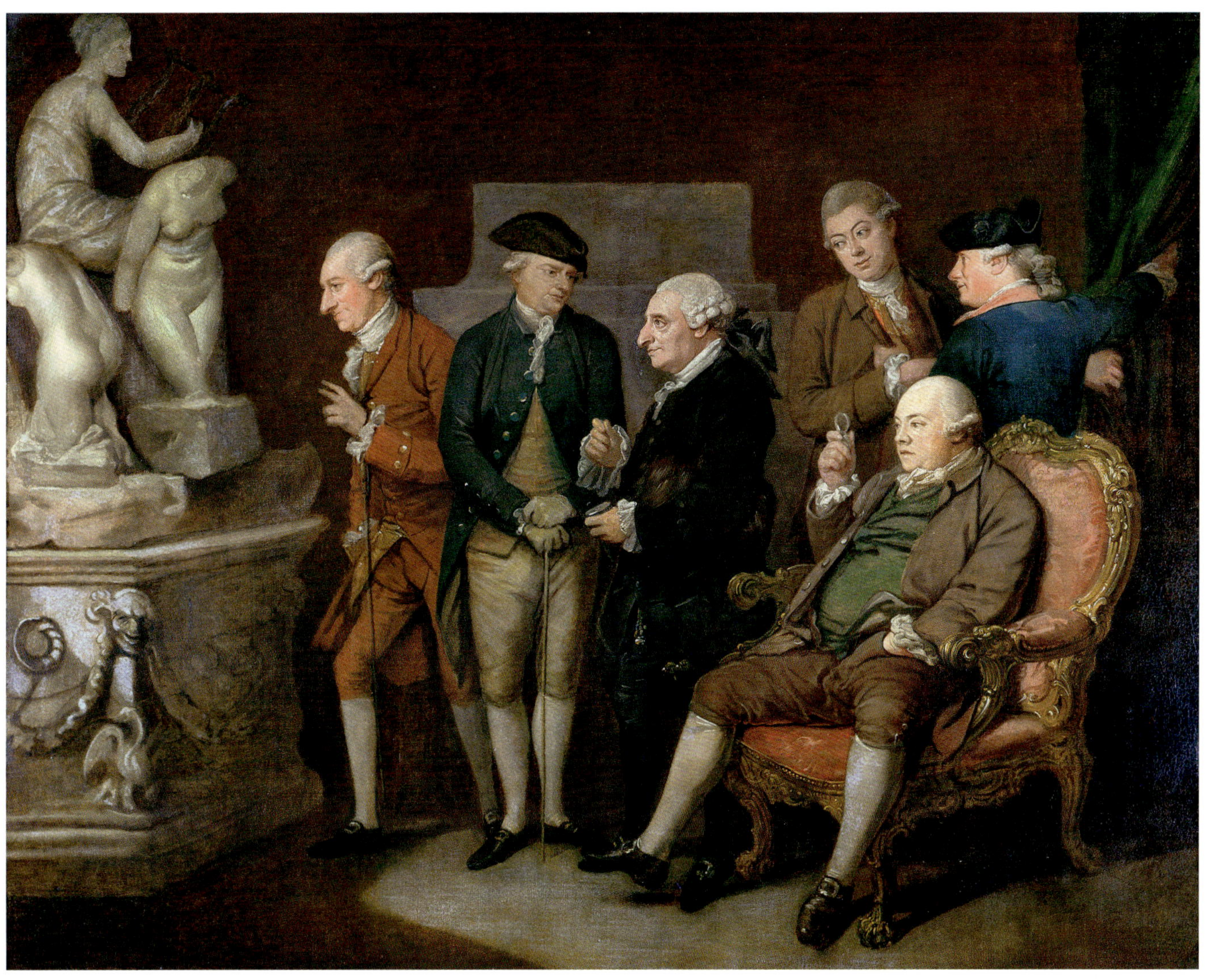

14. A Group of Connoisseurs *by Richard Cosway, 1771–75.*
The dynamic of Townley's circle can be seen in this painting of
the friends, commissioned by Townley just before his second
trip to Italy, and finished on his return. The subject is the
Venus *that Townley had bought in London in 1770, an early*
purchase by mail from Rome, which he kept in the Library at
Park Street. His friends variously leer at the marble statuette,
but Townley (in the green jacket) seems to be in serious
discussion. His interlocutor is 'Dr Verdun', of whom nothing
is known except that he was later committed to a mental
institution.

The mathematician George Shuckburgh arrived
on the street soon after Townley. He had already
been an MP for three years before moving to No. 1
Park Street (now 24 Queen Anne's Gate) in 1783.
Again he would have had common ground with
Townley, preceding him as a member of the Society
of Antiquaries. During his time as Townley's
neighbour, he was at work establishing a universal
standard for measuring a 'yard' by the length of
a pendulum swinging regularly. He moved away
from Park Street in 1788, but would ultimately win
the Royal Society's Copley Medal for this work.

Townley also hosted a cast of itinerant Continental scholars at the house, all with somewhat dubious titles – 'Dr Verdun', 'Baron d'Hancarville' and 'Abbé Devay', successively [14]. They worked from Townley's formidable library and art collection, and in turn provided dinner conversation and the fruits of their own erudition. Verdun and Devay have been lost to history, but the 'Baron' immortalized himself with a series of monumental publications. One of these was written at Townley's house, a treatise explicating the symbolism in the antique sculpture on display there: *Recherches sur l'origine, l'esprit et les progrès des arts de la Grèce* (see Appendix A).

At Park Street, Townley had a view over the most fashionable location in London. In the eighteenth century, during promenading hours, St James's Park was the place to see the fashions of the Georgian age. The birds of Charles II had been replaced by elaborate hats and wigs, which could be seen on the Mall, then a tree-lined path along the north of the park. Outside promenading hours, however, the park had begun to go somewhat downmarket, ever since William and Mary had moved their residence to the quiet of Kensington in 1689. A feature was the 'molly market' for prostitutes of both genders, on the site of Birdcage Walk.[14]

Townley never married, and shared the house only with his Siberian husky Kam [10]. A letter suggests, however, that he had at least one illegitimate child.[15] Sodomy was a capital offence during Townley's life, and there are only oblique references to sexual relationships with men in his surviving letters.[16] The popular story told in almost every biographical account after his death was that Townley claimed his 'wife' to be his famous bust of Isis.[17]

Townley's correspondents often obliquely describe the house as an environment of both scholarship and decadence. One friend joked that mothers 'will even scarce allow their Daughters to come to the park gate'.[18] Another compared it to the palace of the Roman emperor Gordian II, quoting the historian Edward Gibbon: 'Twenty-two acknowledged Concubines and a Library of sixty-two thousand volumes attested the variety of his Inclinations; and from the productions which he left behind him, it appears that both the one and the other were designed for use, rather than ostentation'.[19] No evidence has ever been found for any bacchanals at 7 Park Street. But secrecy is, after all, the whole point of a mystery cult.

Townley was contrastingly open about his religious background. He was not a regular churchgoer, but he identified himself as a Catholic to foreign visitors to his house and collection.[20] Townley's years at Park Street represented a slow improvement in the safety of British Catholics. In 1778 the Catholic Relief Act began the process of removing laws relating to property and inheritance. In 1788 a Roman Catholic Committee, with which Townley was involved, addressed the Prime Minister, William Pitt the Younger. Three years later, with the support of the Whig establishment, most of the legal persecutions were removed. The lack of greater progress was mainly due to King George III, who at one point even forced Pitt to resign from office over the issue of Catholic emancipation. In his later years Townley was openly antipathetic to the king: he displayed a bust of Marcus Aurelius [15], over life size, in the Park Drawing Room, and told visitors that he offered 'supplications to heaven to send the Christians as good a regent as this pagan was'.[21]

The final event in Catholic emancipation was the repeal of laws preventing outsiders to the Church of England from holding government office in 1828. The inclusion of Catholics in this proclamation was in large part thanks to Townley's immediate neighbour, the radical MP William Smith. In 1794 Smith moved into No. 6 Park

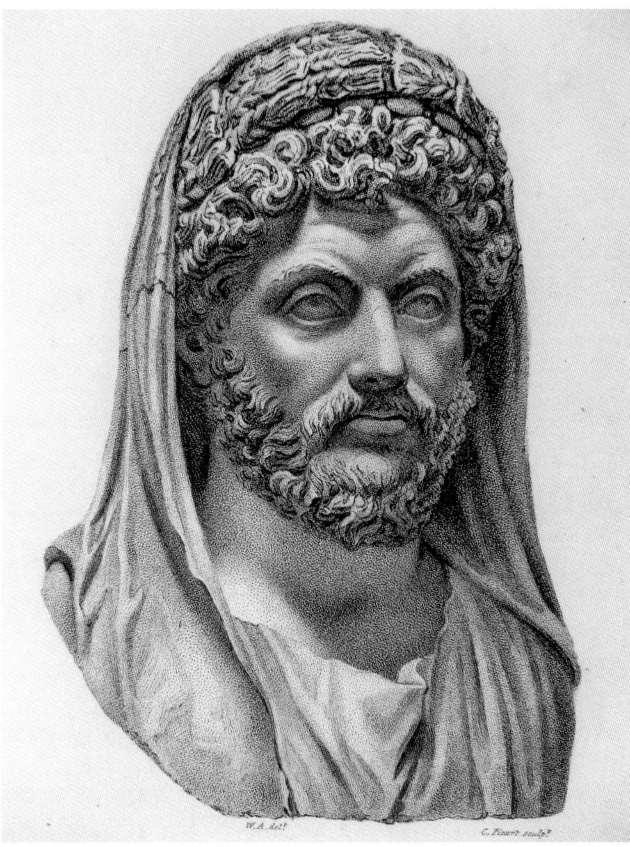

15. *'Marcus Aurelius'. Throughout this book, the titles of the marbles will be those given in the 'Parlour Catalogue' of 1804, created for consultation by visitors to the collection. These often differ from those used later for the works, but in the case of this bust scholars still use Townley's title.*

Street, now 16 Queen Anne's Gate. During his years there he campaigned against slavery, and his work was crucial to the abolition of the Atlantic slave trade in 1807.

By the late 1780s, Charles Townley was the most trusted authority on classical antiquities in Britain. When the Prince of Wales, the future King George IV, needed to decorate Carlton House, his new palace, he went to Townley for advice on what sculptures to buy.[22] No. 7 Park Street was a key aspect of this authority: the Prince made various visits to see Townley there, two of which are recorded in 1786 and 1796.[23] The Prince even authorized the removal of a tree in Birdcage Walk that was blocking the light into the Park Drawing Room.[24]

Townley died in January 1805, in the bedroom overlooking St James's Park on the second floor of No. 7 Park Street. The cause of death is not known, but for years he had obsessively recorded digestive problems in his diary. He was buried in the family chapel at Burnley, and one source wrote that 'so much was he beloved by the country people far and near, that, as his hearse passed, the sides of the road were crowded, and the windows of the town filled, the spectators being all silent and uncovered'.[25] On his tomb was a quotation describing Publius Martius Verus, a general loyal to Townley's favourite Roman emperor, Marcus Aurelius:

χάρις [τε] ἦν ἐπὶ πᾶσι τοῖς πρασσομένοις ὑπ᾽ αὐτοῦ καὶ λεγομένοις, / τὸ μὲν ἀγανακτοῦν ἑκάστου καὶ τὸ θυμούμενον παραμυθουμένη, / τὸ δὲ ἐλπίζον ἔτι μᾶλλον αὔξουσα.[26]

There was a quality of charm about all that he said or did, / a charm that soothed the vexation and anger of everyone, / while raising their hopes even more.

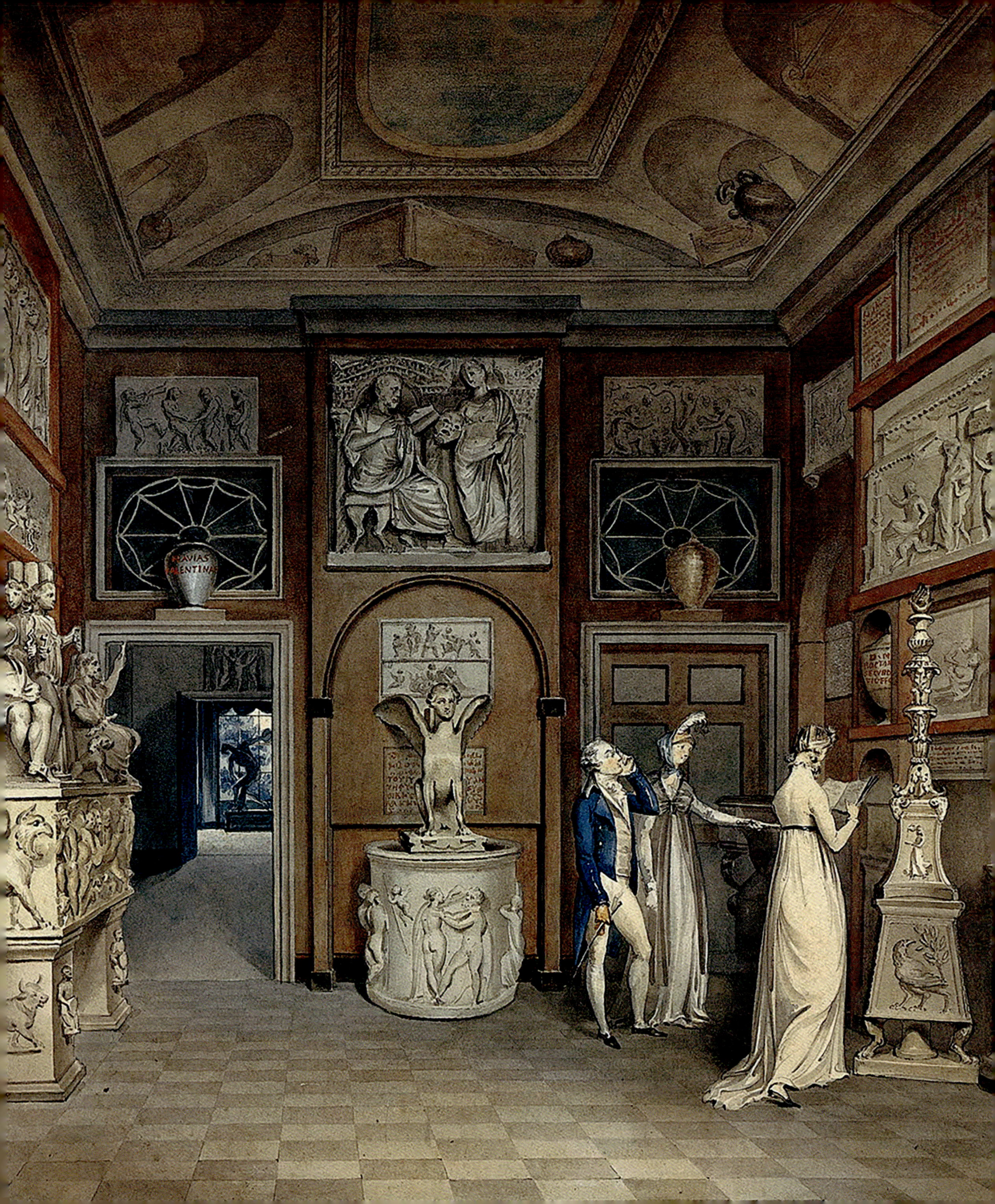

3 . SAMUEL WYATT

THE DESIGN OF CHARLES TOWNLEY'S
house represented an attempt to create in
modern London a temple to Bacchus. At the
time, imagery associated with the god was a
conventionally festive feature of dining rooms,
but No. 7 Park Street contained an unprecedented
programme of Bacchic iconography. Ivy overruns
the design, from the ceilings on the first floor, to
the columns on the ground floor, to the ironwork
on the staircase. Bacchus himself appears at the
centre of the ceiling painting of the Street Drawing
Room. Even the geographical proximity to the
park can be understood in terms of the god,
because the ecstatic frenzy of the Bacchanalia
was staged as a movement from city to nature.

One of the unique features of the house
is the frieze in the Dining Room [17]. This is
decorated with panther heads, ivy and musical
instruments, which were understood to represent
the instruments played during Bacchic orgies.[1]
Music may not seem an obvious feature of an
orgy; however, this was in reference to the violent
dimension to Bacchic sexuality. The Roman
historian Livy wrote that 'violence was concealed
because, amid the howlings and the crash of drums

*16. Detail of a drawing [30] by an unknown artist,
c.1793–1804, showing an unexecuted decorative scheme
for the entrance hall*

and cymbals, no cry of the sufferers could be
heard as the debauchery and carnage proceeded'.[2]

In any other era, such eccentric architectural
intentions would be a recipe for aesthetic disaster.
However, in the 1770s, English taste reached an
apogee that would remain a permanent standard
of elegant design. It had been a swift ascent: only
two decades earlier, a major public building like
Horse Guards (1751–59) still deferred to the
design vocabulary established by British disciples
of Andrea Palladio's architectural treatise. The year
of its completion, a new treatise was published
that introduced French design principles and
new Italian sources, a manifesto for a style that
would come to be known as 'Neoclassicism'. Its
author was a Swedish-born Scot named William
Chambers, who would become the greatest official
architect of the next decades, winning the Swedish
Order of the Polar Star in 1770.

Landmark projects of the 1770s include
Brooks's Club by Henry Holland (1776–68),
Newgate Prison by George Dance the Younger
(1770–80) and Somerset House by William
Chambers (begun 1776). Alongside Chambers,
Robert Adam and his brother James were the most
influential architects of the period, and the energy
behind much of what made the 1770s such a high
point in English taste. At Portland Place, begun in
1773, the brothers designed one of the great urban
developments of European Neoclassicism [18].

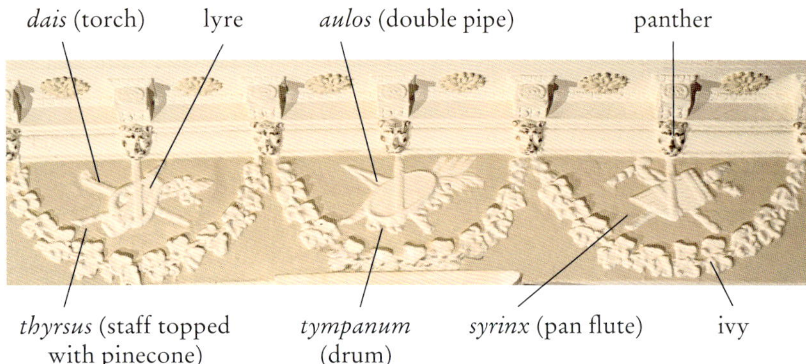

17. *The frieze in the Dining Room is decorated with three repeating motifs of instruments played in Bacchic rites: the* tympanum, syrinx *and lyre.*

The venue for the finest British design of the 1770s was, however, not the public architecture of Chambers's treatise, but the domestic interior. Furniture designers, ceramicists and architects collaborated to create spaces of unparallelled refinement. Names such as Adam, Chippendale, Wedgwood and Sheraton have become synonymous with desirable style. Another name included in that roll-call is 'Wyatt'. This is most often with reference to James Wyatt, architect of the Oxford Street Pantheon and many of the greatest country houses of the era. But his brother Samuel, the architect of Townley's house at 7 Park Street, equally embodied the sophisticated form of Neoclassicism connoted by the name.

Samuel Wyatt [19] was a protégé of Robert Adam at Kedleston Hall near Derby. He had begun work there aged twenty as a carpenter, and within a year replaced an experienced builder as the clerk of all works. The new position involved Wyatt taking up permanent residence on site to supervise the entire staff in carrying out the vision of the architect; he was also to be in constant contact with the patron. Adam explicitly stated that the promotion of the inexperienced Wyatt was so that his own orders would be carried out unquestioningly.[3] It is probable that part of the reason that Wyatt was chosen to design No. 7 Park Street was similar – that Townley had a very clear idea of what he wanted, and did not wish

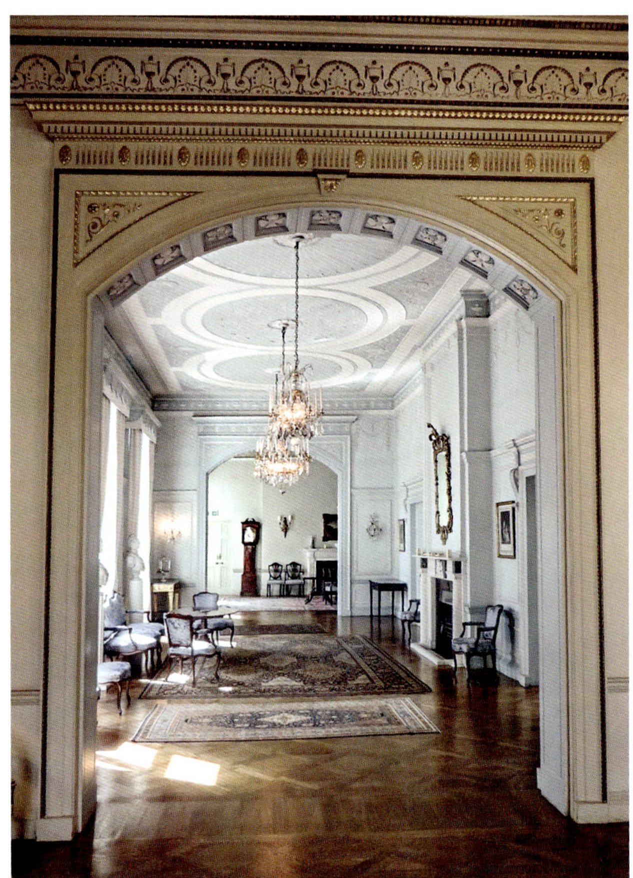

18. *Portland Place was almost entirely destroyed by war damage and property development, but No. 27, now the residence of the ambassador of Sweden, survives intact, preserving the design by Robert and James Adam.*

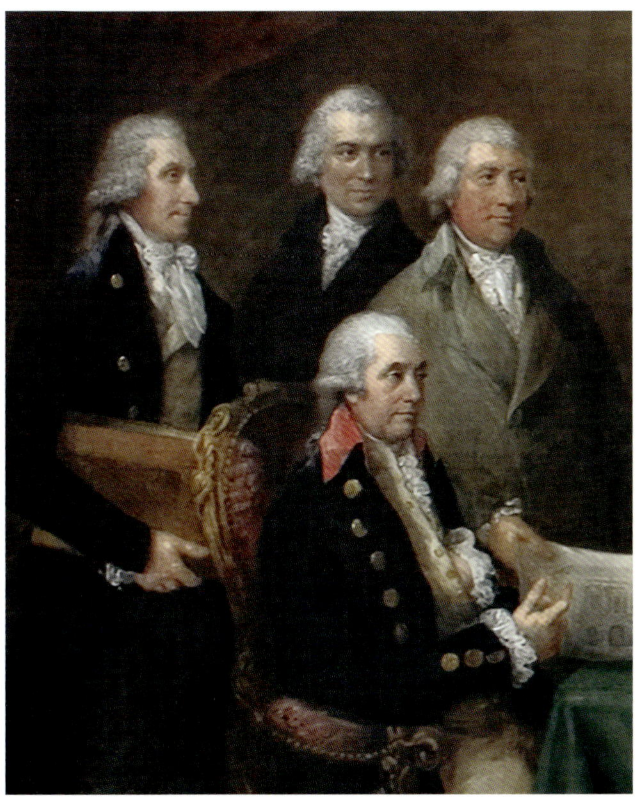

19. The architect Samuel Wyatt (1737–1807) is shown here, wearing a green jacket, in a group portrait of 1794 by Gainsborough Dupont. He is delivering his designs for Trinity House in the City of London; they are received by the Elder Brethren of the Corporation, who were, and remain, responsible for the nation's lighthouses.

to have to battle an egotistical architect. Indeed it is Wyatt's subtlety that is the most distinctive feature in his work. He designed country houses that, even by the standards of early Neoclassical architecture, are exercises in restraint: the exteriors of houses like Doddington Hall in Cheshire (1776) and Coton House in Warwickshire (c.1785) are almost defiantly unforthcoming, rejecting any style other than the plainest classicism.

The houses on Park Street show how Wyatt could characterize his buildings within this narrow formula. The end house, No. 7, is clearly the principal façade, being set just ahead of the others, with a slightly higher string-course, and an

entablature over the door. Most of all there would have been the colour, with the facing of natural Malm brick, rather than the usual grey stock of the other houses. Malm had been introduced only a few years earlier, and would have given the house a rich sulphurous yellow [8]. The cornice and other details were of Portland stone.[4] The house now stands out differently, having been refaced on both sides in a rich red brick, flanked by other houses refaced in modern artificial Malm.

The absence of overt external flourish allowed Wyatt to focus on his favourite part of design – internal planning. Wyatt's plans are among the most complex ever devised for domestic buildings, reconfiguring rooms within difficult existing spaces, and using elaborate geometry to incorporate unusual shapes. This too would have been a reason for Townley's choice of architect. He had a clear vision that his house required a top-lit sculpture gallery, and had rejected a house by Robert Adam in Portland Place for this reason.[5] To incorporate one into a terraced house in London required extreme ingenuity, and Wyatt was up to the challenge.

Another planning issue was how to incorporate extensive servants' quarters into a narrow site with lots of floors, where servants needed to be able to move freely from their rooms in the attic to the workplace in the basement without a visitor being aware of their presence. Wyatt's solution was to incorporate a 'small circular back staircase' behind a wall next to the grand staircase, lighting it from above with a skylight. Wyatt then concealed it further by creating a 'staircase fronting Park Street' within it, possibly in the manner of a double helix, rising from the Hall to the Street Drawing Room.[6] A fake fan sash was even painted above the door in the Hall to create symmetry with the opening to the passage on the left side.

Like Townley, Samuel Wyatt embodied the contradictory forces of Britain in the late

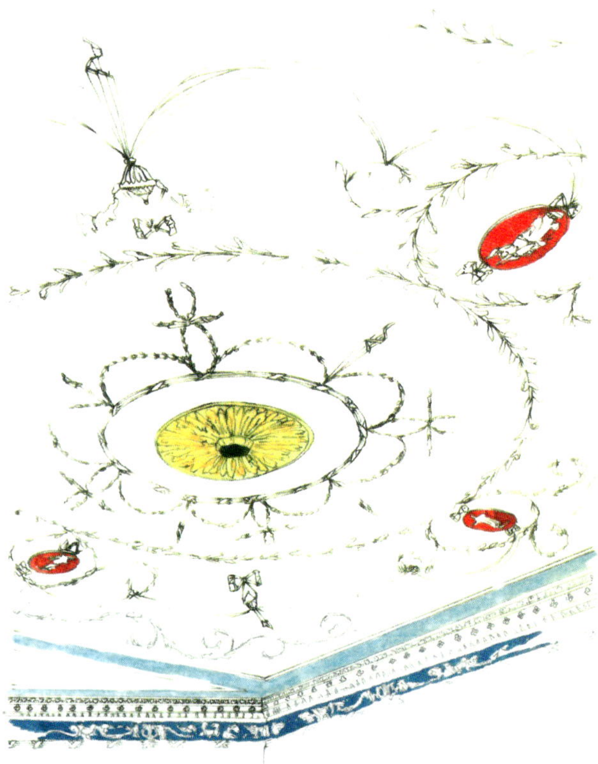

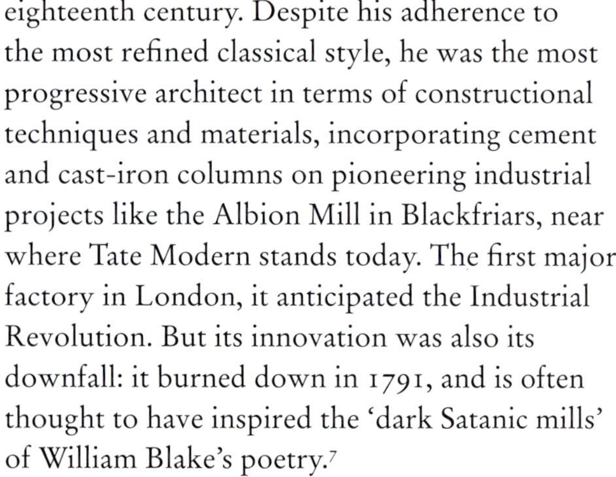

20. *This sketch, made in 2013, recreates the ceiling of the Park Drawing Room as it was originally decorated, on the basis of scientific analysis of the lowest layer of paint.*

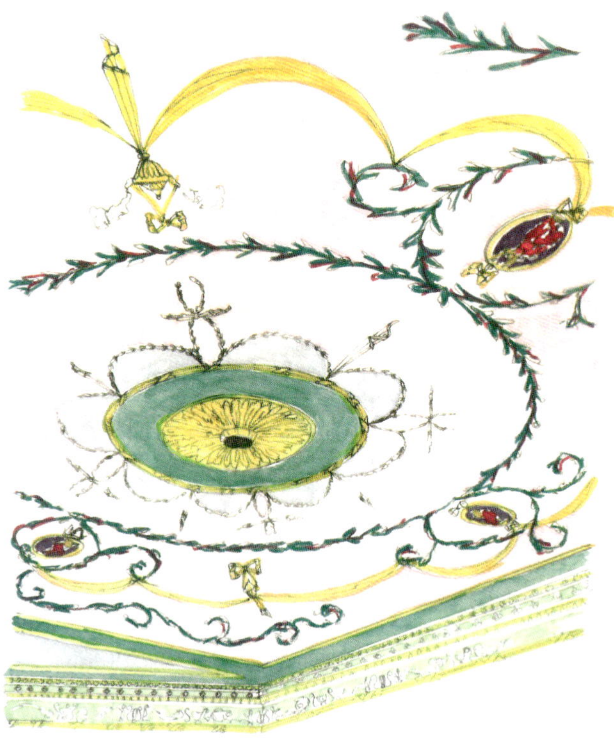

21. *This sketch shows the same ceiling as it was repainted, on the basis of scientific analysis of the second-to-lowest layer of paint.*

eighteenth century. Despite his adherence to the most refined classical style, he was the most progressive architect in terms of constructional techniques and materials, incorporating cement and cast-iron columns on pioneering industrial projects like the Albion Mill in Blackfriars, near where Tate Modern stands today. The first major factory in London, it anticipated the Industrial Revolution. But its innovation was also its downfall: it burned down in 1791, and is often thought to have inspired the 'dark Satanic mills' of William Blake's poetry.[7]

In terms of construction, Wyatt was particularly adept as a carpenter, his original role at Kedleston and the source of his nickname, 'the Chip'.[8] This may have been the most important

factor in his commission to design the Park Street house, because a major part of Townley's vision was for sculptures and terracottas to be installed directly into the wall [24]. Indeed, it was stated in the developer Michael Barrett's contract that he would carry out these unconventional elements without complaint.[9] Having been disappointed by Portland Place, Townley may have discovered that Adam's protégé had arrived in London in 1774 and could be the perfect person to fulfil his requirements in a suitable style.

Ceilings were a major decorative feature of Neoclassical design in Britain, and the Adam style had been popularized by the *Works in Architecture of Robert and James Adam*, the first volume of which had begun publication in 1773, as well as

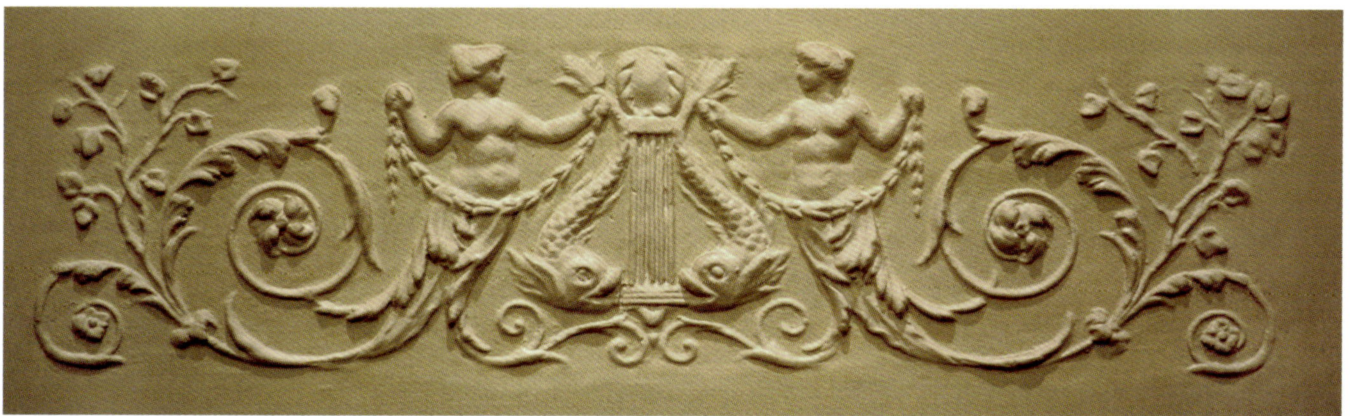

22. Decorative motif of a lyre and ivy used multiple times on the first floor of the house. The design may be referring to the Dionysiac poet Arion, who according to Herodotus was saved from drowning by music-loving dolphins.

a book of ceilings by one of their draughtsmen, published in 1776. Wyatt's ceilings, however, refine its vocabulary in a way that, in the words of one critic, 'makes Adam's seem almost gross by comparison'.[10] Furthermore, they incorporate naturalistic imagery, particularly ivy, contrasting with the more geometrical designs of Adam. Modern analysis of the paint in the drawing room has shown that, while the colour scheme was subdued, the central rose was entirely gilded [20]. This also distinguished the design from those of Adam, who would have filled the ceilings with bright contrasting colours.

The house as built had four floors (ground, principal, chamber and attic) plus a basement. The plan of the ground floor remains mostly as it was, with the entrance hall, referred to simply as 'the Hall', now divided into the vestibule and reception office, and the spiral staircases replaced with a lift. The office now on the other side of the west wall was a larger space, used as a dressing room, and was accessed by a door opposite what is now the lift. On the same side, in the position of the present secretary's office, was an alcove.

The main room on the ground floor was the spectacular dining room [31, 52, 57, 88, 92], which has not changed in plan except for the addition of a second door on the entrance side into the office. The walls were painted blue, interrupted by columns of a dark red in an evocation of a Roman peristyle. The stated plan was that this colour scheme would present sculptures to their best advantage.[11] The strange design of the capitals is a copy of one discovered by Vincenzo Brenna at an archaeological site while Townley's party were returning back to Rome from Naples in 1768 [23]. Its symbolism was understood to denote a temple of Bacchus and Ceres, who are represented by ivy and corn respectively.[12]

The first floor was the principal storey, fifteen feet high, with a library and two parlours, known as the Street Drawing Room and the Park Drawing Room [26, 27]. The main innovation about the house's design was its incorporation of top-lighting into the otherwise windowless library, an elegant maximizing of wall space.

The second floor was the chamber storey, ten feet high, for Townley's private apartment. The

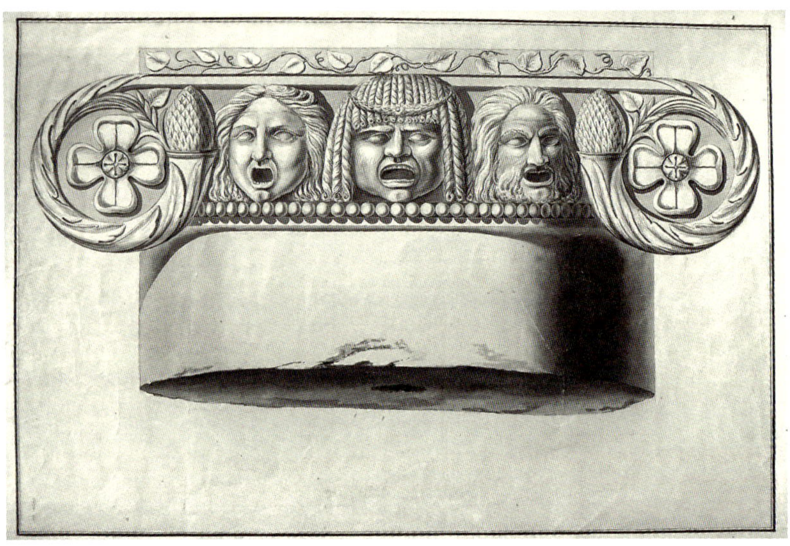

23. *Townley annotated this drawing, now in the Victoria and Albert Museum: 'This capital, lying amongst the ruins of an antient temple at Anxur, now called Terracina, was discovered and drawn by Vincenzo Brenna arhi:t in our journey to Naples Mar: 1768'. The design was used for the capitals in the Dining Room.*

24. *The sculptural installation at the house has all been removed, and only survives in sketches such as this one for the Entrance Hall, made by an anonymous hand, c.1786–93.*

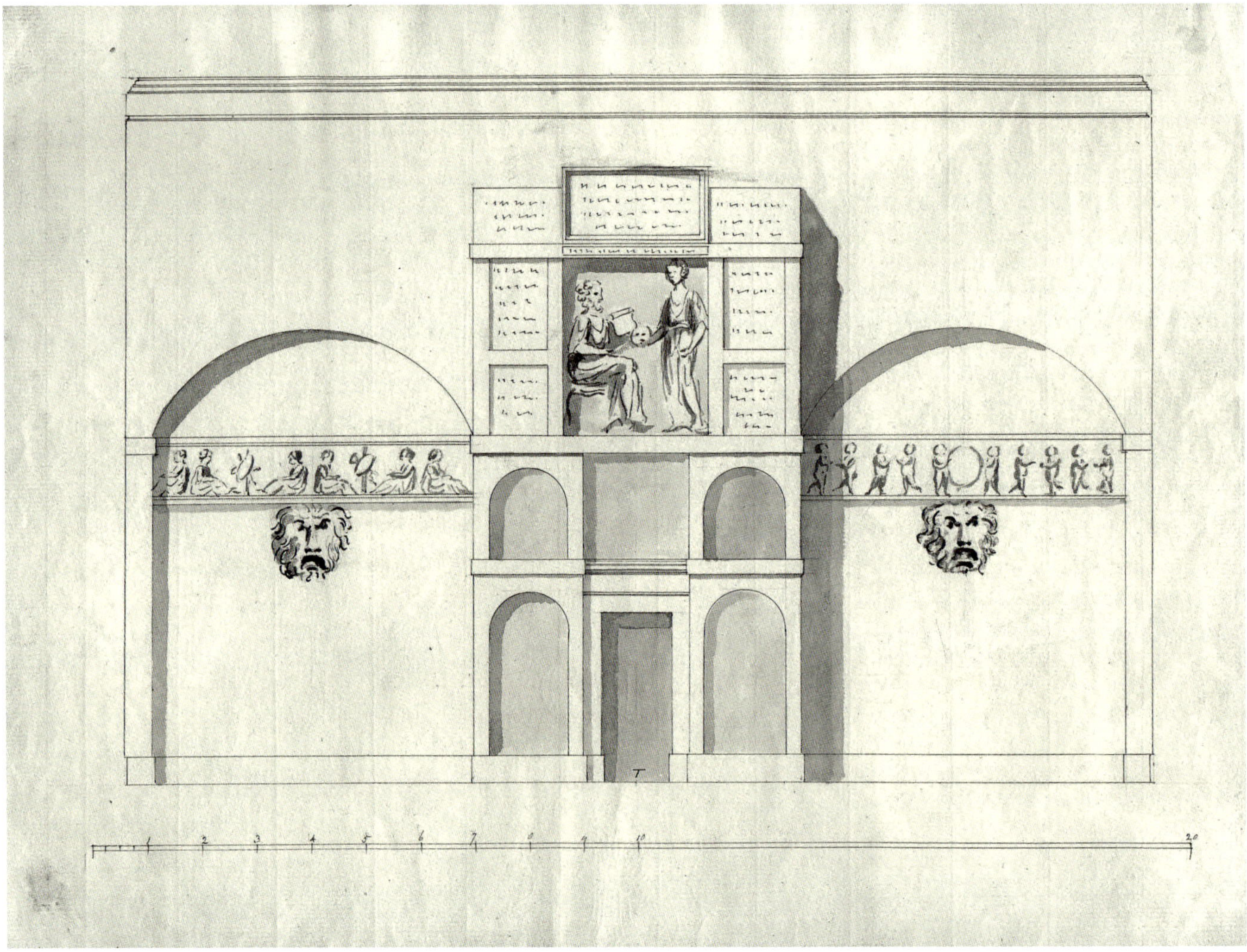

bedroom faced the park and the dressing room faced the street, and they corresponded in plan to the drawing rooms below. They were connected by a passage, and both contained a chimneypiece of veined marble.

At the front and back of the house were two attics, eight feet high, one above the dressing room, the other above the bedroom. The street attic was the residence of the servants. Above it, in the centre, was a small 'cockloft' with a door that led back on to the roof.

A spiral stair led all the way down from the attic storey to the servants' workplace in the basement. This extended under Park Street, making it the largest single floor. Space was allocated for a kitchen, a housekeeper's room, a larder and two wine cellars. Dishes and utensils were stored in a pantry and cleaned in a scullery. As was customary, due to the needs of eighteenth-century mens' fashion, Townley's wigs were allocated their own space, the 'powdering room'.

The other feature to be built was a coach house [25]. Its location is not known, but it was of considerable size, thirty-six feet in width. Initially it housed a coach and a cart, but later Townley sold these to make more storage space for his sculptures.[13] A coach was not necessary, as so much of his social circle was nearby, whether on Park Street itself or across the park in St James's.

In 1774, when the design had all been set out in the contract with Wyatt, the intention had been that the top-lit Library would be the principal space for the display of sculpture. Townley's collection did not then contain many life-size items, but that changed the next year, when several became available. Townley ordered his dealer in Rome by post to purchase them and send them to London; he must have known that they would certainly not fit in a single room on the house's first floor, so the original vision for Park Street was reconceived.

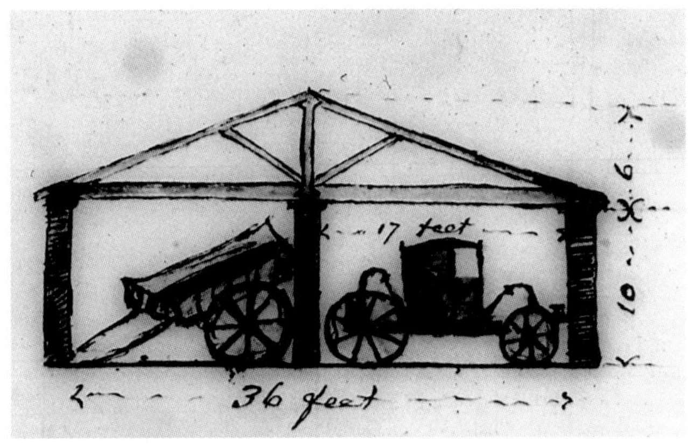

25. *An undated and unattributed design for a coach house among the Townley papers at the British Museum, annotated in the hand of Charles Townley*

Before, during and after his next shopping spree in Italy, Townley considered moving on from the house altogether, either by erecting a new gallery at Towneley Hall or by finding a new residence in London.[14] But, having explored these options, he decided in the late summer of 1777 to stay in the house as he had originally planned. Townley's antiquities dealer in Rome, Thomas Jenkins, was pleased with the decision, describing the Park Street house as a 'Palace in London' and commenting that to 'have such a Place as the Park for your Garden, in such a Capitol as London now is, is a most interesting circumstance'.[15]

The plan then became for the sculptures essentially to take over both the ground and principal storeys. Another antiquities dealer wrote that 'it is the same in every elegant feast; all the nice morsels must not be served up at once; some will like the roast beef & others prefer the macharone pie & so unlike one another as not to bear a comparison … if all the fine things of the Villa Borghese were to be arranged in one great room, exclusive of the rest, the whole would not be so entertaining'.[16] It must have been at this point, with the decoration to the house not yet complete, that the theme of Bacchic occultism was

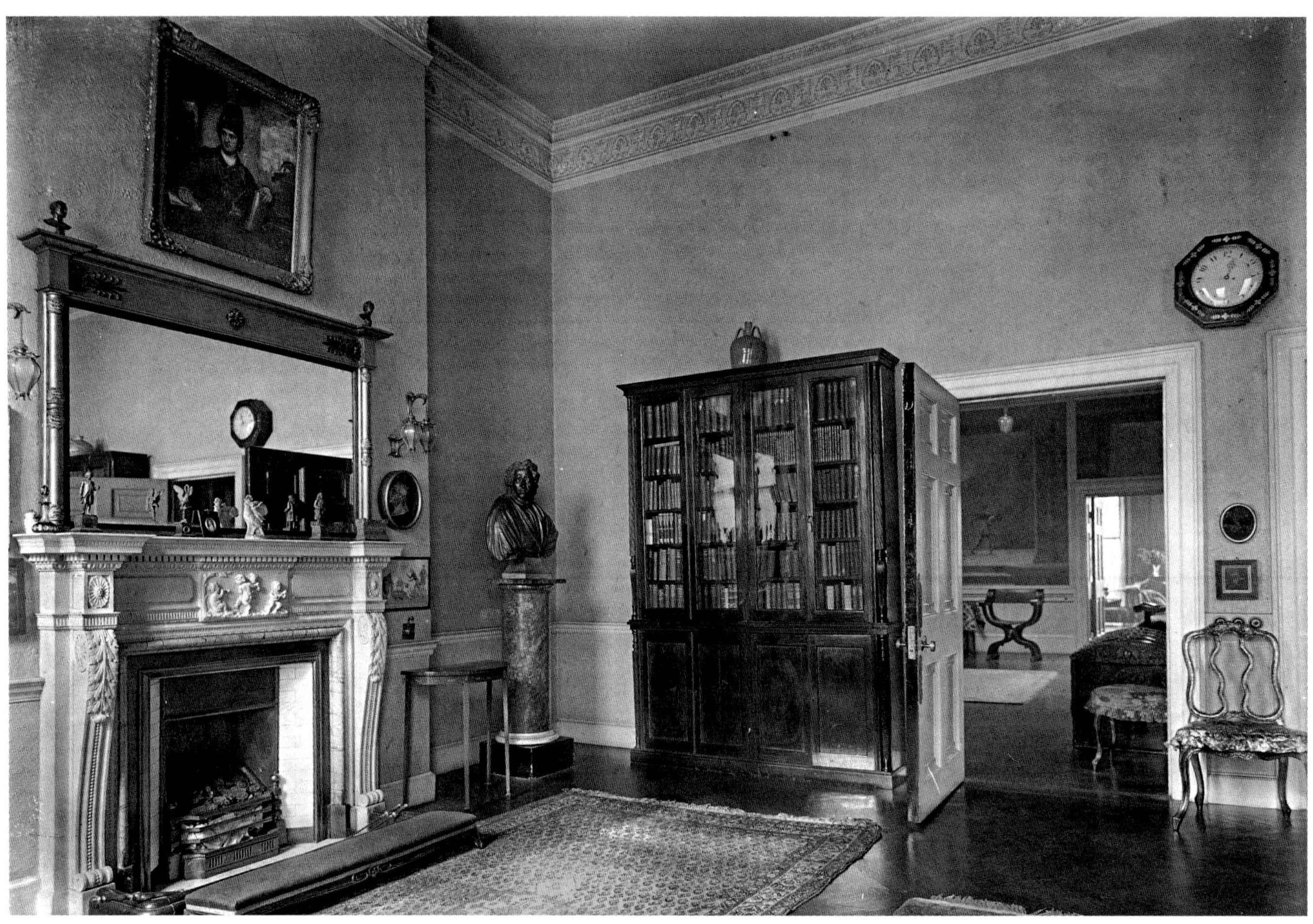

26. *The Street Drawing Room in 1915. The chimneypiece has since been moved to the Dining Room downstairs.*

conceived for the ground floor, with objects of *virtù* above.

In January 1778, the firm of Richter and Bartoli was commissioned to add scagliola to the Dining Room peristyle. This may have been inspired by the work of Robert Adam, including the internal peristyles of full columns in the marble hall at Kedleston (1763) and the anteroom at Syon House (1765), the latter including scagliola. The elegant version with half-columns was Wyatt's own, and in 1794 he adapted it for the entrance hall at Shugborough, in Staffordshire, where antique marbles were also displayed.

The original specifications for the construction of the house required rooms like the library to be '<u>all richly</u> ornamented'.[17] However, Townley's taste in decoration seems to have become more restrained over time. Though parts of the niches and ceilings were gilded, he rejected the heavy gilding of Cardinal Albani's sculpture gallery in Rome.[18] He also rejected the Adam style, which had been employed in the most lavish new sculpture gallery in Britain, at Newby Hall. Townley visited in 1779, and criticized it in a lost letter to Jenkins for its excessive ornamentation.[19] By contrast the Bacchic iconography of No. 7

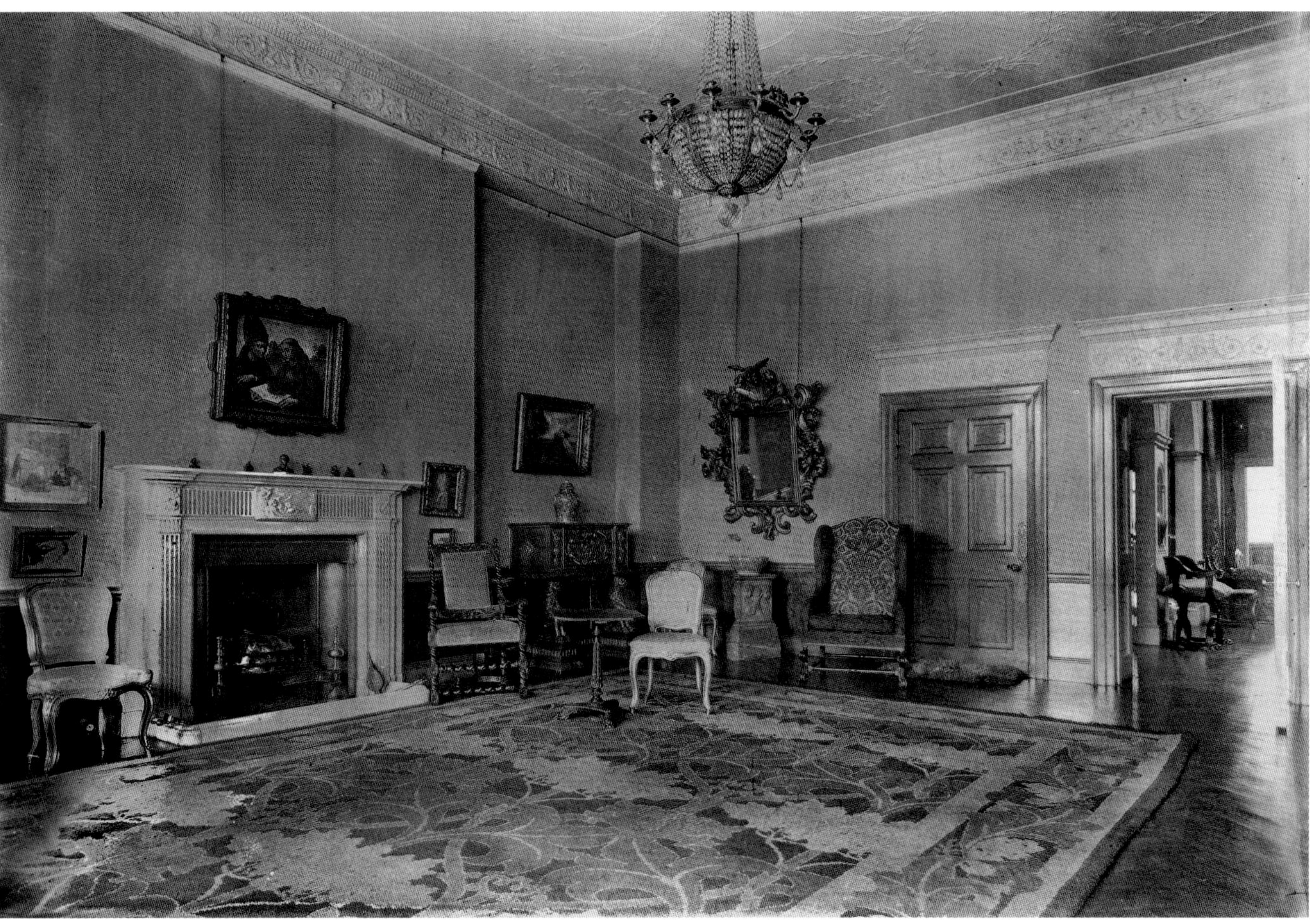

27. *The Park Drawing Room in 1915. This image and the one opposite are the only record of the full enfilade that Samuel Wyatt created along the first floor via the Library.*

Park Street was carefully chosen and unobtrusive, almost as if it were a secret code.

Architectural work and sculptural installation seem to have been completed in 1780, when the first visitors to the collection began to arrive. One of the final touches may have been the repainting of the ceiling of the Park Drawing Room [21]. This was much more colourful than its predecessor, but in a naturalistic manner, not in the Adam style. Instead of large blocks of bright artificial colour, the new scheme was illusionistic, filling in the vines with green. The intention was apparently to emphasize the Bacchic trails of ivy,

creating continuity with the view outside the window.

The repainting of the ceiling of the Park Drawing Room may be contemporary with the surviving paintings in the Street Drawing Room. Townley decided on a level of display unusual for the small front room of a Georgian townhouse, with the ceiling painted with five roundels depicting figures from classical mythology [29]. The paintings were executed by a certain William Hamilton (unrelated to the famous collector).[20] The large central roundel is copied from a decorative painting at the Domus Aurea in Rome,

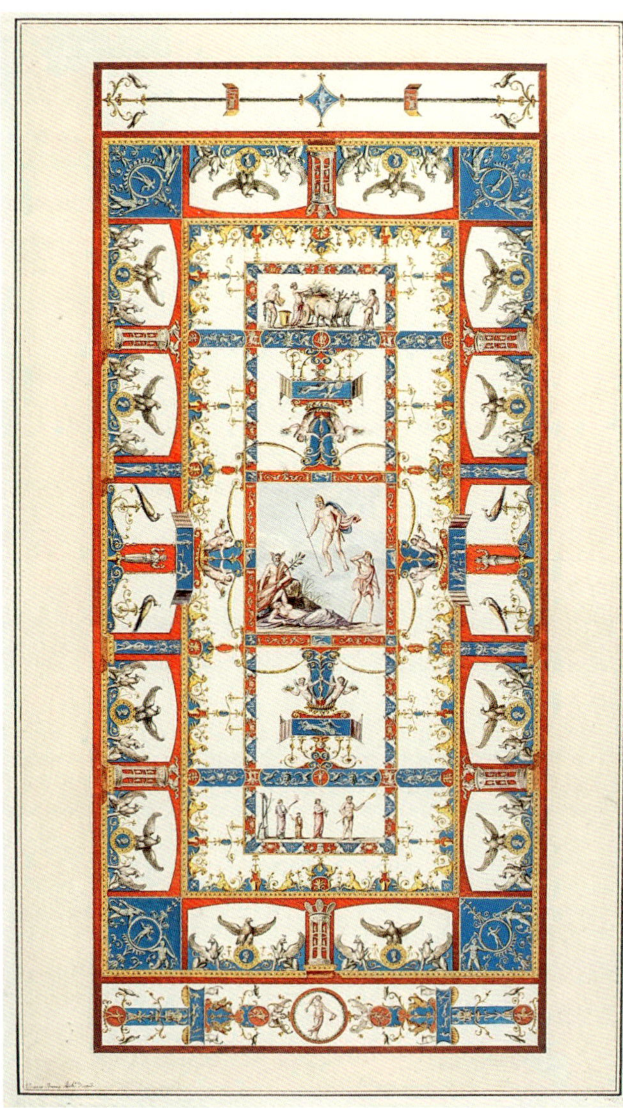

28. Vincenzo Brenna's spectacular watercolour drawing is thought to represent the lost vault of the Eagle Room at the Domus Aurea, with the scene of Bacchus and Ariadne at its centre

a composition believed to represent the discovery by Bacchus of Ariadne abandoned on Naxos.

The Domus Aurea, the palace of Emperor Nero, was built from AD 64, and frescoed with arabesque ornament, fantastical figures and mythological scenes such as this one. After the emperor's death and the partial destruction of the palace by fire, the Baths of Trajan were built on top, leaving the remaining palace interiors preserved underground for a millennium and a half. In 1480 they were rediscovered, and artists including Raphael went down under the baths, into the subterranean spaces below, looking for fresh source material for their own works of interior decoration. The spaces were like caves or *grotte*, so the resulting style was named *grottesca*, or 'grotesque'.

The frescoes of the Domus Aurea have now deteriorated, but in the later eighteenth century they were still spectacular tourist attractions. After their opening for excavations in 1772 they were visited by Casanova and the Marquis de Sade, among others, and probably by Townley as well. The connection with Nero's palace had not been made, so they were erroneously known as the ruins of the Baths of Titus. Townley had a personal connection with the site through Brenna: after accompanying Townley on his first Grand Tour, Brenna worked on a lavish publication recording the frescoes. With the paintings' subsequent deterioration, *Vestigia delle terme di Tito* (1776–78) remains an important record of their original state. Hamilton's source, however, was probably not the book but Brenna's original drawings, some of which were owned by Townley. His spectacular watercolour of the vault of the Eagle Room shows a scene of Bacchus at the centre [28].

The four other roundels stylistically derive from Brenna's original. Jupiter, the father of Bacchus, brandishes a lightning bolt and rides an eagle, inspired by the birds that feature as the

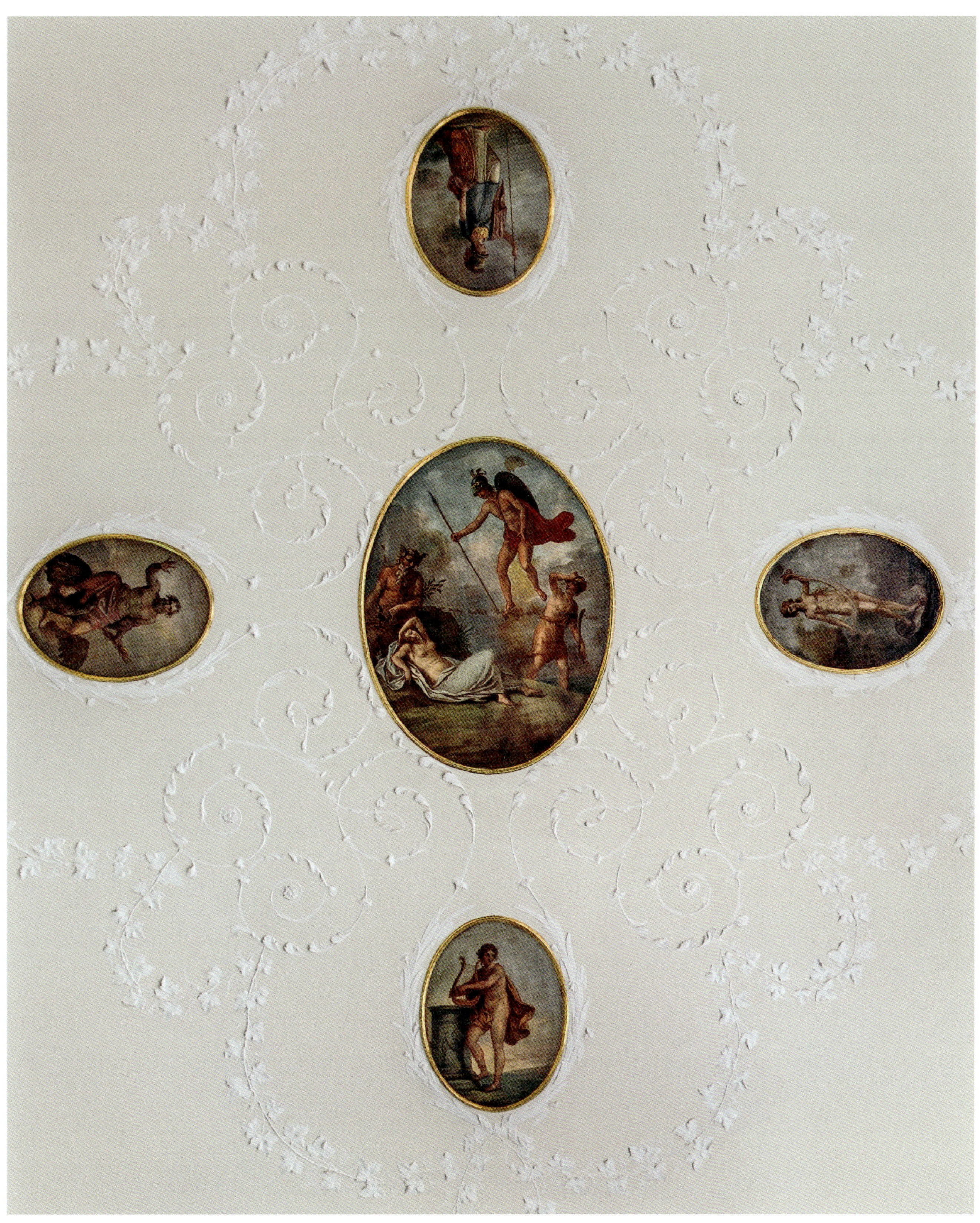

29. *The ceiling of the Street Drawing Room*

principal motif of the 'Eagle Room'. With his right
hand he gives a gesture of benediction. During
the subsequent use of the room for the display
of Indian sculptures, the viewer would have
been reminded of the *mudra*s of Hinduism and
Buddhism, as well as the hand gestures of classical
rhetoric.

The other roundels depict Venus, Athena and
Orpheus, who are chosen for their relationship
to Bacchus. Venus was the mother, by Bacchus,
of Priapus, while Athena saved Bacchus's heart
after his death, bringing about his resurrection.
These stories derived from poems traditionally
attributed to Orpheus, who was also believed to
be the inventor of the Bacchic mystery cult. In
the painting, he leans against a plinth decorated
with the same motif of instruments that features
in the frieze of the Dining Room downstairs. This
suggests that the paintings postdate the original
decoration of the house, and may be contemporary
with the repainting of the Park Drawing Room.

The two most reproduced images of Townley's
house are a pair of watercolours whose date,

authorship and purpose are unknown [30, 31].
They have been attributed to the draughtsman
William Chambers, unrelated to the architect,
on the basis of a reference to a 'drawing of the
Hall' in Townley's expenses.[21]

The watercolours depict an idealized view
of the Hall and Dining Room. The ceiling of
the Hall has a *trompe-l'œil* painting of funerary
vases and sarcophagi seen from below, while the
Neoclassical ceiling of the Dining Room has been
replaced with rectilinear beams, emphasizing the
regular symmetry of the sculptural arrangement.
Neither accords with either the present state of
the ceilings or an account of them by a visitor in
1784.[22] The drawings may visualize a redecoration
scheme that could have been executed if Townley
had lived longer. Together they show an essentially
antiquarian scheme for decoration, one that
develops the work by Michelangelo Simonetti
for Pope Pius VI at the Vatican, where antiquities
were to be displayed not in modern rooms but in
evocations of their original locations.

30 & 31. *Drawings by an unknown artist, c.1793–1804,
showing unexecuted decorative schemes for the entrance
hall and Dining Room*

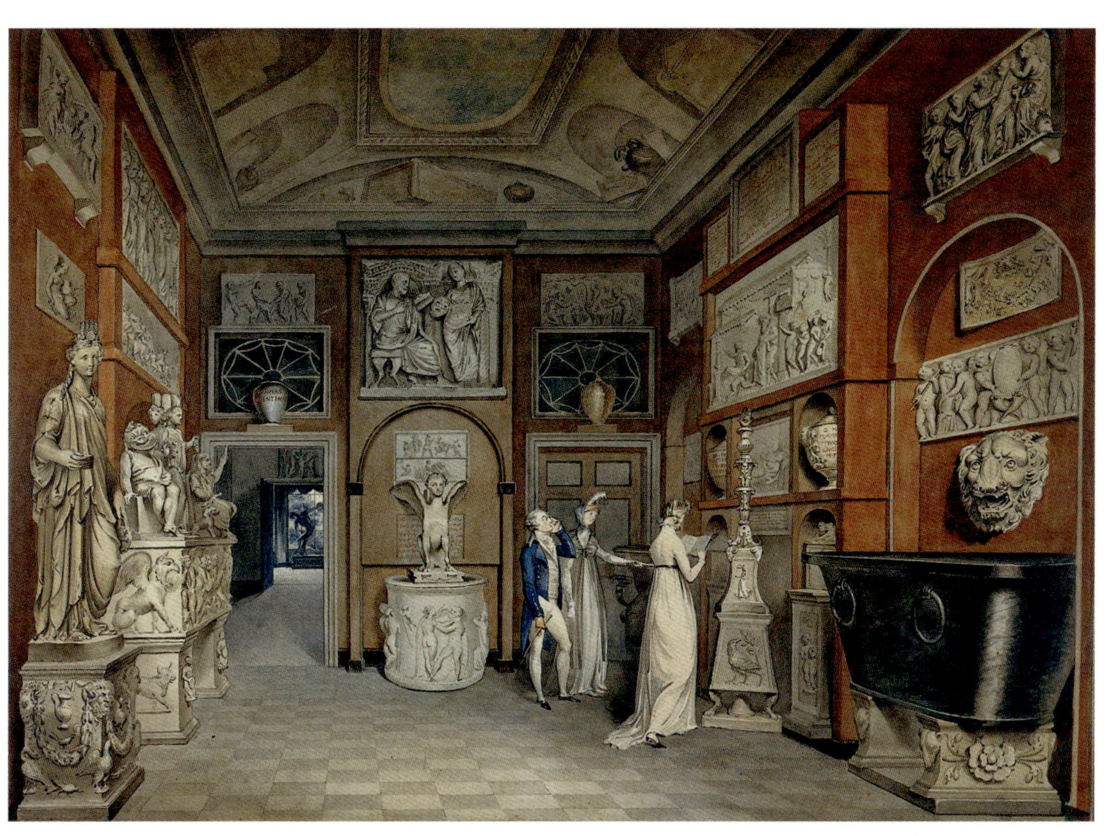

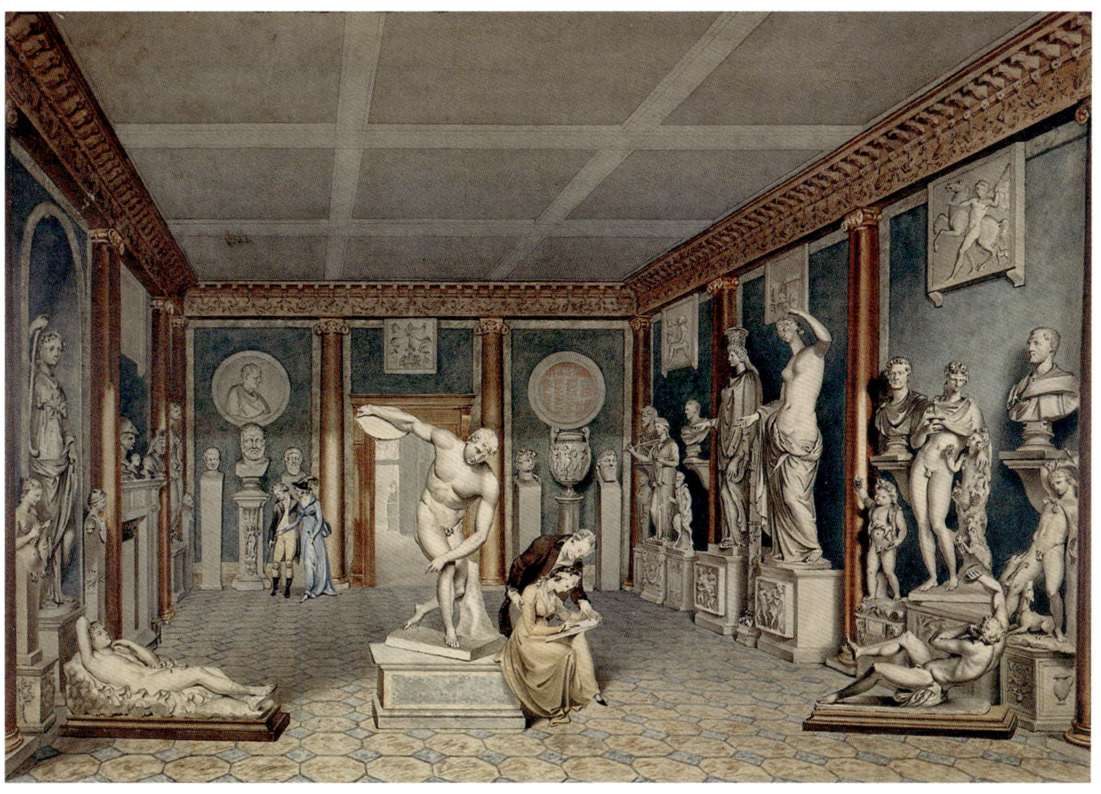

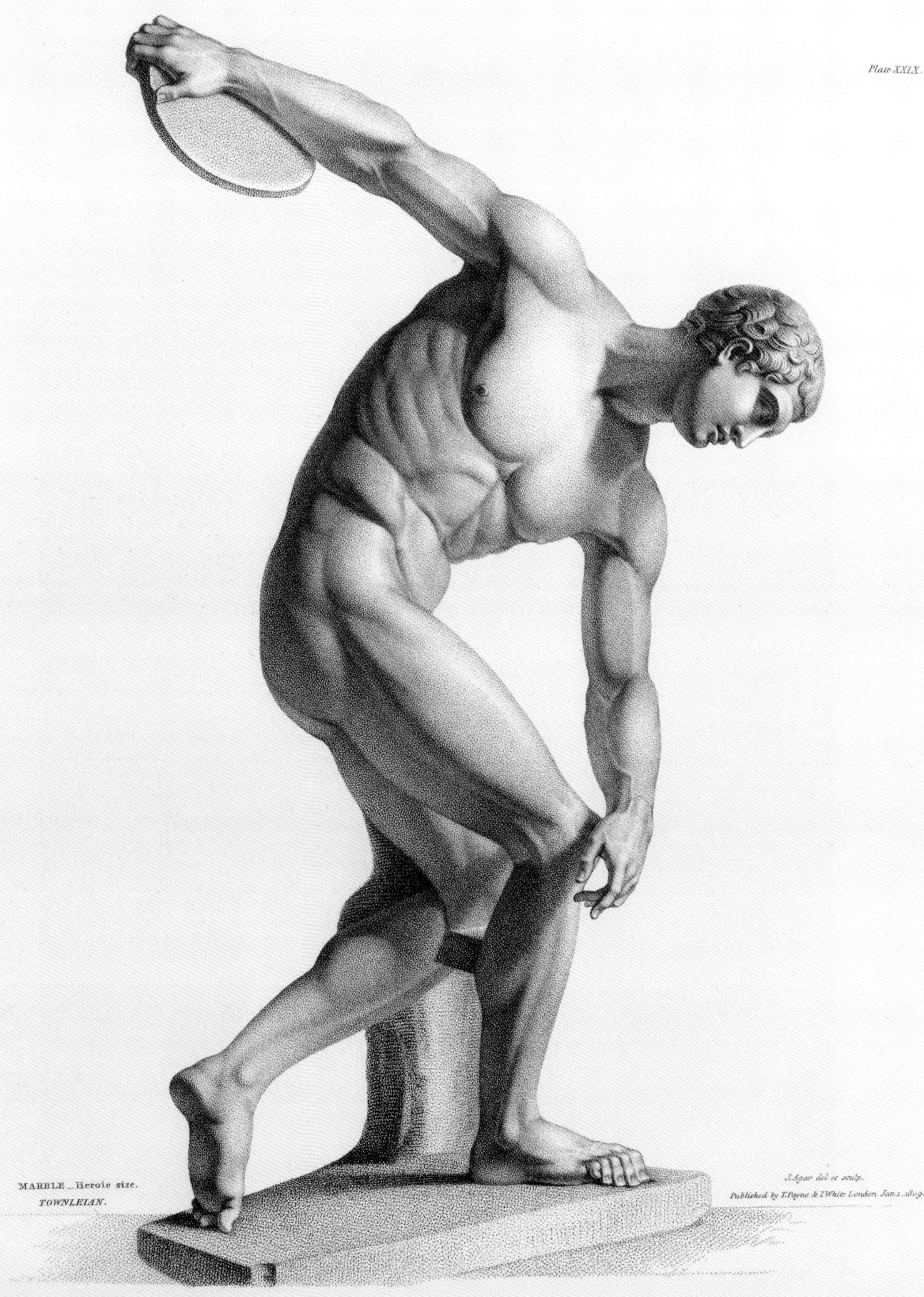
MARBLE __ Heroic size.
TOWNLEIAN.
J. Agar del et sculp.
Published by T. Payne & I. White London Jan.1.1809.

4. THE TOWNLEIAN COLLECTION

SEVEN PARK STREET WAS DESIGNED FOR THE display of one of the greatest art collections in Europe. It included non-Western and contemporary works, but the most prominent part was a group of over a hundred and fifty Roman marble sculptures. Not unique artworks in the modern sense, these were copies of lost Greek originals, preserving designs that are now otherwise known only from verbal descriptions. The sculptures represent an eighteenth-century attitude to art that has itself become lost to modernity.

Townley's distinction as a collector was threefold. First, he was more speculative in his perspective on the past, interested in mystery cults rather than social life or political history. Secondly, he was not exclusively interested in classical antiquity: indeed, he was the only European before the twentieth century to own a major work of Indian erotic art.[1] Thirdly, Townley took an unprecedented interest in aesthetic quality, and in collecting ancient copies rather than modern ones. His marbles were 'the cream, rather than the skimmed milk', in the words of other collectors.[3]

Historians often present Townley's collection as homogenous, but there seems to have been a distinction between the objects sacred to Bacchus and those sacred to *virtù*. The latter were on the first floor; objects with fine craftsmanship were in the Park Drawing Room, and those more interesting for the detail of their iconography were in the Library. The objects of mystery cult ritual were broadly on the ground floor, with the theatrical showpieces in the Dining Room. These differing priorities need to be registered, otherwise viewers are likely to be disappointed by the aesthetic dimension to the 'iconographic' works. One modern critic wrote that the navel of the Townley *Venus* [56] 'will distress both the lover of beauty and the historian of taste'.[2] Such a judgement is less likely to be made about the works displayed in the Park Drawing Room.

Anticipating modern taste, Townley was concerned to preserve as much original craftsmanship as possible. A visitor to the house recorded her feeling of being able to sense 'that inimitable character of the chisel of the Greek artists'.[4] At the time, most collectors would have fragmentary works freely finished by professional restorers, a practice that had been standard since the Renaissance. Townley was pioneering both in the value he placed on the hand of the artist and in the scrutiny with which he judged restorations [33]. In this he anticipated the prohibition on tampering with fragmentary originals that began in the nineteenth century. Even the 'Elgin Marbles'

32. *'Statue of a Discobolus' (Parlour Catalogue: Dining Room). The work, here engraved for* Specimens of Antient Sculpture *(1809), later became known as the* Townley Discobolus.

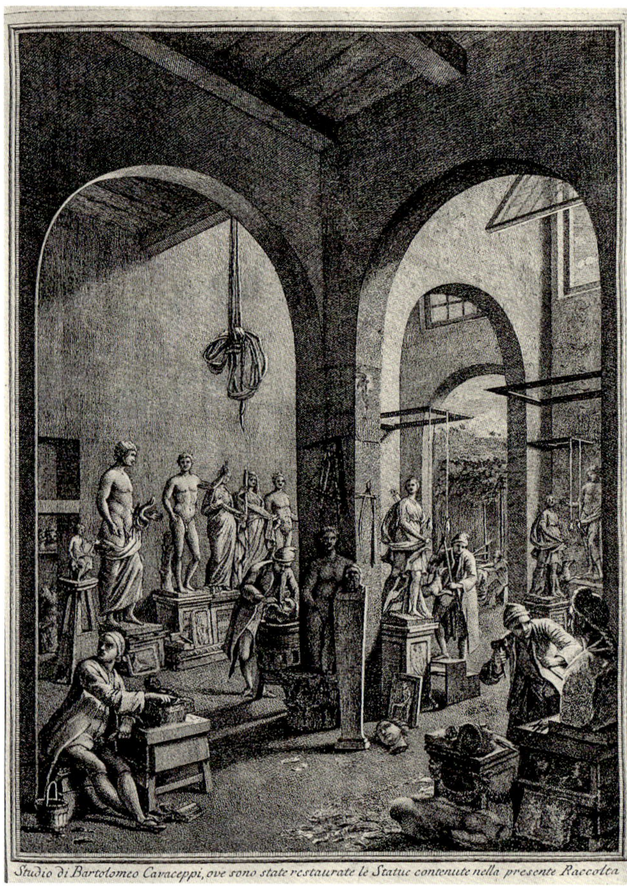

33. *Carlo Albacini executed most of the restoration of Townley's sculptures. He was trained in this workshop, run by Bartolomeo Cavaceppi.*

would have been restored had the sculptors John Flaxman and Antonio Canova, both visitors to Townley's house, not persuaded the British Museum in 1818 to leave them in their original state. It is probable that, if he had lived on until then, Townley himself would have joined them in this campaign.

Townley's collection was formed in various ways. The art market in London was already a major force, and some purchases were made at Christie's from the sales of other collectors. He also bought through dealers in Rome, most notably the rivals Thomas Jenkins and Gavin Hamilton. They sent drawings and descriptions,

corresponding extensively with Townley, who purchased by a kind of mail order. Another type of collecting was in person, during Townley's three trips to Italy. These visits demonstrate three stages of his progress as a collector.

The first trip began conventionally, a Grand Tour as anyone in his aristocratic position would be expected to conduct, although Townley was a little older than would have been common. He departed London in August 1767, travelling through Paris for the first time since his adolescence. He then went on to Florence, and at the Uffizi would have seen the original of the *Dancing Faun* and Medici *Venus*, familiar from the entrance hall of Towneley Hall. He arrived in Rome on Christmas Day, and remained there until August 1768, with the exception of a month in Naples and a visit to the sublime ruins of Paestum. His return trip took him through the remaining major cities of northern Italy, before arriving in London in November.[5]

During his first Grand Tour, Townley's patronage was mostly conventional and diffuse: he bought bound collections of engravings, Baroque paintings, and drawings of art and topographical ones of architecture that he commissioned. This was the course of most previous Grand Tourists, purchasing marbles while in Rome, and then returning to Britain never to trouble oneself again with the pursuit of *virtù*.

The itinerary of the second tour was quite different, and marked Townley out as a collector with unprecedented vision, energy and means. In particular he had his sights set on Sicily, which was important to him for the opportunities it offered for purchasing Greek coins. He left London in November 1771, arriving in Rome in February 1772, going on to Sicily in May, via Naples. On a return trip to Naples he purchased the bust best known as '*Clytie*' [34] from the collection of the Duke of Laurenzano, which would become the

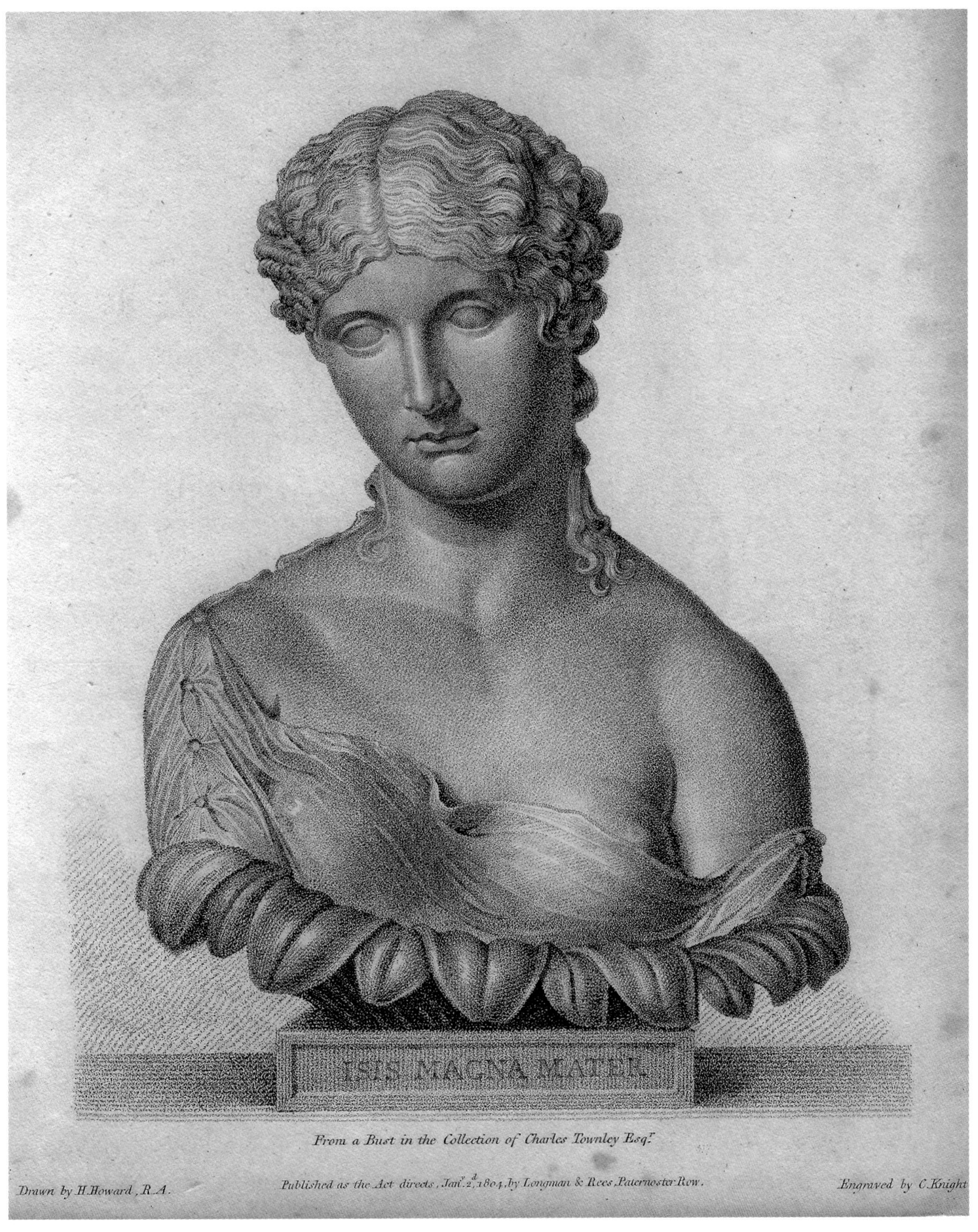

34. *When this bust arrived at Park Street from Naples, it was known as
'Agrippina'. By 1781, however, it was known as 'Clytie', a character in
Ovid's* Metamorphoses *who turns into a flower. Townley changed his
mind soon after, and referred to it as 'Isis' until the end of his life. It is
now in the British Museum, and contemporary scholars believe it is a
portrait, possibly of Mark Antony's daughter. This engraving, from a
drawing by Henry Howard, was published in 1804, and later appeared
as an illustration for the entry on drawing in Rees's* Cyclopædia.

most famous object in his own collection. He returned to Sicily in October, and stayed until the new year, acquiring over 1,500 coins. After a further bout of coin shopping in Naples, he returned to Rome in February 1773, where he remained until November. He stayed in Florence and arrived in Paris in February 1774, staying there until May, when he returned to London.[6] The coins that characterize the purchases on the second tour were a major part of Townley's collection but have often been overlooked. One reason for his interest was that they offered a chance to see authentic Greek craftsmanship, without the Roman filter that applied to sculptures. They were also relatively dateable, and therefore offered a chance to reconstruct the chronological progress of iconography in the ancient world. The majority of illustrations in d'Hancarville's *Recherches* (see Appendix A) are not the famous sculptures but the designs and iconography of Townley's medals.

Townley's first two trips to Italy were exploratory, but his third and final one had a much more specific objective. Pius VI became Pope in 1775, and was keeping a closer eye on exports, so that Townley's dealer Gavin Hamilton had to hide the best objects and sell them as 'contraband'.[7] Townley could not send an object back from London to Rome if he did not like it, and so had to be sure before making an expensive purchase. In November 1776 he had to decide about a double purchase amounting to £1,000 – two figures that came to be known as '*Thalia*' [53] and the 'Townley *Venus*' [56]. He departed from London, going directly to Rome, and arriving by mid January. Apart from a week in Naples in March he stayed in the Eternal City for his whole visit, before leaving in April, having confirmed the purchase, and making many more.[8]

A fourth visit was planned in 1779, but the Anglo-French War (1778–83) made this impossible, and indeed limited Townley's

collecting ability because of the damage it caused to the economy. Most of his income came from the rents from his estates, and with a war these rents started falling. The Catholic Relief Act of 1778 may have started removing penalties on Catholics, but a double land tax was still enforced. As a result, the majority of Townley's collecting took place in the single decade between 1768 and 1778. Afterwards, book collecting was his priority: a posthumous account describes his time as 'chiefly occupied in arranging a library, which comprised almost every curious work on the subject of the arts'.[9] Nevertheless, there were many notable purchases made while Townley was in residence at Park Street. Townley's dealers in Rome would send drawings to London of the latest discoveries, possibly made with a camera obscura. Townley was offered first refusal among the collectors of the city, as happened when a *Discobolus* [32] and a *Hercules* were discovered together. Townley chose the former, and the latter went to the next most powerful collector. This situation required some diplomacy when his rivals were more aristocratic and richer than himself. In this case he broke the news gently by letter, framing the *Hercules* as his rival's first choice, when in fact it was his second.[10]

What then was the moment of revelation, transforming Townley from a conventional Grand Tourist, albeit an especially educated and wealthy one, to the most powerful collector outside Italy? The answer must be the visit to Naples that Townley made from Rome in March 1768, during his first tour. There he would have discovered the fresh excavations of Herculaneum and Pompeii. Excavations at the former had begun in 1738 and at the latter only in 1755, with constant new discoveries relating to Roman daily life. During this visit, Townley bought black-market copies of the books published about the recent excavations, as well as subscribing to a treatise on the collection of William Hamilton by Baron d'Hancarville.[11]

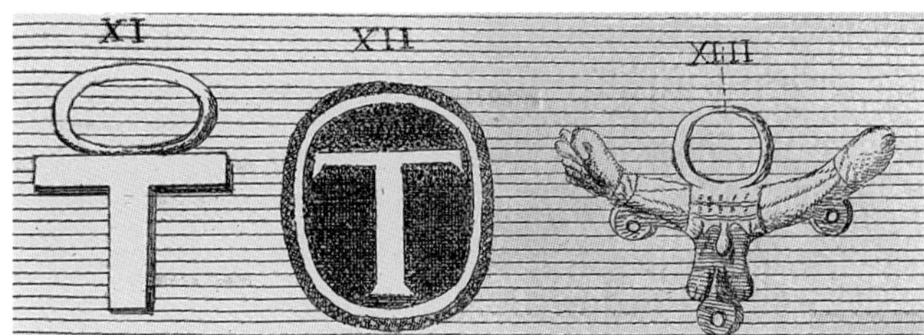

35. The priapic works that Townley acquired from Cardinal Albani are unlocated in the collection of the British Museum, but the curators believe that they may be a group of horse-trapping phalluses, of which one is illustrated here in d'Hancarville's Recherches *(I, p. 183). It is used to demonstrate one of the book's more provocative theories, that a phallus, joined with a hand giving the fig sign, was the source of the ankh, and by implication the Christian cross.*

The great collector of vases William Hamilton had been British Envoy in Naples for four years, during which he devoted unprecedented attention to antiquities. Hamilton was not present during Townley's visit, but Townley met the circle of scholars that centred on the Palazzo Portici, which contained a museum of antiquities. The palace was the home of the Bourbon Prince Felipe, the son of Charles III of Spain, who had been excluded from royal succession owing to a mental illness that manifested in a sexual mania.

The Portici scholars had an unusual interest in erotic art, and the museum contained the first dedicated room for such works, which survives to this day. Townley acquired the Portici scholars' interest in prohibited imagery, and indeed one of his first purchases on returning to Rome was a group of depictions of the phallic god Priapus.[12] These were from the collection of Cardinal Albani [35], whose librarian was Johann Joachim Winckelmann. Fortuitously, Winckelmann was away from the city at the time, and the purchase was made through Albani's mistress, who was not friendly with the Prussian scholar.

Over the next few decades, Townley purchased hundreds of marbles, many of which were primarily notable for unusual iconography that

he interpreted in terms of ancient mystery cults. When his collection was donated to the British Museum it contained many more works with sexual themes, and these became part of the 'Secretum', a special collection analogous to the 'Enfer' at the Bibliothèque nationale and the 'Private Case' of the British Library. The Secretum was segregated some time in the late 1830s, and became officially codified in 1865.

When Townley's collection became a public part of the British Museum in the nineteenth century, mention of its sexual dimension was mostly expunged. Contrastingly, it is often claimed in modern discussions of Townley that his entire approach to antiquarianism was sexual, based around Priapism. However, it was Bacchus, not Priapus, who was the presiding deity of No. 7 Park Street, with Priapus playing an important but secondary role as Bacchus's son. The modern view seems to be based on the assumption that an open attitude to sexuality must necessarily overwhelm a multifaceted personal mythology. This assumption makes the modern view arguably as inhibited as the nineteenth-century one.

Aside from his collection of marbles, there was a significant collection of Old Master paintings and drawings. This included works by Salvator Rosa, Guido Reni and Jusepe de Ribera. The highlight, at least in twenty-first-century estimation, was *The Destruction and Sack of the Temple of Jerusalem* by Nicolas Poussin [36]. Commissioned by Francesco Barberini, it was first owned by Cardinal Richelieu. The painting must have stayed in Rome, because when Richelieu died it made its way into the hands of Thomas Jenkins, who then sold it to Townley.

Townley's paintings were sold by his family after his death, and the *Destruction* disappeared until 1994. Unfortunately for its owners, it lost its authorship in the intervening two centuries, being listed as 'attributed to Pietro Testa' at auction. Sold

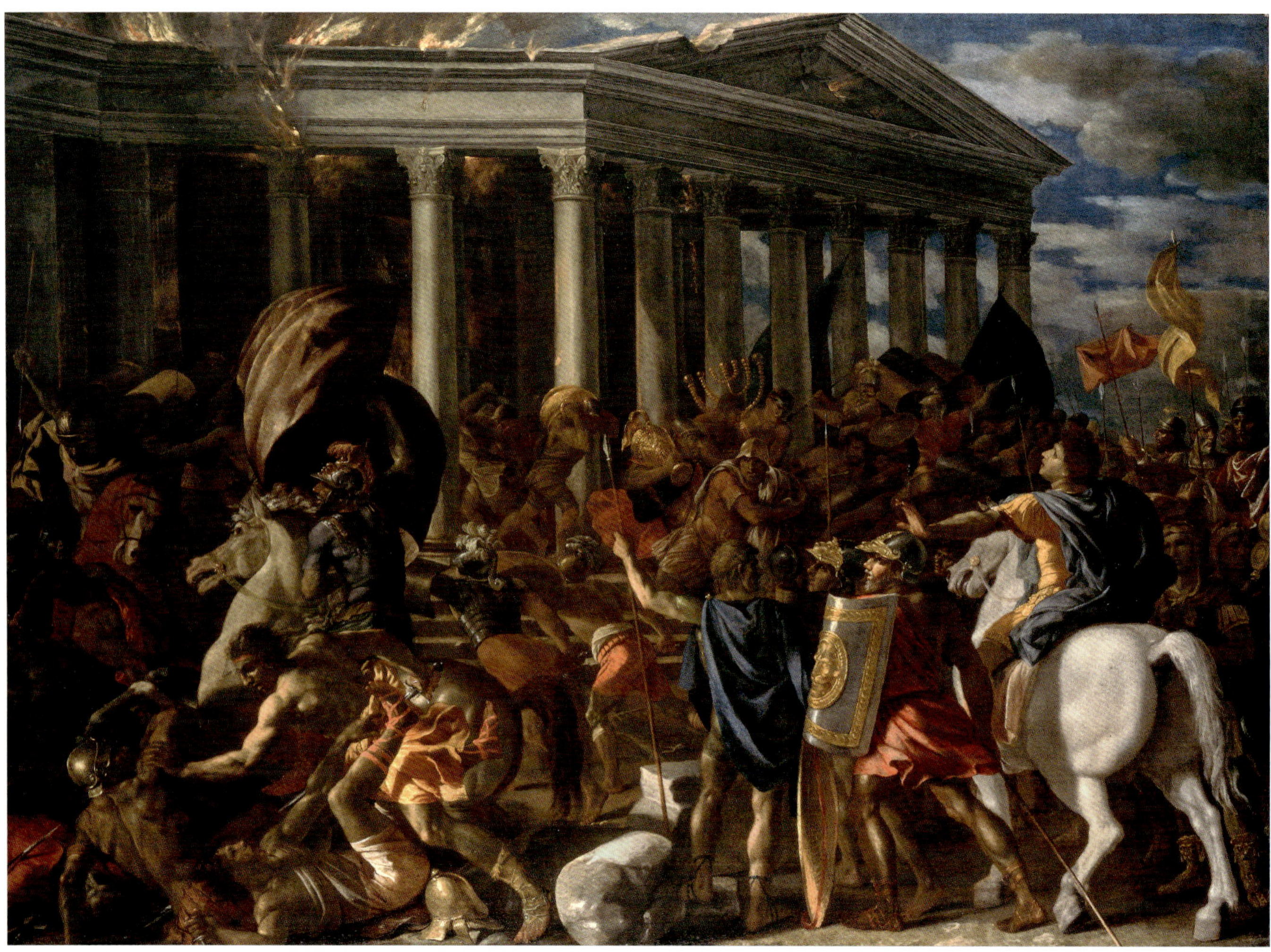

36. The Destruction and Sack of the Temple of Jerusalem *by Nicolas Poussin, 1625–26. Poussin depicts an unprecedented subject: Titus, later Roman Emperor, attempts unsuccessfully to prevent the ruin of Jerusalem by his soldiers in AD 70. Townley's purchase of the work may have been inspired by his lifelong opposition to religious bigotry.*

for a fraction of its value, it was then cleaned and reattributed to the French master. In 1998 it was bought for the Israel Museum in Jerusalem for £4.5 million. The connection to Townley has not previously been made: if it had, it seems likely the painting would have sold for even more.

Townley's collection was also an instrument by which its owner rose to gain entrée into the highest circles of the intellectual establishment. This took many years: during his first few years at Park Street he was mostly involved in assisting Baron d'Hancarville on the *Recherches* and he was comparatively isolated. He still had fashionable friends, such as Richard and Maria Cosway: he gave away the bride at their wedding in 1781.[13] But the late eighteenth century was an era of clubbability, and Townley was not yet a member of either the Society of Antiquaries or the Society of Dilettanti, despite being more erudite than most of their members. But, with the *Recherches* finished and the Baron departing late in 1785, Townley could focus on the London scene, joining

in the following year both the clubs of which he
was a glaring absentee.

First, in February 1786, he became a fellow
of the Society of Antiquaries, proposed by the
President, George Townshend, Earl of Leicester,
and seconded by Joseph Banks. Banks had
risen to fame as the official botanist on the first
circumnavigation of the globe by James Cook
in 1768–71, and at this time was in charge of
government policy on the sciences as President
of the Royal Society. Townley's Catholicism may
have been problematic to the Society's patron,
George III, but both Townshend and Banks would
have seen in him a kindred spirit, born into wealth
and status but using his means to further human
knowledge. The Society of Antiquaries was then
based at Somerset House; today it is located at
Burlington House.

The other key club to join was the Society of
Dilettanti [37]. This was a rather different milieu to
the Antiquaries, a strange mix of dining club and
scholarly publishing house. Their meetings were
above a pub in Pall Mall, but the wealth of the
members sponsored such landmark projects as the
archaeological work of James Stuart and Nicholas
Revett, published as *Antiquities of Athens* in 1762.
The club survives today within Brooks's Club.

Townley was proposed for the Society of
Dilettanti in June 1786 by Richard Payne Knight;
the election was unanimous. Townley's earlier
absence may seem surprising, but a large part
of the Society's early activity was a ridiculing of
Catholicism. That generation of Dilettanti was
dying off in the 1780s, and it may have been their
absence that permitted Townley's admission.
Furthermore, in 1785 Richard Payne Knight was
using ideas from the *Recherches* for an essay titled
Discourse on the Worship of Priapus, published
through the Society in 1787. He may have
wanted his mentor's support for the provocative
publication.

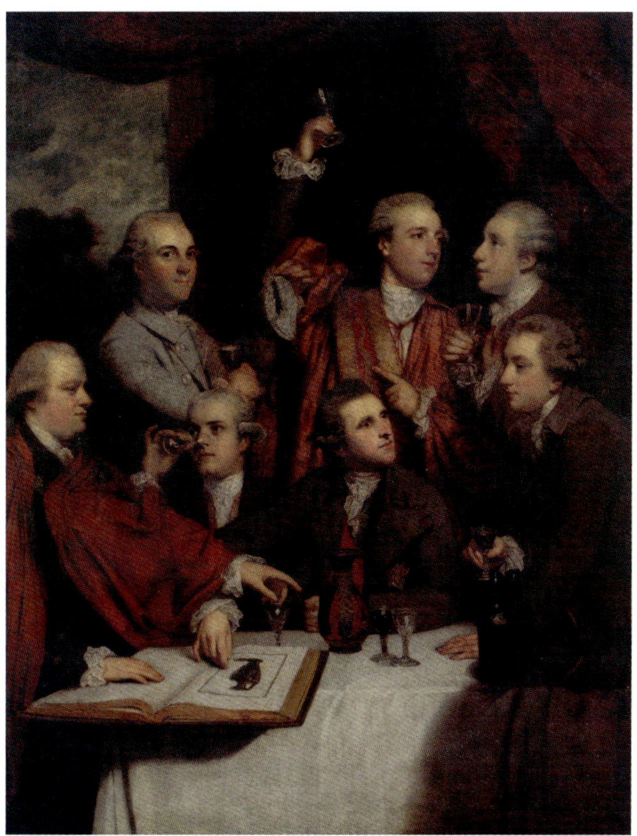

37. *Joshua Reynolds painted this group portrait of the
Society of Dilettanti in 1777–79. William Hamilton is in the
centre, displaying the first volume of d'Hancarville's treatise
on his collection. On his jacket he wears a star, referring to
the name of the tavern where the Society met – The Star
and Garter, on Pall Mall.*

Through the Dilettanti, Townley met the first
President of the Royal Academy, Joshua Reynolds.
The Academy had been founded in 1768 by a
group of painters, sculptors and architects as an
art school and exhibition society, and immediately
it became the most important institution in the
British art world. Reynolds had painted two group
portraits of the Dilettanti in 1778, which are
now in Brooks's Club. In 1788 he was to paint
another, with Townley, Payne Knight and the 11th
Duke of Norfolk (a distantly related successor
to Mary Howard's husband), but it was never
executed.

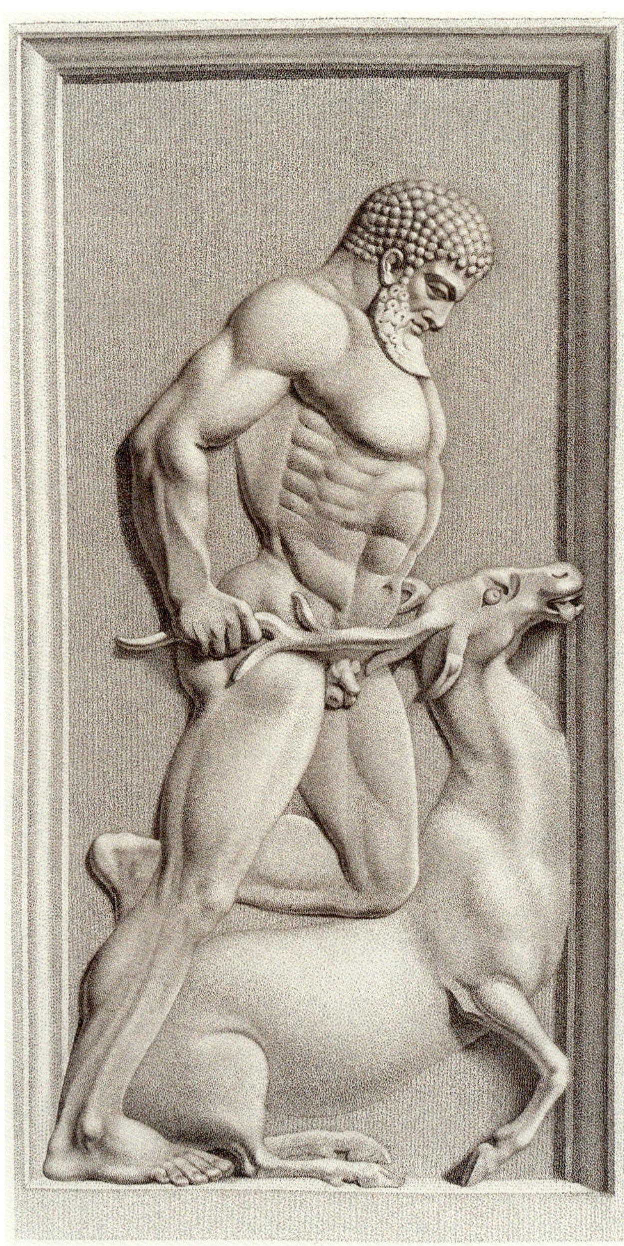

38. *The illustrations to* Specimens *(1809) were supervised by Townley: in his notes to the plates, Richard Payne Knight often criticizes them for privileging aesthetics over accuracy. In the case of this relief, showing 'Hercules & the deer', the engraving shows the work complete, when in fact the original was cracked and imperfect. The engravings are the major interest of the whole project, and have been described as 'the finest ever made of sculpture' (Clarke, Penny [1982], p. 149).*

Nevertheless, Reynolds became a regular fixture of the social life at Park Street. Townley's Sunday dinners became famous social occasions, attended by Reynolds, the painter Johan Zoffany and the sculptor Joseph Nollekens among others. These were apparently less formal that most dinners of this milieu: Nollekens was usually not invited on account of his famously profane conversation. When Reynolds died in 1791 Townley attended his funeral, though he was not a pallbearer, as has sometimes been claimed.[14]

Townley's last major addition to his antiquities was the *Discobolus*, or discus-thrower [32].[15] Since work on the Museo Pio-Clementino began in 1771, the energy and power of its curators, the Visconti family, had dominated the trade in ancient marbles. The availability of the *Discobolus* in 1792 seems to have been in some way political: according to the dealer who sold it to Townley, the Pope was hoping to secure British support against the threat of Napoleonic France.[16]

Another version of the lost bronze by the Greek sculptor Myron already existed, the Massimo *Discobolus*, later purchased by Adolf Hitler. However, Townley's was slightly different: in particular, the head on the figure faces away from the discus. This became the authoritative version of the work: when a third version, in the Vatican, was restored, the head of Townley's was used, rather that of the Massimo version.[17]

Townley was appointed to the Society of Dilettanti's Committee of Publication in 1799. The result was *Specimens of Antient Sculpture* [38], which presented spectacular illustrations of works from the collections of Townley, Knight, Hope, Lord Lansdowne and other British collectors. In terms of its argument, the publication refrained from discussing religious and symbolical meanings that were such a major part of the research of Townley and Knight, leaving that for another volume. Instead it embodied their *virtuoso* side,

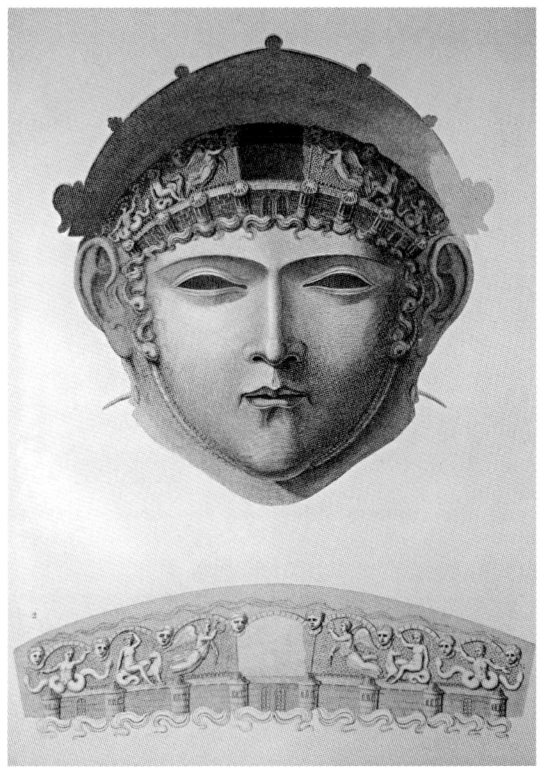

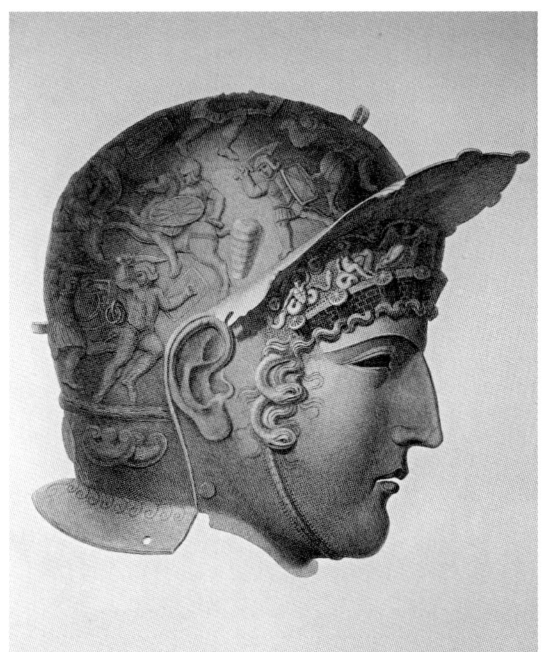

39. *Two engravings of the 'Ribchester Helmet' from Townley's article of 1799. Although it was extensively decorated, he was mainly interested in the visor, interpreting the three figures as representing Venus, Cybele and Medusa.*

focusing on the objects in terms of their execution and preservation.

Townley did not live to see the project to its completion in 1809. Knight took advantage of Townley's absence to fill the book's text with critical stories, disparaging the opinions of his former mentor. At this time Knight was in the process of decimating his scholarly reputation by arguing against the artistic merit of the 'Elgin Marbles', and the text of *Specimens* offered him another public forum in which to posture intellectually.[18] Townley's reputation has certainly suffered greatly from this mercenary friendship, even if Knight ultimately proved a worse enemy to himself.

Townley was at work on another book, describing the collections of ancient marbles across Britain. Like *Specimens*, it was finished by someone else – James Dallaway, as *Anecdotes of the Arts in England* (1800). It was the first such project, though until recently Townley's pioneering work had gone unrecognized.[19] Townley's only completed publication in his lifetime was a discussion of a bronze helmet discovered in Ribchester [39], not far from his family home in Lancashire. This appeared as a pamphlet in April 1799, and gave a public glimpse of his interest in the occult.[20] In it he proposed that the helmet was created in honour of Isis, the 'Magna Mater', representing her aspects as a generator (Venus), preserver (Cybele) and destroyer (Medusa).

Townley finally reached the summit of intellectual prestige when he was made a Trustee of the British Museum in 1791. Again, Joseph Banks was the instigator of his appointment. For the rest of his life Townley's diaries show him attending trustee meetings, although his appointment seems to have come at first as a surprise: he wrote to one of his proposers that 'I have no pretensions to it either from rank or the requisite abilities'.[21] But he must have been a success, and he became on

particularly good terms with the Revd Richard
Penneck, Keeper of the Reading Room, who
bequeathed Townley a Persian manuscript on his
death in 1803.

Townley's trusteeship and Penneck's death give
a window of a little over a decade in which one
of the most colourful acquisitions arrived at Park
Street. In the second chapter we left the head of
Francis Towneley at the top of a pole in Temple
Bar, covered in pitch, a warning to Catholics of the
consequences of sedition. The great-nephew of the
head's former owner was understandably unhappy
to have such a landmark still in his home city, and
so formed a plan. Townley waited for a particularly
stormy night and then went to Temple Bar with
a few companions including Penneck. The party
removed the head from the pole, so that people
would assume the storm to be responsible. Before
its interment in the family chapel at Towneley Hall,
the head was kept in secret at the house on Park
Street, where it would have joined a number of
other severed heads, albeit made of marble.[22]

Townley's expertise was sought regarding not
only historical works of art but also contemporary
ones. In 1802 he was appointed to the new
'Committee of Taste', which supervised the
design of public sculpture commemorating naval
and military victories. Every new monument in
St Paul's Cathedral had to pass their scrutiny.
He was thus central to the establishment of the
concept of 'simplicity', which would cause conflict
with sculptors in later decades.[23] Nevertheless,
Townley's appointment is evidence that he did not
see the antique simply as a window on to another
world. It was also a mirror of our own, in the spirit
of his motto that 'knowing the old things, you will
understand the new'.

Townley made a will in November 1802 that
bequeathed all of his collection to the British
Museum, provided they 'exhibit these Antiquities
to the public to the greatest advantage'.[24] He added

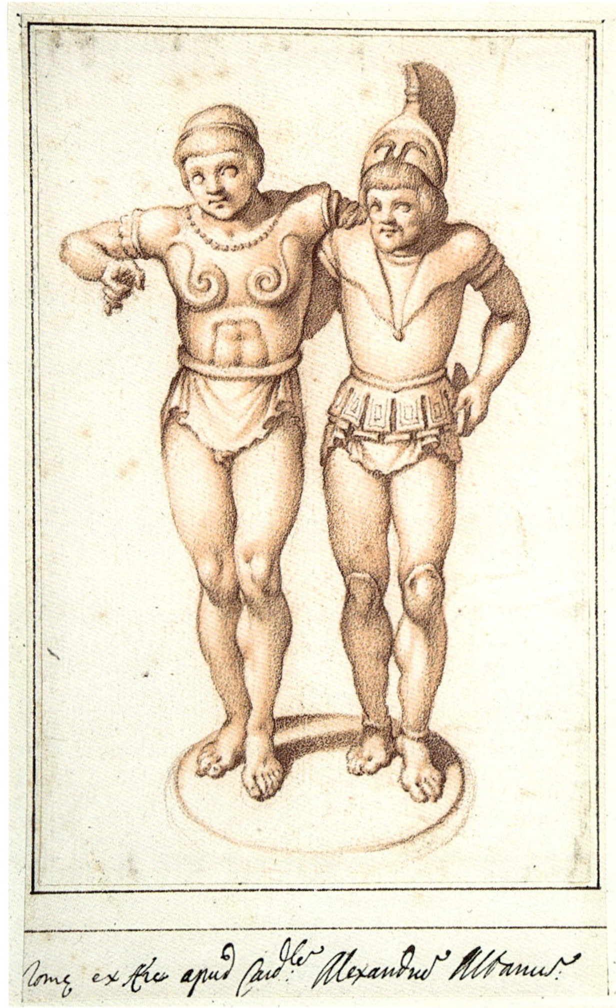

40. *A drawing in red chalk of an Etruscan candelabrum
finial, c.1620–40, from one of Townley's volumes of
Cassiano's* Museo Cartaceo

a codicil in December 1804 giving his heirs five
years from his death to build an equivalent private
gallery before the marbles were given to the nation.

Townley's final major purchase came in
1804 – four albums from the Paper Museum of
Cassiano dal Pozzo. The Paper Museum (*Museo
Cartaceo*) was assembled by the seventeenth-
century scholar and patron as a visual assembly of
human knowledge [40]. It was not unlike the many
drawings and engravings that Townley himself

commissioned of his own objects and those of others. Most of Cassiano's Paper Museum had been shipped to England by George III in 1762, from which shipment Townley's four volumes derived.

After Townley died, the trustees of the British Museum mobilized to persuade the Towneley family not to follow the course laid out in the codicil to the will. The museum purchased the marbles for £20,000, a vast sum which may also have been symbolic, as the museum had bought its founding collection from the heirs to Hans Sloane for the same amount. The Towneley family were left the remainder of the collection, including the bronzes, the volumes of Cassiano's Paper Museum, and Townley's own commissioned drawings. His brother Edward was given a trusteeship to the museum, with his uncle John to follow upon Edward's death. Nollekens remembered that John looked forlorn at being denied the opportunity to bring the marbles to Towneley Hall.[25] The Prime Minister William Pitt was in favour of the purchase, and in June a petition was 'very favourably received' in the House of Commons, indicating the popular esteem that the collection had achieved by the end of Townley's life.[26] A committee was appointed the following February to organize the transport of the marbles from Park Street to Bloomsbury. They were installed in the building intended for the Egyptian antiquities, and the new gallery was opened in June 1808.

The conventional narrative in historical accounts has been that the 'Elgin Marbles' immediately overshadowed Townley's collection. These had already been on display at Lord Elgin's house from 1807; they were shown at Burlington House from 1811, and finally at the British Museum from 1817. The 'Elgin Marbles' represented original Greek art, rather than Roman copies, and made for a more immediate aesthetic experience. A less discussed but arguably

more important factor in the ascendance of the 'Elgin Marbles' was that they could be used as an instrument of British nationalism, treating them as a model of craftsmanship. The idea was that, by studying the hand of ancient Greek genius, modern British artists could acquire their skills, advancing beyond their Continental contemporaries. This required the erasure of all cultural content, so no such use could be made of the Townley collection.

However, the abruptness of the change in esteem has been overstated by scholars of the period. In 1828, the Keeper of Prints and Drawings at the British Museum wrote that it was only the professors who preferred the 'Elgin Marbles'. Ten years after the Townley collection had been supposedly rendered irrelevant, the general public still preferred it.[27] In 1836 and 1846 the Townley marbles were the subject of a major two-volume catalogue by the museum's librarian.[28] In 1854, Gustav Waagen described Townley's collection of antiquities as 'the most important of all' in his *Treasures of Art in Great Britain*.[29] In the late Victorian period, bronze copies were made of works from the collection, including the Townley Vase, of which two are currently at 14 Queen Anne's Gate (see Appendix B). It is certainly true that the Townley marbles became less of a cultural icon over the following decades, but there was no simple cause and effect.

Townley's reputation reached its nadir in the mid twentieth century. In 1950, he was judged not to be of sufficient merit to warrant a blue plaque at his former home.[30] However, this changed in 1977, when the Wolfson Foundation made an award to the British Museum to create a gallery for the Roman antiquities in the Townley collection. The gallery opened in 1983, in rooms directly below the Duveen Gallery that hosts the 'Elgin Marbles'. The rooms, however, were not regarded as a curatorial success, and were criticized in the press

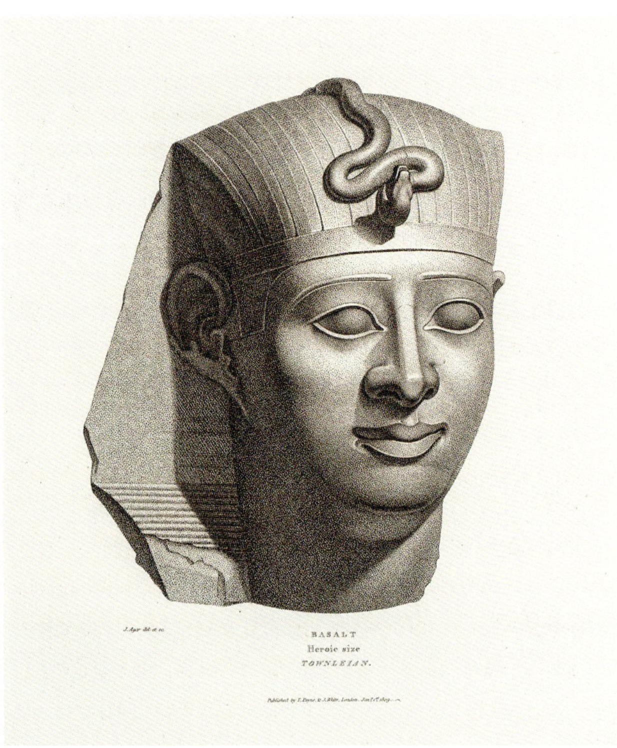

41. *'Isis in Basaltes' (Parlour Catalogue: Street Parlour), engraved for* Specimens of Antient Sculpture *(1809). It is a green siltstone head, now thought to be a portrait of Nectanebo I, from Townley's collection of Egyptian sculpture, now at the British Museum.*

for their aesthetic insensitivity.[32] Knowledge of this part of the collection was advanced through several publications by the Keeper of Greek and Roman Antiquities, Brian Cook. In 1985, a blue plaque was finally installed on 14 Queen Anne's Gate. Today the address is one of the most significant parts of London in terms of blue plaques – six on a single street.[31]

The Townley bequest uniquely features in every curatorial department of the British Museum, but the resulting divisions are the antithesis of Townley's syncretic approach. All but the most spectacular examples of Roman antiquity remain in the galleries of 1983, which were permanently closed in 2000. At the time of writing, almost all Townley's non-Roman art is in storage. The dispersal and entombment of the Townley collection at the British Museum has been controversial, inciting vitriolic emotion from scholars in the otherwise placid field of eighteenth-century antiquarianism.

Some might be tempted to wonder if it would have been better for the collection never to have gone to the British Museum. The trustees certainly meant well; on becoming one in 1814, Knight would bequeath his own collection in the same manner. But if Townley's family had been able to build the kind of private gallery imagined in the 1805 codicil, whether it was in London or Lancashire, the collection would have preserved its identity, immune from the expansions, rebuilding and modernization of the British Museum, as well as the vicissitudes of popular taste.

However, considering the circumstances, it may be that the museum was ultimately the best place for the collection. The Towneley family was rich, but perhaps not quite rich enough to build a lavish sculpture gallery. Even if they had, collections that remained in a family were precarious, in constant danger of being sold off. The collection of Townley's rival, the 2nd Earl of Shelburne, 1st Marquess of Lansdowne, stayed in the family, but the sculptures were dispersed at a sale in 1930, and the Lansdowne *Hercules* is now the pride of the Getty Villa in Los Angeles.

Even when a quasi-museum was established, there was still no guarantee of survival. Townley's friend Francis Douce owned a collection of Gothic ivory carvings that could be described as the counterpart to Townley's collection in the world of Gothic sculpture. Like Townley's, Douce's interest was in using the works to reconstruct the beliefs of lost societies. Unlike Townley, his dream of being survived by an independent museum was realised in the 'Doucean Museum' at Goodrich Court. In the 1870s, however, the whole collection was sold and dispersed; the British Museum has been gradually retrieving it ever since.

When Townley's uncle and heir John died, his son Peregrine needed to raise money for building projects at his new inheritance of Towneley Hall. He sold his father's library and the remaining antiquarian objects of Charles Townley's collection in 1814. Drawings, prints and books were sold in a series of separate sales from 1812 to 1817, and the British Museum chose not to acquire them, resulting in their dispersal. The remainder of the *'biblioteca Townleiana'* was sold in 1883.[33] That sale was described as 'one of the most deplorable dispersions of an old family library'.[34]

In fact the timing of the 1814 sale was arguably the greatest stroke of fortune for the unity of the antiquarian objects, because Townley's reputation at the British Museum was still at its zenith, and the institution bought the entire collection. If the sale had been made later, when Townley was no longer the pre-eminent benefactor to the museum, it is probable that no effort would have been made to acquire diverse objects, many of them of little material value. Instead, the miscellany remains under the same institutional umbrella as the marbles, united by their shared presence at Park Street. With its Egyptian and Indian works, the geographical diversity of the Townley collection was an importance aspect of its character that has also been preserved [41, 42].

The forecast for the collection at the British Museum is surely hopeful. *The Burlington Magazine* recently proposed uniting the Roman antiquities in the vacant Reading Room.[35] Reminiscent of the Pantheon, and the Sala Rotonda at the Museo Pio-Clementino, this arrangement would certainly meet with Townley's enthusiastic approval. Unlike the 'Elgin Marbles', his collection never became an instrument of nationalism, making it also an ideal means with which to articulate a non-isolationist British heritage. The long-term future of the 'Elgin Marbles', meanwhile, is increasingly uncertain: for the sake of public

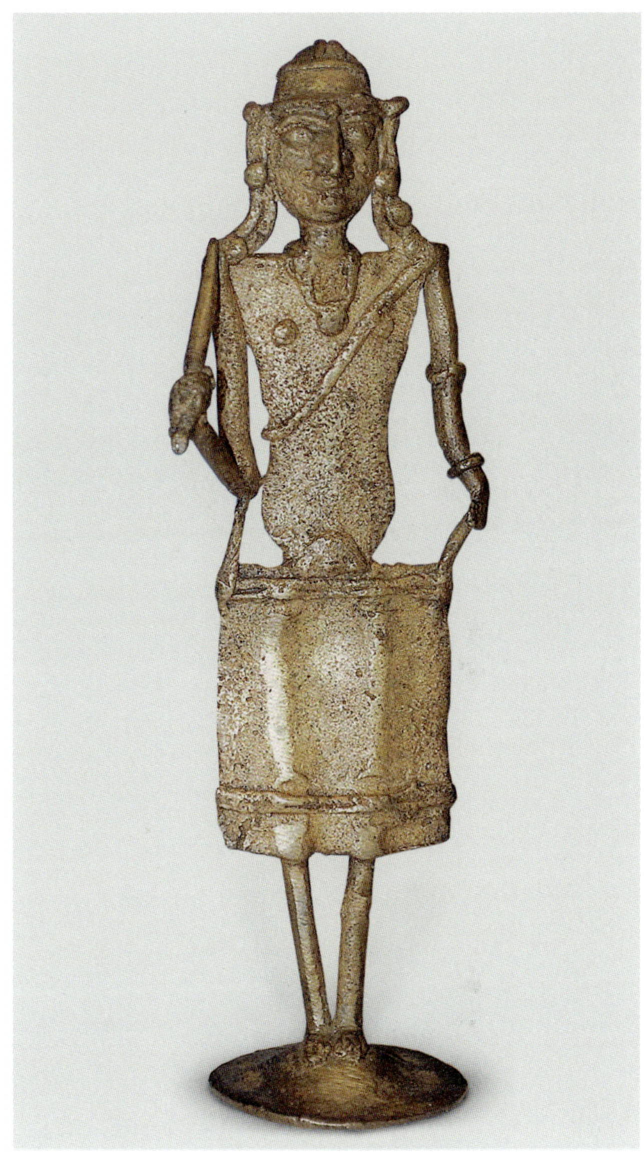

42. *A bronze figure from Townley's collection of Indian sculpture, now at the British Museum*

prestige, European goodwill and private funding, it seems a matter of time before a request is received from the Greek government for a loan. The institution could then rediscover its founding collection of antiquities. Until then, the vast and diverse Townley collection remains united at the museum, awaiting its moment.

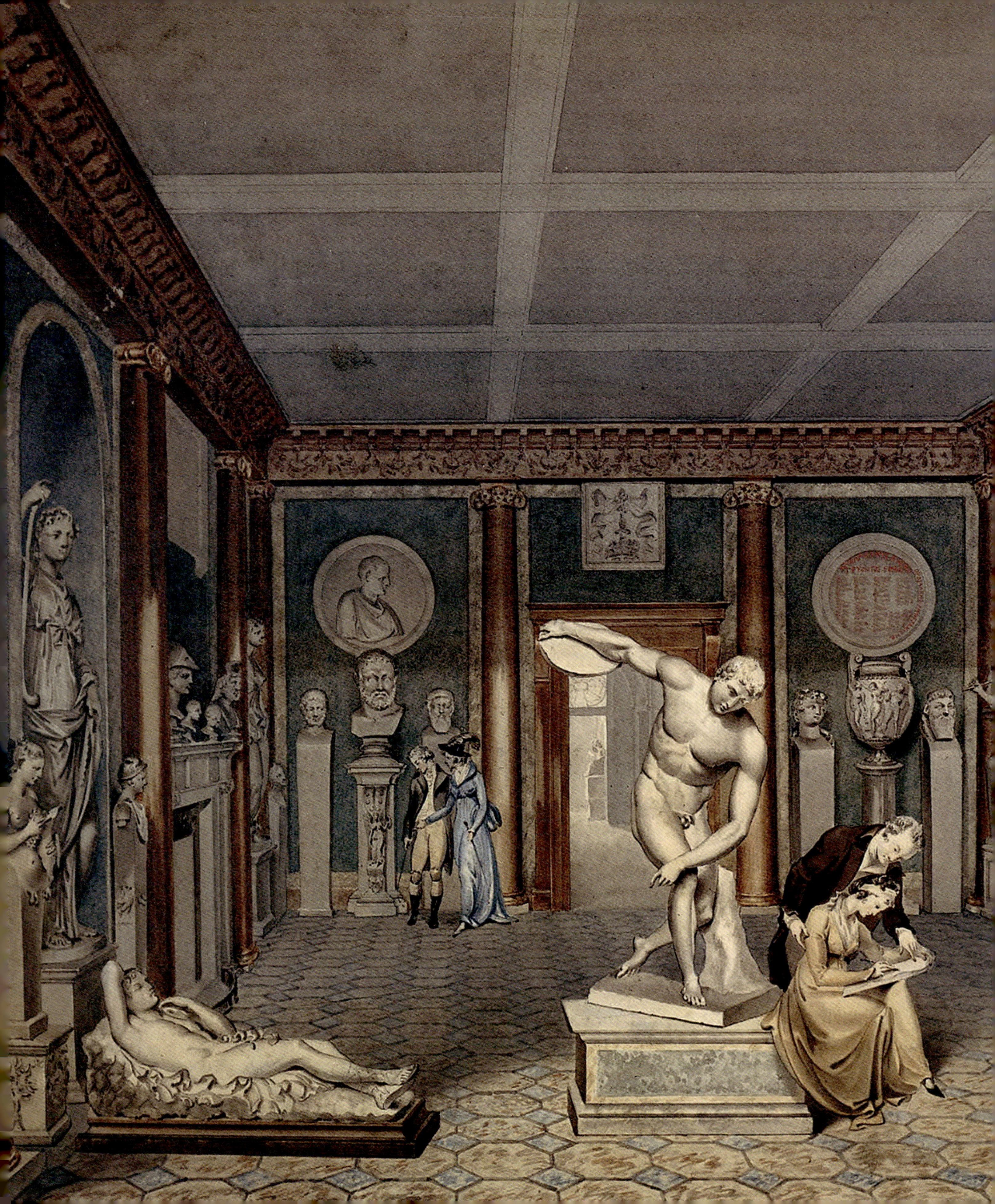

5. THE TOWNLEIAN MUSEUM

A VISITOR ARRIVING AT 7 PARK STREET IN the late eighteenth century could have heard about the house through guidebooks to London, which recommended it as 'the finest collection of antique statues, busts, &c. in the world'. Superlatives were also used abroad: in April 1804, the *Allgemeine Zeitung*, published in Ulm, described Townley as the proprietor of the most magnificent private museum in Europe ('*der Besitzer des prächtigsten Privatmuseums in Europa*').[1]

Townley also advertised the house with a card, which he gave out to a chosen few [44]. Antiquities dealers in Rome directed young potential customers to visit, and foreigners were brought in the company of Townley's cosmopolitan friends, such as Joseph Banks and Maria Cosway. Without a personal connection, one would write a letter to Townley himself, and he would reply with the hour of public admission.

Walking into the entrance hall it is hard to know what a visitor would have expected, but it was probably not a series of rooms arranged around the the initiation ritual of a Bacchic mystery cult. Nevertheless, this is what the ground floor of the display comprised, reflecting

Townley's deep fascination with esoteric practice in general, and the rites of Bacchus in particular.

Mystery cults are a tantalizingly obscure feature of the ancient world. Their power was derived from secrecy: the name comes from the Greek '*myein*', to close. By antiquarians like Townley they were believed to have preserved the earliest theological principles of human civilization. Their rituals involved, in the words of one historian, 'passing beyond the limits of morality in as many directions as possible'.[2] The mysteries operated outside official religious institutions, independent of such central authority as the Roman *pontifex maximus*. The most revered were the Eleusinian mysteries near Athens, devoted to Demeter and Persephone, and the Roman Empire later produced its own mystery cult in the form of Mithraism.[3]

The most widespread mystery cult was that dedicated to Bacchus, known in Greece as Dionysus. *The Bacchae* of Euripides represents the establishment of the rites in the blighted city of Thebes, at a time when the rituals were restricted to women only, known as maenads. The cult emerged in the sixth century BC, lasting until the fourth century AD, and individual personal initiation into a group of worshippers (*thiasos*) was a standard ceremony. Before a novitiate could participate in the orgiastic ceremonies devoted to the god, they had to progress from death to rebirth

43. Detail of a drawing [31], showing the Dining Room with a decorative scheme that was never executed

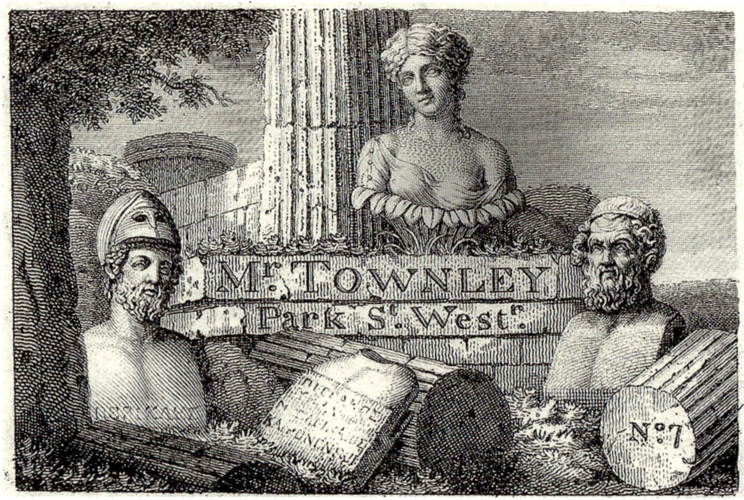

44. *Townley's visiting card depicts his busts of Pericles, Isis and Homer. Later, one acquaintance wrote that 'this elegant performance, always considered a great rarity, was left only at the houses of particular persons, so that an impression of it is now greatly coveted by the collectors of such bijoux': Smith [1828], p. 265.*

during initiations (*teletai*) that took them from darkness into light.

The project of recreating such a ceremony can be understood as analogous to the initiation rituals of freemasonry, an iconic aspect of late eighteenth-century culture in Europe. Mozart's *Die Zauberflöte* (1791) directly invoked the initiation into the mystery cult of Isis that was another of Townley's obsessions. However, the mystery dimension of freemasonry was antithetical to Townley's occultism: it was explicitly Christian in its values where his was pagan, and focused on numerical symbolism rather than animal. Most of all, the object of masonic ceremony was scientific rationality, rather than sensory disorder; its bacchanals were convivial rather than ecstatic. In the terms of *Die Zauberflöte*, Townley would be more of a Queen of the Night.

The first stage of Bacchic initiation was the descent into the underworld (*katabasis*), represented by the first room, the Hall [30].

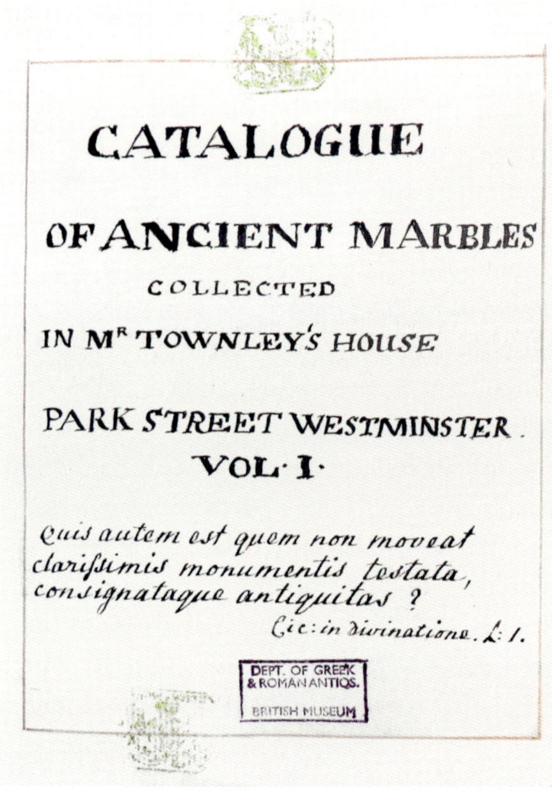

45. *The epigraph to the catalogue is taken from a defence of divination. As the character cites ancient sources for his argument, he asks 'is anyone unmoved by famous relics, signed and sealed by antiquity?': Cicero,* De divinatione, *I, XL*

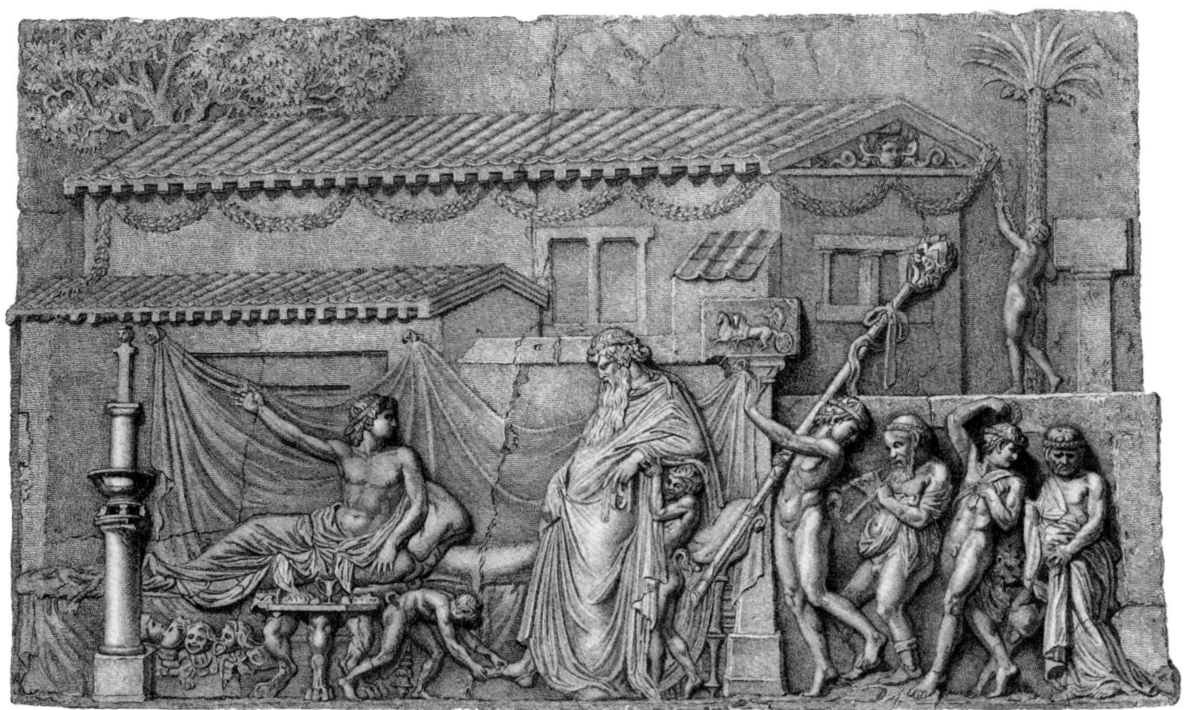

46. *'Large bas relief of Bacchus &c' (Parlour Catalogue: Hall)*

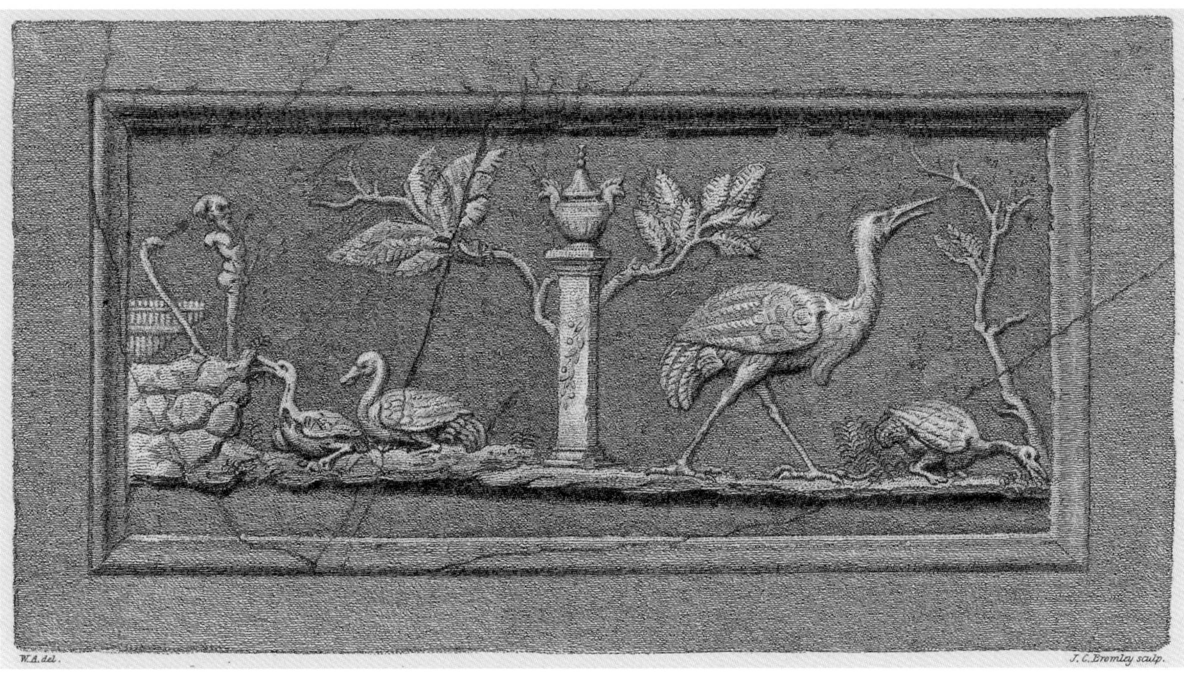

47. *'Bas relief with Terminus &c' (Parlour Catalogue: Hall)*

Here the visitor was presented with Townley's collection of *cineraria*, beginning among the effects of death. The first object a visitor would see was the seven-foot-long sarcophagus that was placed on the left of the door.[4] Elsewhere were cinerary urns and gravestones, one of which featured a skeleton in relief.[5]

Bacchus himself appeared on various works around the room. The main one was the relief at the centre of the chimneypiece [46].[6] For Townley it depicted a ritual involving 'an unwieldy figure of Bacchus', like many in his own collection.[7] It suggests a self-consciousness about the role of sculpture in ritual, and there was similar work above and to the left – a relief showing a landscape in which stood a terminus of Bacchus's son Priapus [47].[8]

The two largest works in the entrance hall, and indeed the whole collection, had been owned by Christina, Queen Regent of Sweden. They were displayed symmetrically either side of the chimneypiece, recalling their shared provenance. On the right was a green basanite bath and on the left a granite basin.[9] Townley described the latter as

a '*periranterion*' (*perirrhanterion*), an object 'placed in a particular part of the temples to hold the water, in which it was necessary to purify the hands, to gain admittance at the sacrifices'.[10] Another work also recalled the idea of purification – the puteal that came to be known as the 'Townley Well-Head'. This showpiece had only been displaced from the dining room by the arrival of the *Discobolus*.[11] The placement of these three works in the entrance hall suggested the preparation and purification at the beginning of initiation.

The other room that faced the street was the Street Parlour. The presiding god here was Ceres, and the goddess was represented by a veiled *terminus* [49]. Townley believed that her union with Bacchus gave life and animation to the world, and so the room was filled with sculptures of animals, including a goat-legged Pan, an acrobat on a crocodile, and a pair of tauroctonies (depictions of Mithras in the act of sacrificing a bull).[12]

The other remarkable feature of the Street Parlour were the walls, in which were installed Roman terracotta reliefs for architectural decoration (now known as 'Campana' reliefs). D'Hancarville discussed these in the *Recherches* as an unusually public display of the symbolism of the mysteries.[13] Of them the painter Giovanni Battista Cipriani said that 'they afforded him so much pleasure that he never knew when to leave them'.[14] Campana reliefs were little known at the time; it was not until 1842 that they were first published, by the collector who gives them their name.

Beyond these rooms was the windowless transitional space at the bottom of the staircase, with an alcove containing the catalogue to the collection, as well as a head of Isis.[15] Above the entrance to the Street Parlour was a mosaic, and above the entrance to the Dining Room was a marble relief of a Roman marriage ceremony [50].[16] It might seem surprising for an unmarried

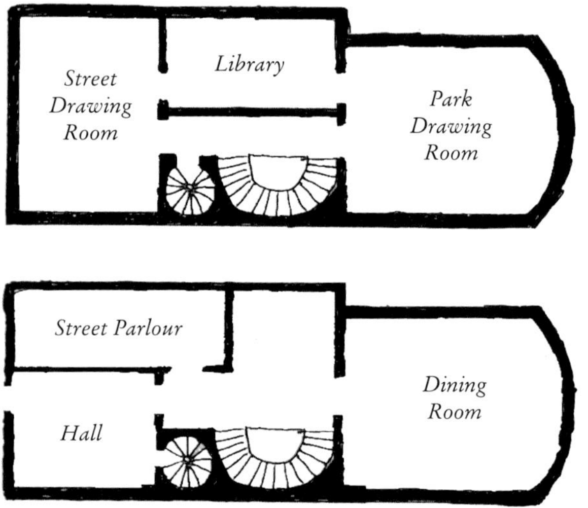

48. A modern reconstruction showing the probable layout of the rooms that were open to visitors, c.1780–1805

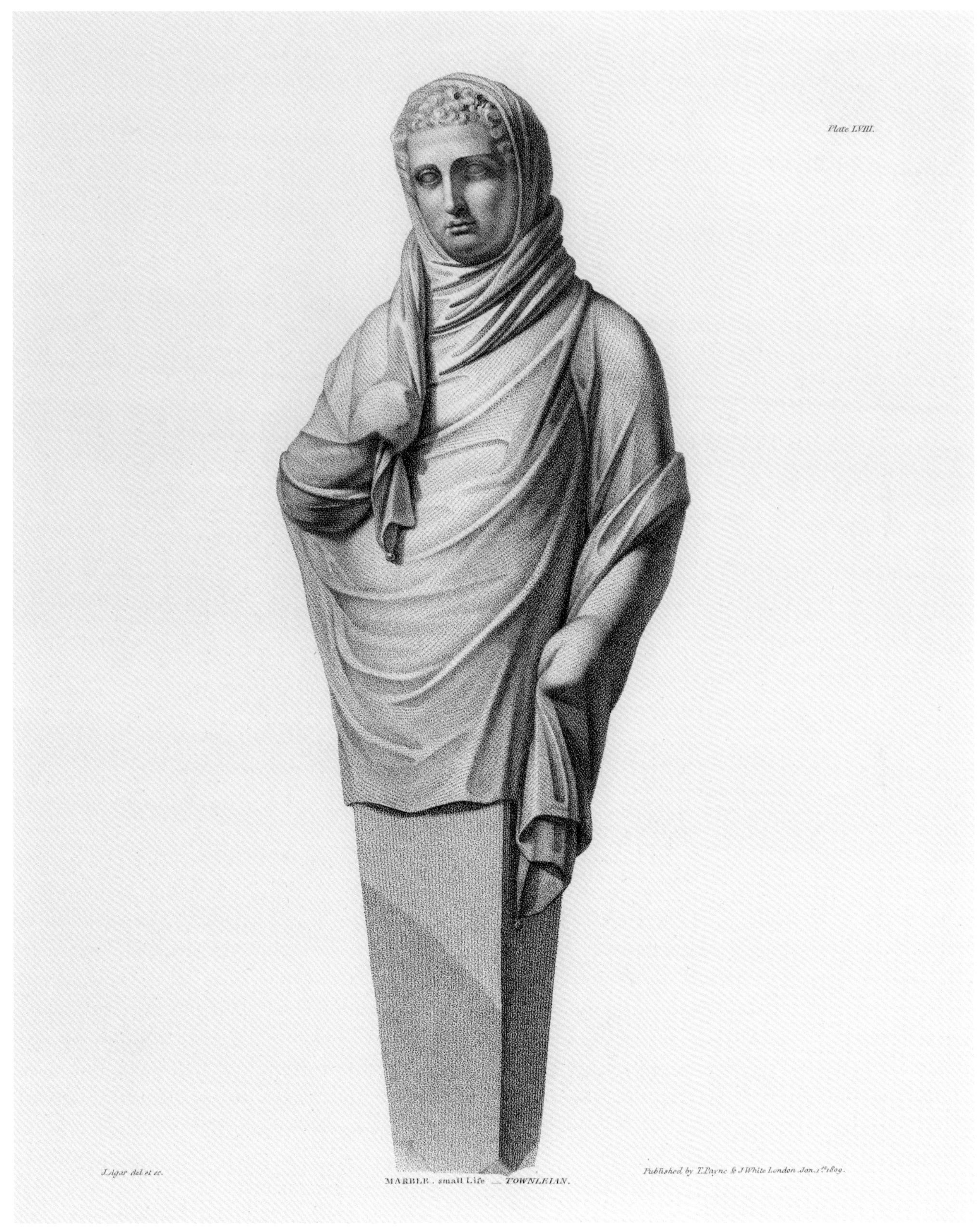

49. 'Terminus of Ceres' (Parlour Catalogue: Street Parlour),
engraved for Specimens of Antient Sculpture (1809)

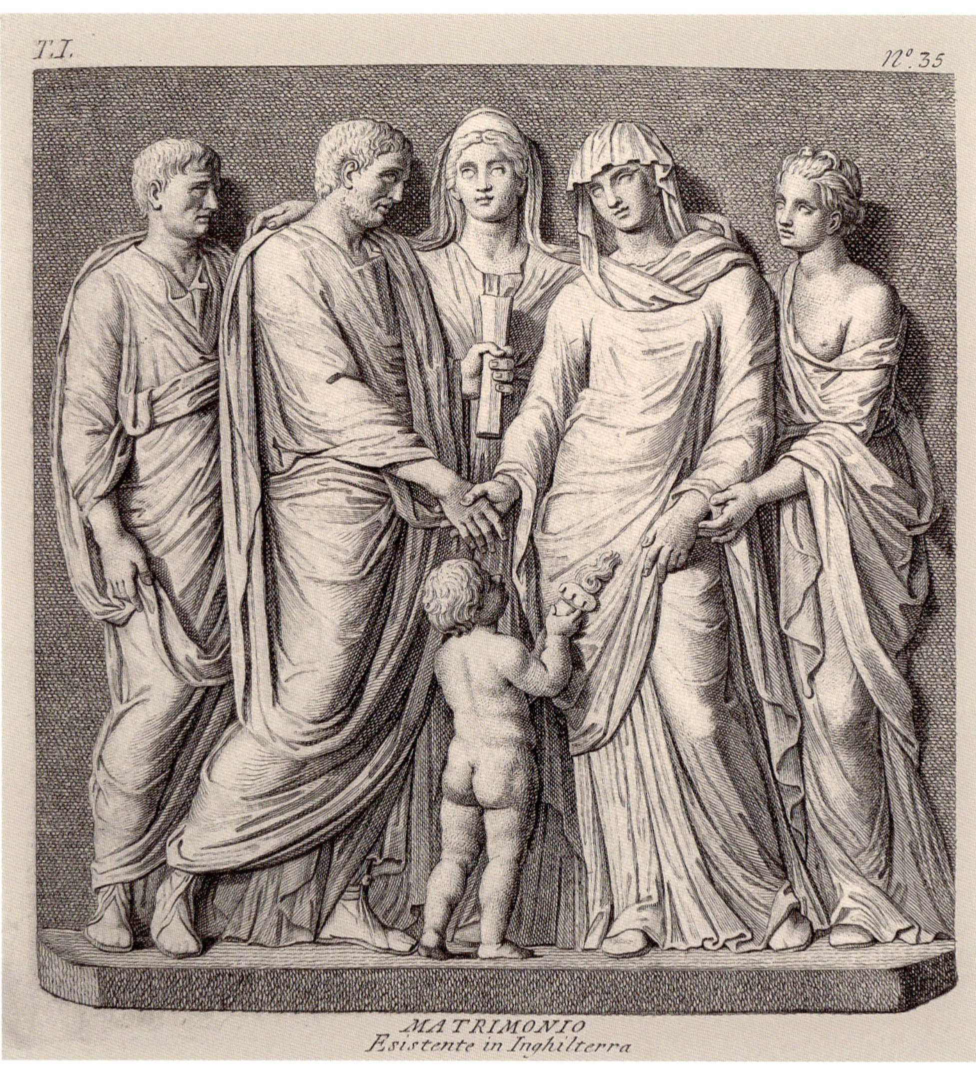

50. *'Bas relief of a marriage' (Parlour Catalogue: Staircase)*

man like Townley to display a marriage scene so prominently. However, it was not to be taken literally, but in terms of the visitor's ceremonial progress through the rooms: it represented the mystical marriage (*hieros gamos*). Having passed beyond death, the neophyte was brought into union with the god, as the mortal Ariadne had been with Bacchus.

The culmination of the progress through the mysteries was the sanctuary's central hall or *telesterion*. At Park Street, this was the Dining Room, where the full-length figures were displayed around the walls [31]. In this manner, the initiates to the mysteries would move out of the unlit spaces into the bright *telesterion*, finally meeting the priests. For an eighteenth-century visitor who had not experienced classical art first-hand, the effect must have been overwhelming. The most famous text on the emotional experience of mysteries was the speech by Socrates in the *Phaedrus*, where the climactic arrival is an analogue for the revelation of truth through visual beauty.[17]

The two large niches flanking the fireplace each contained a female figure with spectacular drapery: the one on the left was identified by Townley as the pastoral muse *Thalia* [53], that on right as *Diana throwing a Javelin* [54].[18] Facing them, paired between the two central columns of the room, were the works that now bear their owner's name, the 'Townley Caryatid' and the 'Townley *Venus*'.[19] These were not, however, the identifications that Townley knew them by: the caryatid was '*Regina Isis*' [55], Bacchus's female counterpart, and the *Venus* was Bacchus's wife *Ariadne* [56].[20] The latter was considered by Canova to be the most beautiful female figure in England.[21] The Townley Vase was on the left of the door as one entered (see Appendix B). Above it and to the right, on the wall, was the only major piece of Greek marble carving, the monument of Xanthippus [51].[22]

The sculpture of *Silenus recumbent* [58], on the ground by the window, was discussed in the *Recherches* for Silenus's significance as the father of Bacchus, representing the importance of induced derangement in the rites. For Townley, his example was the most beautiful to survive of Silenus, showing the god in a transitional state between drunkenness and sleep, suggesting the conclusion to the rites and the end of the visitor's progress across the ground floor of the house.[23]

Having become an initiate, the visitor would then proceed up to the first floor, a more intellectual environment, closer to *virtù* and the modern idea of an art gallery. The largest room was the Park Drawing Room, with its great view over St James's Park, and here were contained works attributed to specific Greek sculptors and others notable for their fine aesthetic quality rather than their mystical function.

On the ground by the door was a work attributed to Polyclitus, the *Astragalizontes* [59], a sculpture of a boy biting another after arguing

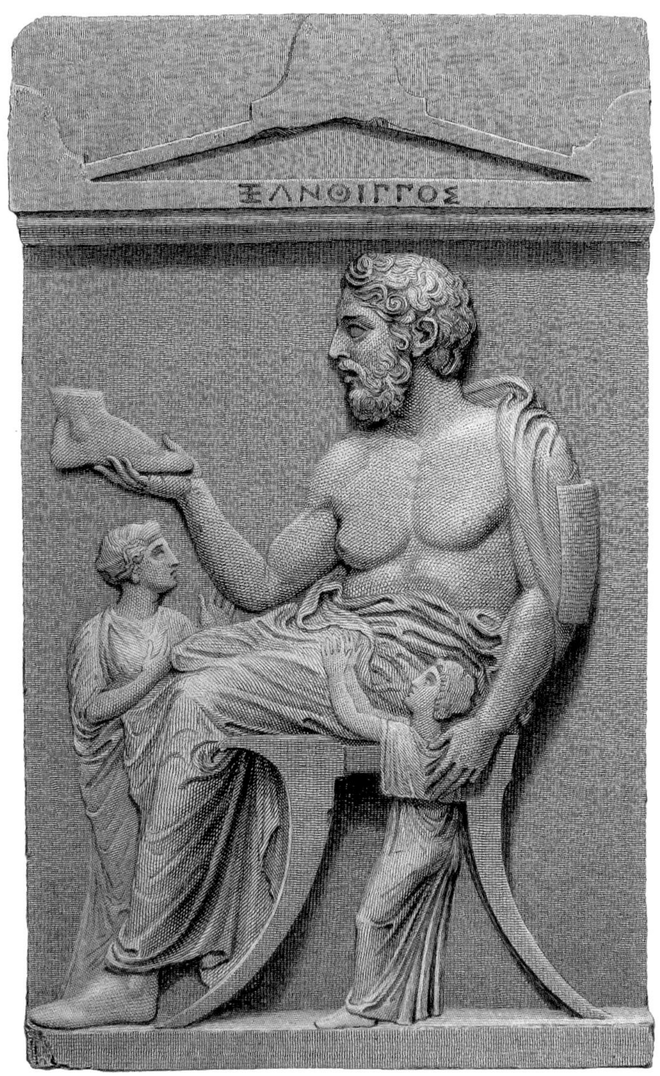

51. *'Monument of Xanthippus'*
(Parlour Catalogue: Dining Room)

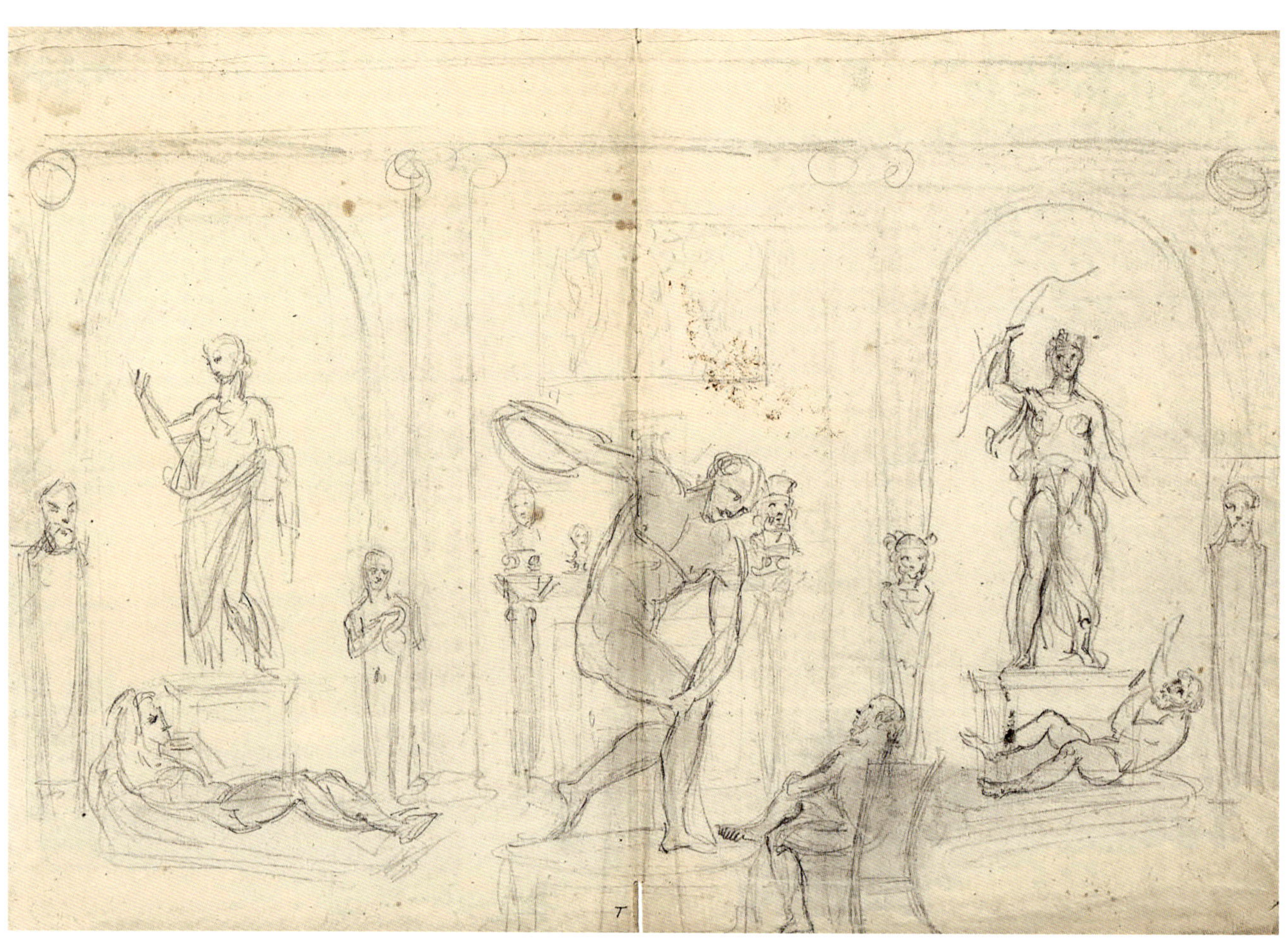

52. *Sketch of the east wall of the Dining Room, attributed to Joseph Nollekens, c.1793, with Thalia and Diana in the niches, and the Discobolus in the centre*

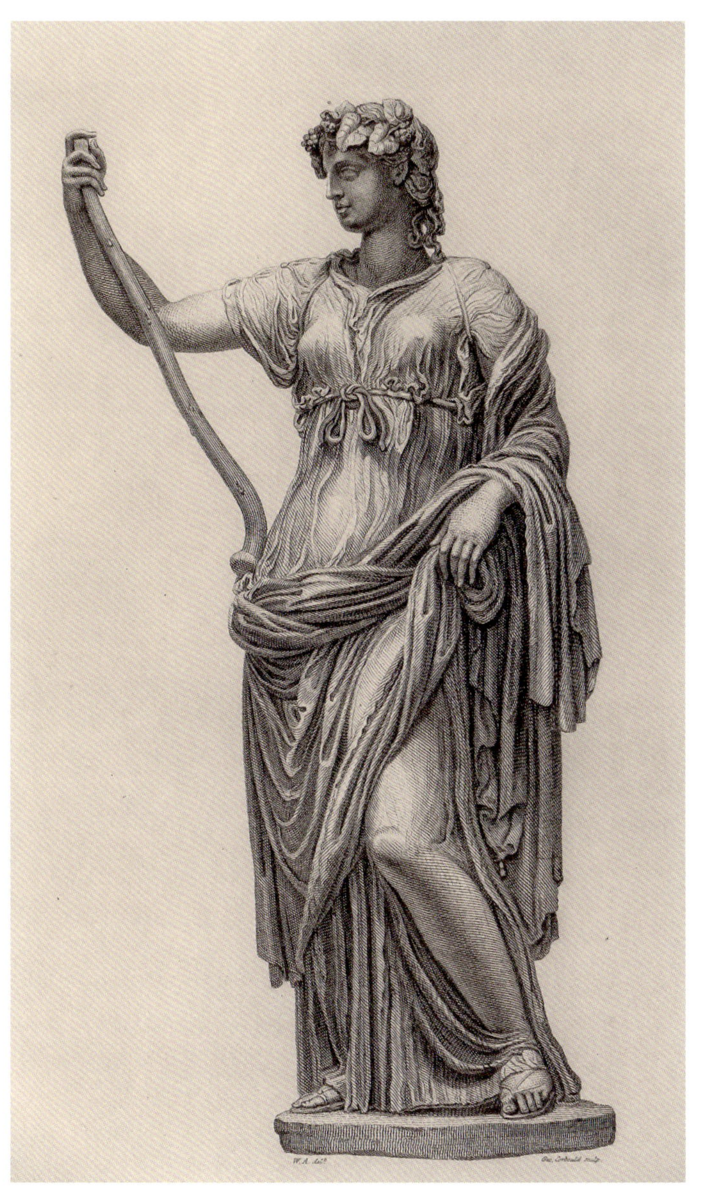

53. 'Statue of Thalia'
(Parlour Catalogue: Dining Room)

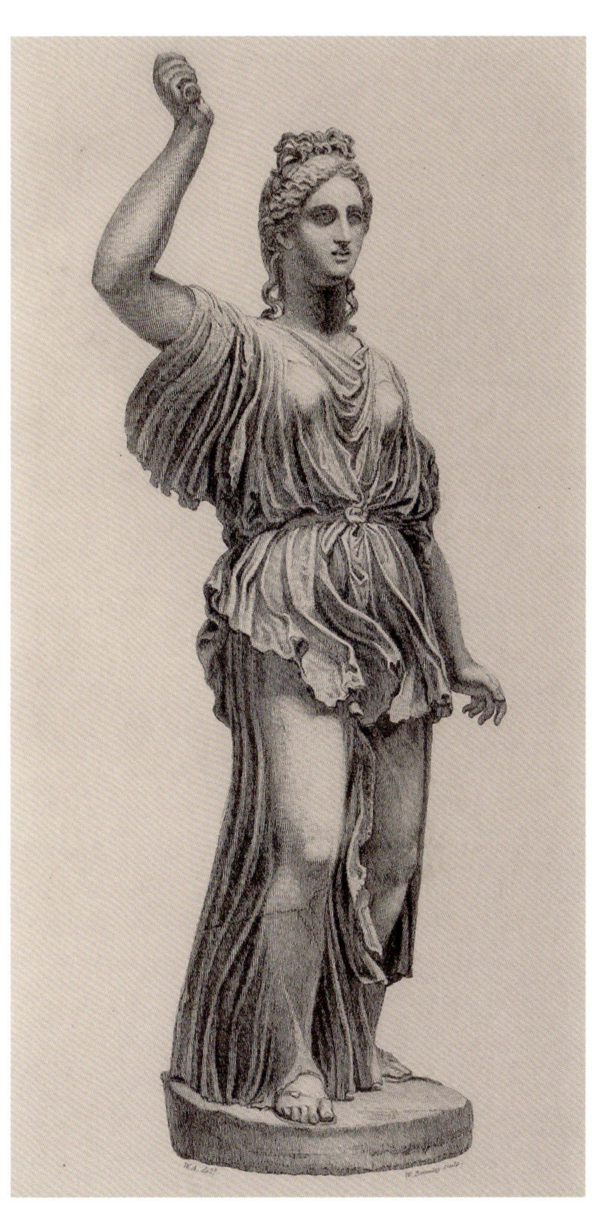

54. 'Statue of Diana'
(Parlour Catalogue: Dining Room)

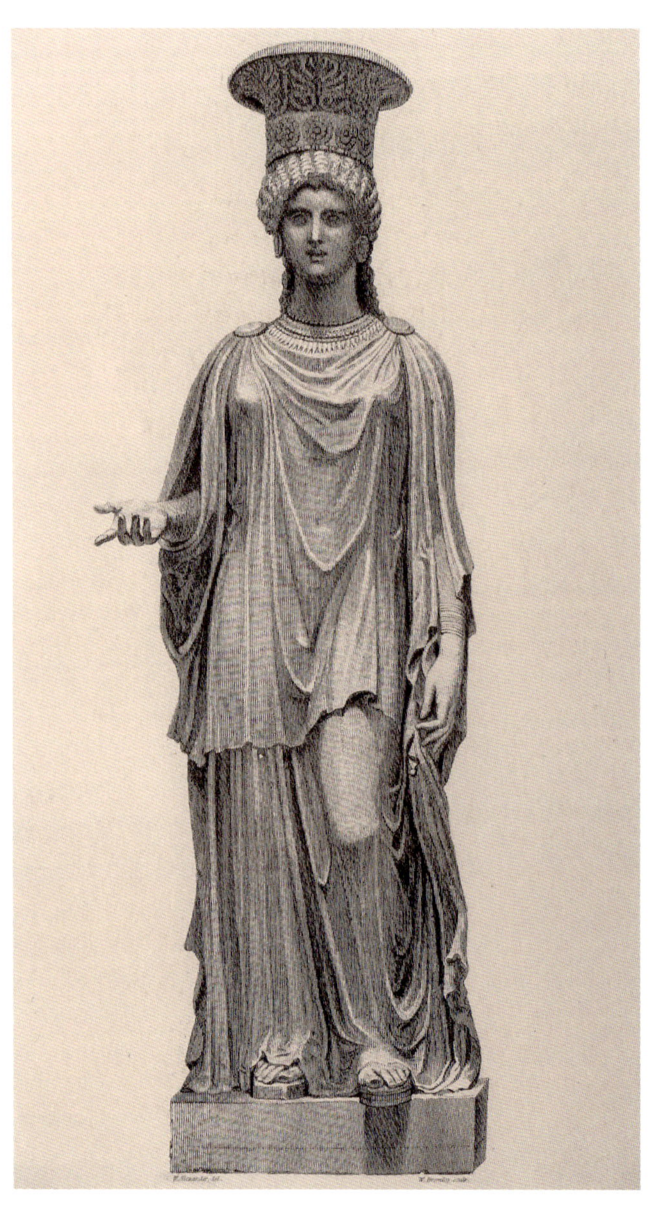

55. *'Regina Isis'*
(Parlour Catalogue: Dining Room)

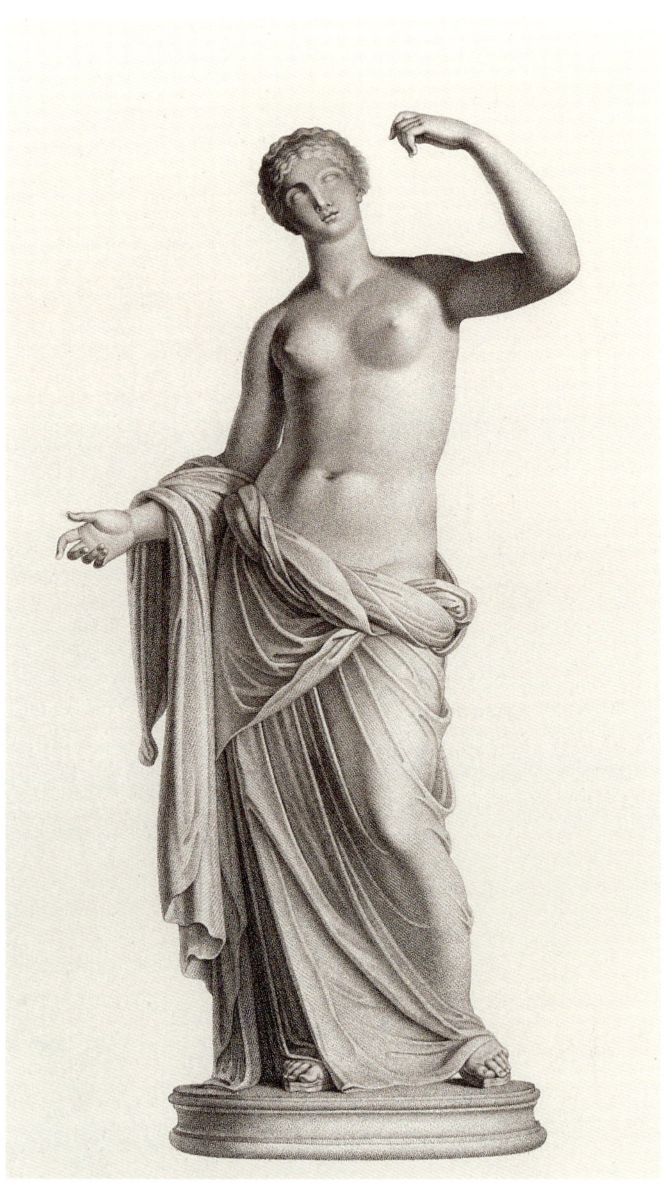

56. *'Statue of Ariadne'*
(Parlour Catalogue: Dining Room)

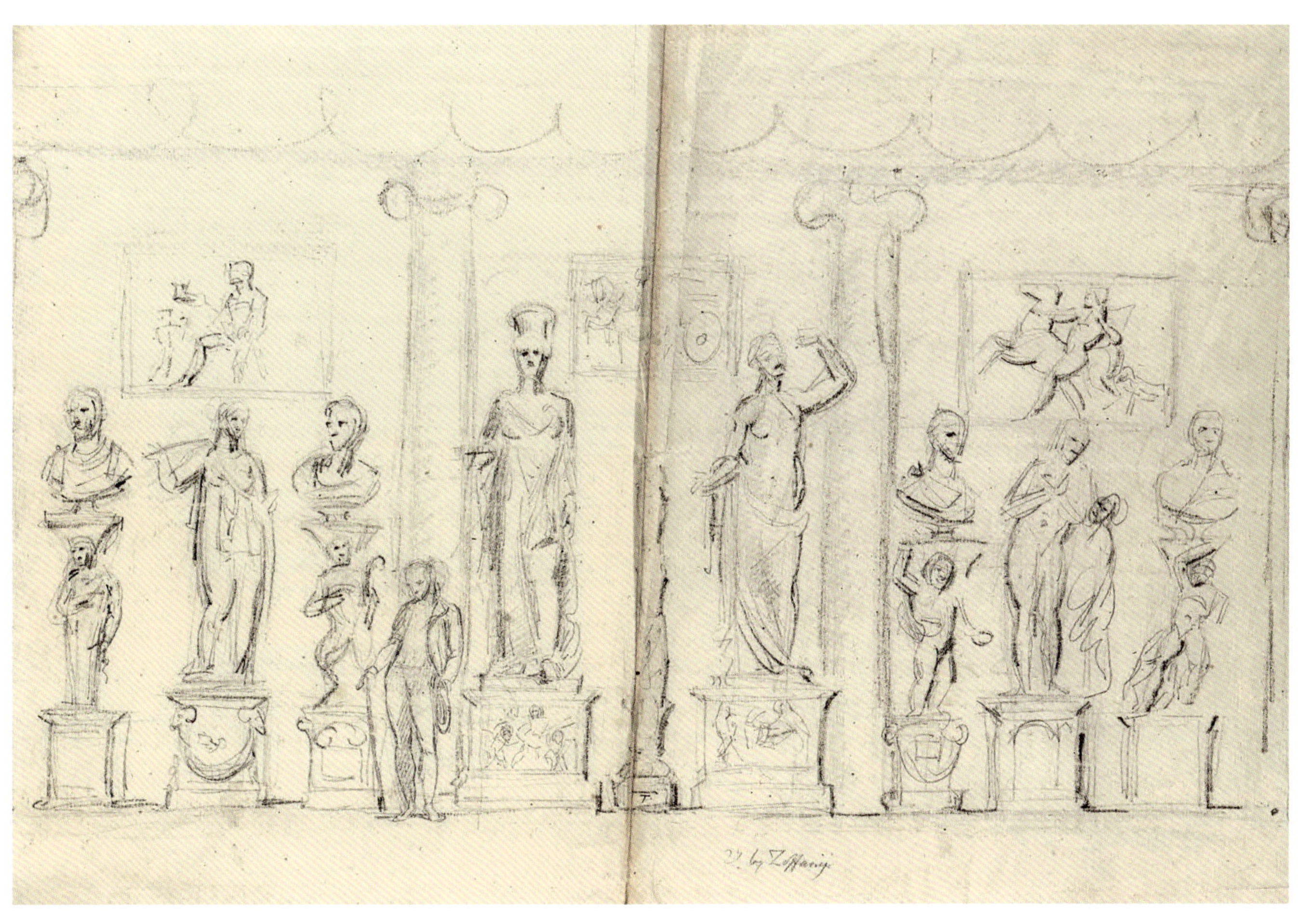

57. Sketch of the west wall of the Dining Room, attributed to Joseph Nollekens, c.1793, with Regina Isis and Ariadne between the central columns

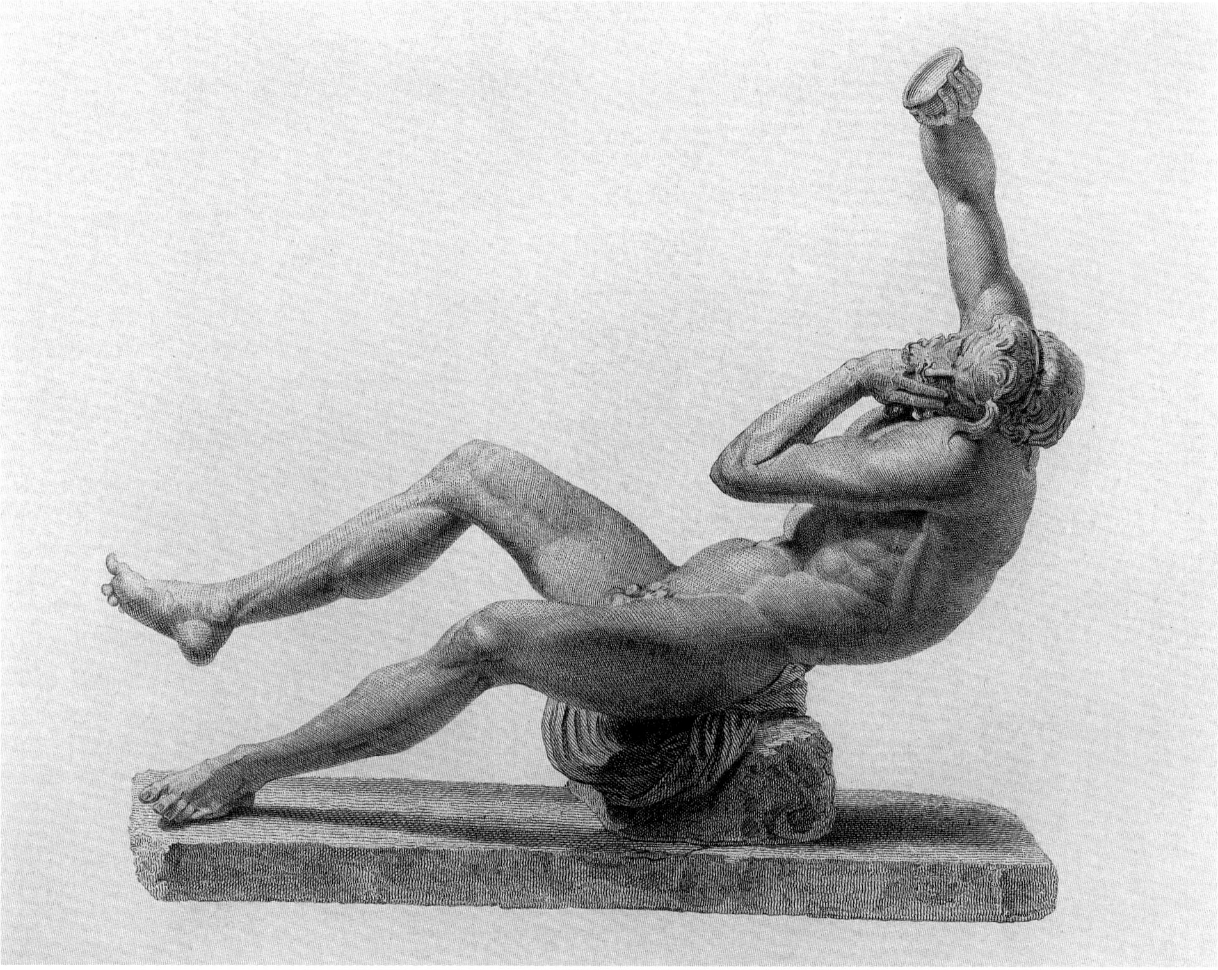

58. ‘Silenus recumbent’ (Parlour Catalogue: Dining Room)

59. *In Zoffany's painting [75], d'Hancarville and Townley
are discussing the marble* Silenus *with reference to this page
from the official catalogue of discoveries at Herculaneum.
The engraving illustrates a bronze that became part of
the collection of the Palazzo Portici. It was an important
comparison for Townley, and he also referred to it in the
public catalogue: Townley (1804), I, p. 34.*

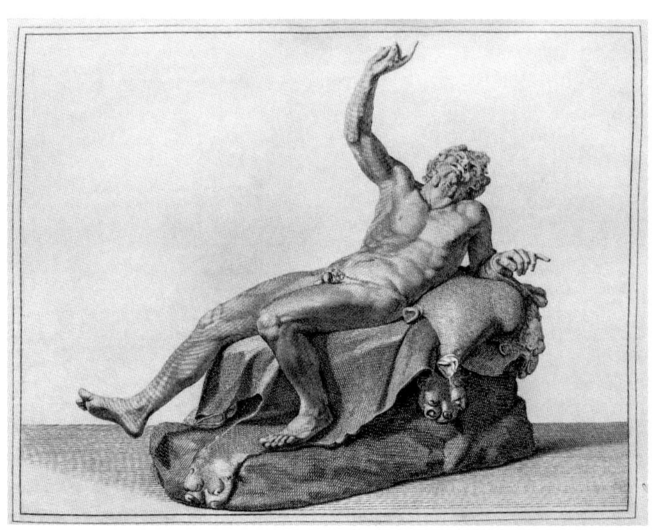

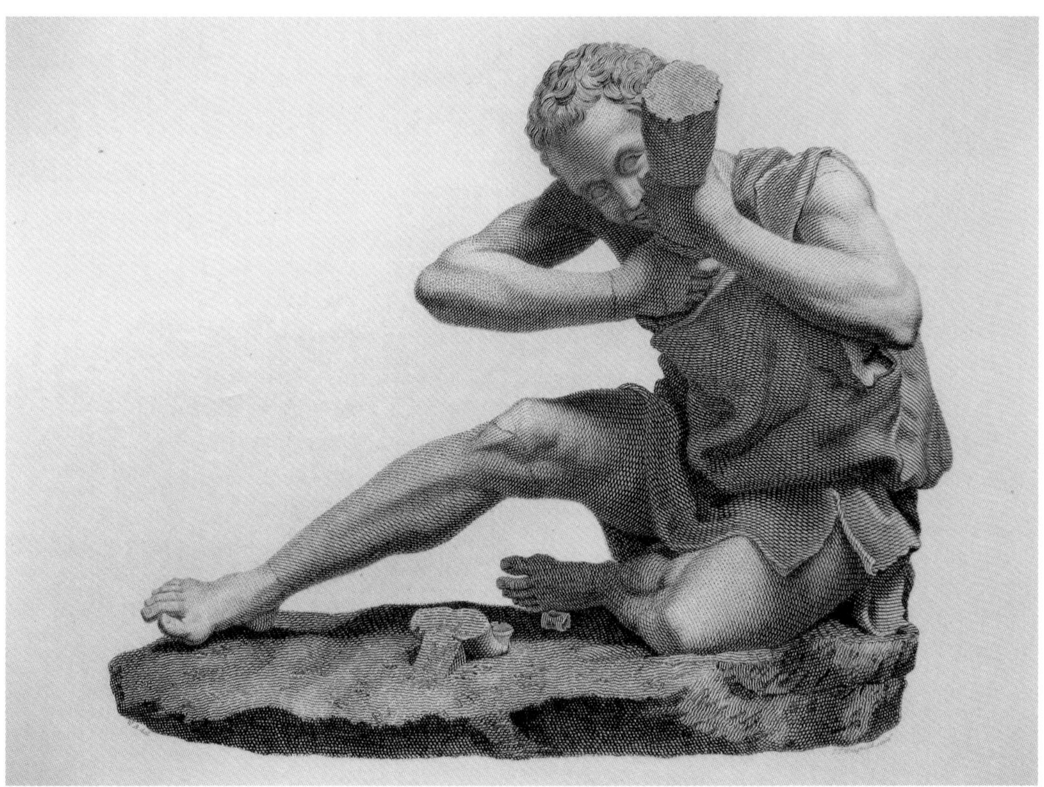

60. *'Astragalizontes'*
(Parlour Catalogue: Park Drawing Room)

over a game of knucklebones.[24] Because only the hand of the bitten boy survived, for a long time the hand was supposed to be severed, and the figure represented to be a cannibal. That story was probably facetious, but it was only when he discovered a knucklebone clutched in the hand that Winckelmann was able to make the connection to an ancient description of a lost work on the subject by Polyclitus.

The other attributed works were two nearly identical figures that Townley believed to be by Praxiteles.[25] They represent a young boy holding a cup, and accord with a description of a satyr that, according to legend, was one of the two works that Praxitiles himself prized above all others, giving it the name *Periboeton* ('the renowned') [61]. D'Hancarville had retold the story of Praxiteles

in the *Recherches*, and used the statue to discuss the bi-gender portrayal of Bacchus.[26] He also identified Praxiteles as an artist who would have undergone initiation into the mysteries.[27]

On the mantelpiece was placed the most popular work, a female head emerging from a lotus, identified by Townley as *Isis* [34]. When John Towneley lived at the house, following his nephew's death, he purchased a copy of the bust by Nollekens and placed it in the same position as the original had stood.[28] Townley had first encountered the cult of Isis during his first visit to Naples in 1768, when the Pompeian temple of Isis was being excavated to general astonishment. To its left on the floor was a lion whose head also emerged from a lotus [62].[29] The carving of its mane was a highlight of sculptural technique, and

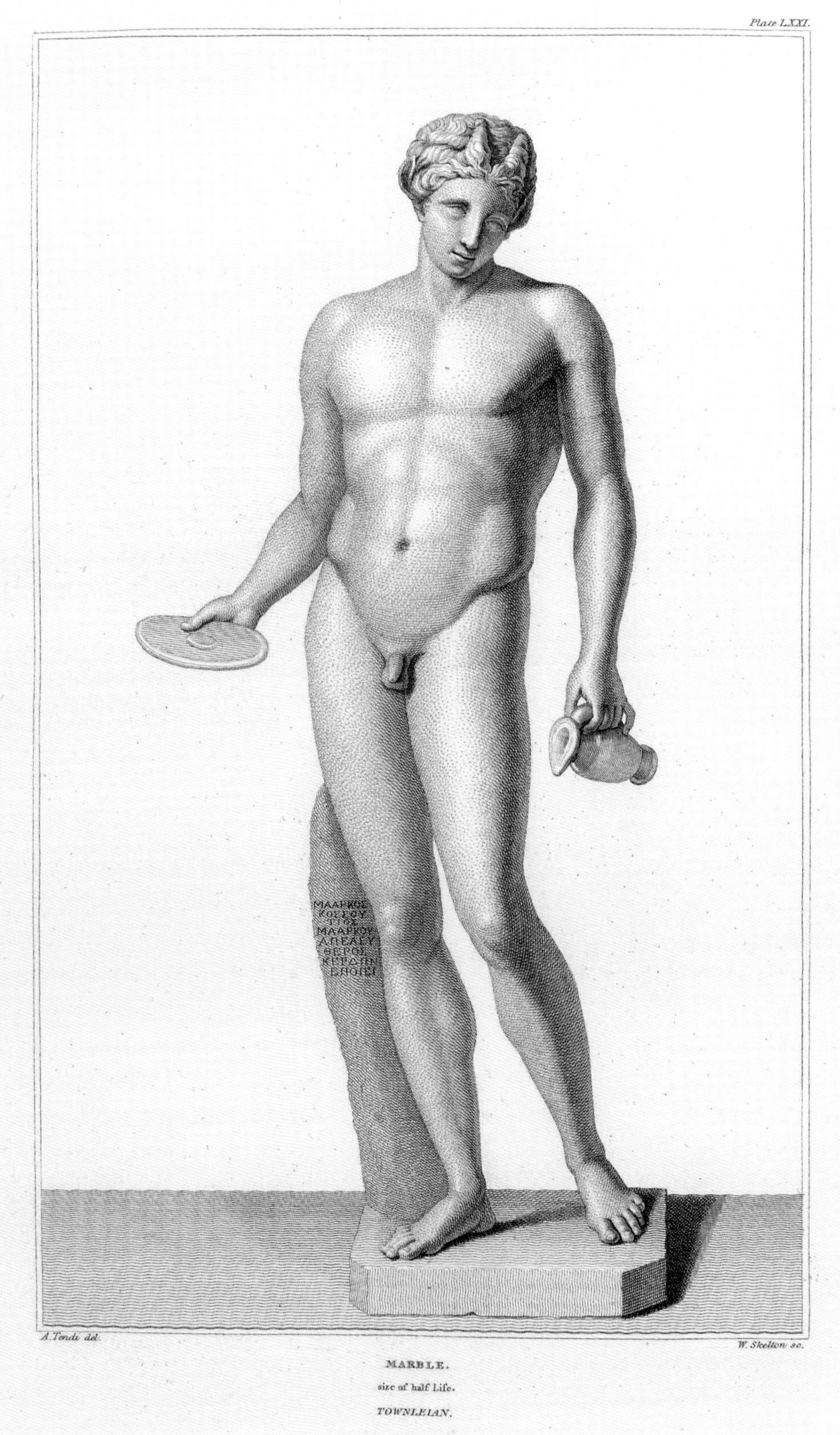

61. *'The Periboeton' (Parlour Catalogue: Park Drawing Room), engraved for* Specimens of Antient Sculpture *(1809)*

it was apparently a major inspiration for the great
portrait sculptor Francis Chantrey.[30]

Existing accounts of the famous Portland Vase
do not discuss its whereabouts between 1790 and
1810.[31] However, in 1794 a visitor to No. 7 Park
Street recorded 'the Portland Vase' in a 'small
cabinet' at the centre of the Park Drawing
Room. This may be simply referring to a copy in
jasperware: Josiah Wedgwood had made his first
successful copy late in 1789. But the note does say
'the Portland Vase'. It is possible that the work's
owner, the third Duke of Portland, had put it
in Townley's possession once Wedgwood was
finished with it; the original could then be put on
public display while the duke was preoccupied
as Home Secretary. The vase had been William
Hamilton's finest and best-known possession,
and Townley would reasonably be honoured to
have it, even if it was not officially part of his
collection. Indeed, he was taking on the role that
the British Museum would later play, as from
1810 it was exhibited there while officially still the
property of the duke. The vase would have been
safer, however, at Park Street: in 1845, a visitor
accidentally smashed it into over two hundred
pieces.

From the second door in the Park Drawing
Room, the visitor would go into the Library [63],
the inner sanctum, apparently intended for the
study of the collection rather than spectacular
showpieces. A sense of mystery was conjured by
a sculpture that Townley called the '*Angerona*', a
Roman goddess who held a finger up to her lips.[32]
For Townley this goddess was really Isis, and in
the *Recherches* the gesture had been discussed as
an embodiment of the secret mysteries of ancient
religion.[33] In the Library, detailed study could be
made of specific mystical symbols. A feature of
the room were the figures of satyrs: one could be
seen in a niche to the right of the chimneypiece,
while another was adjacent on a pedestal, attacking

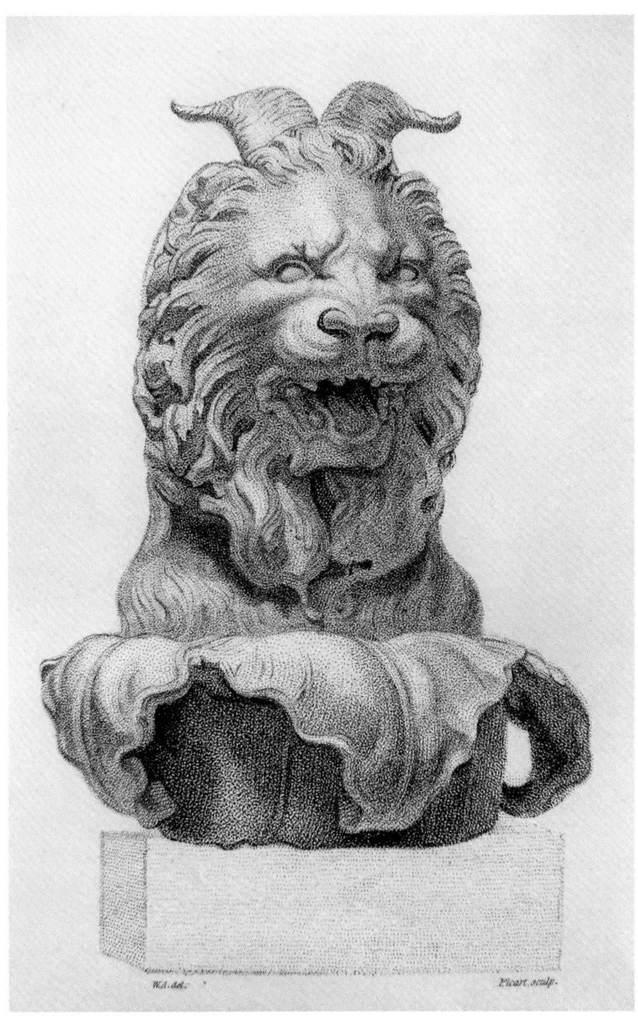

62. *'Lion's head with horns'*
(Parlour Catalogue: Park Drawing Room)

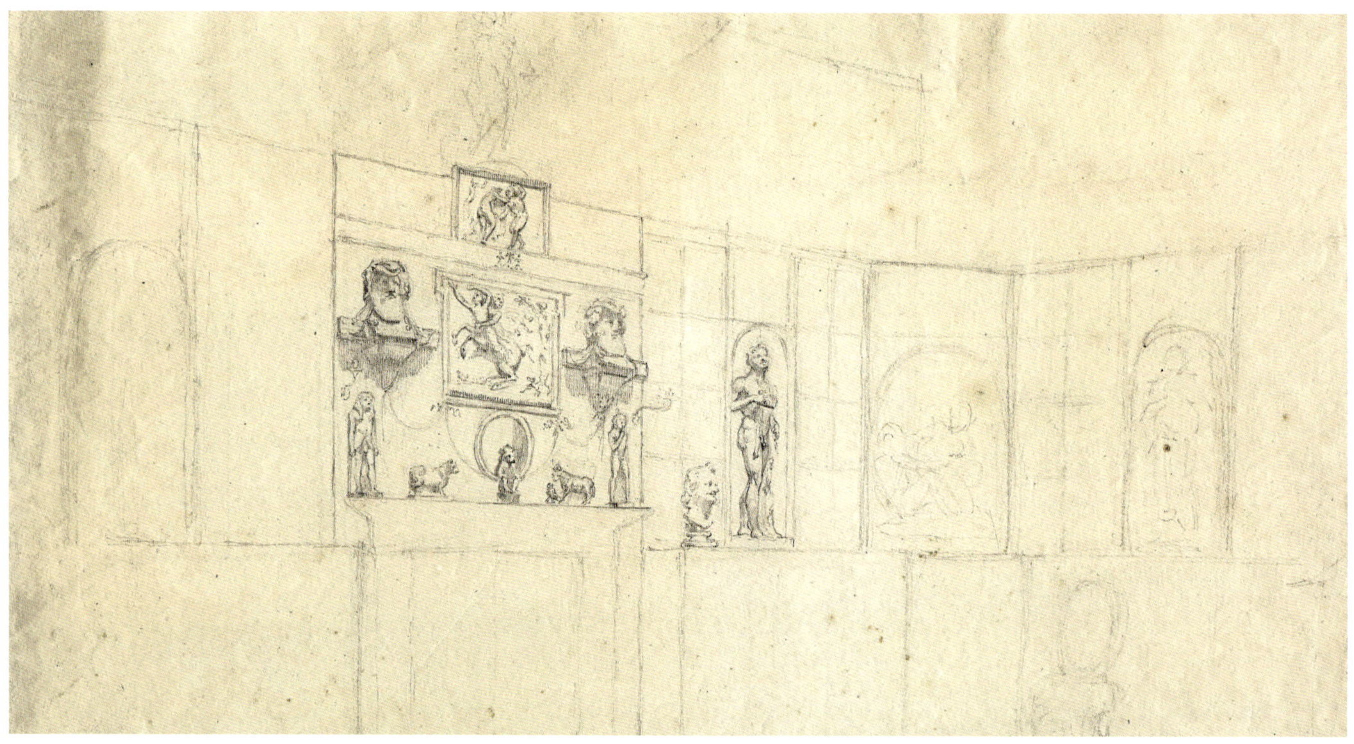

63. *This sketch by an unknown hand shows the Library in the early 1780s*

a nymph.[34] In d'Hancarville's *Recherches*, this arrangement had been promoted to readers as a way to compare the way both satyrs had the attributes of young goats (*chevreaux*), which in turn held symbolic meaning.[35] The fact that Townley kept the two satyrs in the same position for twenty years suggests that he did not find these ideas far-fetched.

Aside from the more esoteric works, the other feature of the room was busts, a traditional decoration for libraries. These included *Jupiter* [64], *Diana* [65] and a *Dioscurus* [66], but the most famous was of Homer [67], which had been made immediately iconic by its engraving in 1788 by Francesco Bartolozzi.[36] The original stood opposite the chimneypiece. Another bust of Homer, portrayed slightly younger, was displayed in the Dining Room, and Townley chose the Library to show the poet 'represented in the more advanced age, and in a more sublime and animated character'.[37] One of the prizes of his library was a manuscript of the *Iliad* dating from the eleventh century, which was among the oldest medieval examples to survive.[38]

The final room on the tour was the Street Drawing Room, overlooking Park Street. Here could be found some art that was not from ancient Greece or Rome. First, there was something contemporary, a terracotta by Joseph Nollekens over the chimneypiece, based on the relief above the entrance to the Dining Room. In his catalogue, Townley took the opportunity to promote his friend as 'the best English sculptor of his time'.

Secondly, there was a work of the Italian Renaissance, a giant terracotta head by Guglielmo della Porta. The sculptor is best known for his restoration of antique works like the Farnese *Hercules*, a practice now much maligned but that

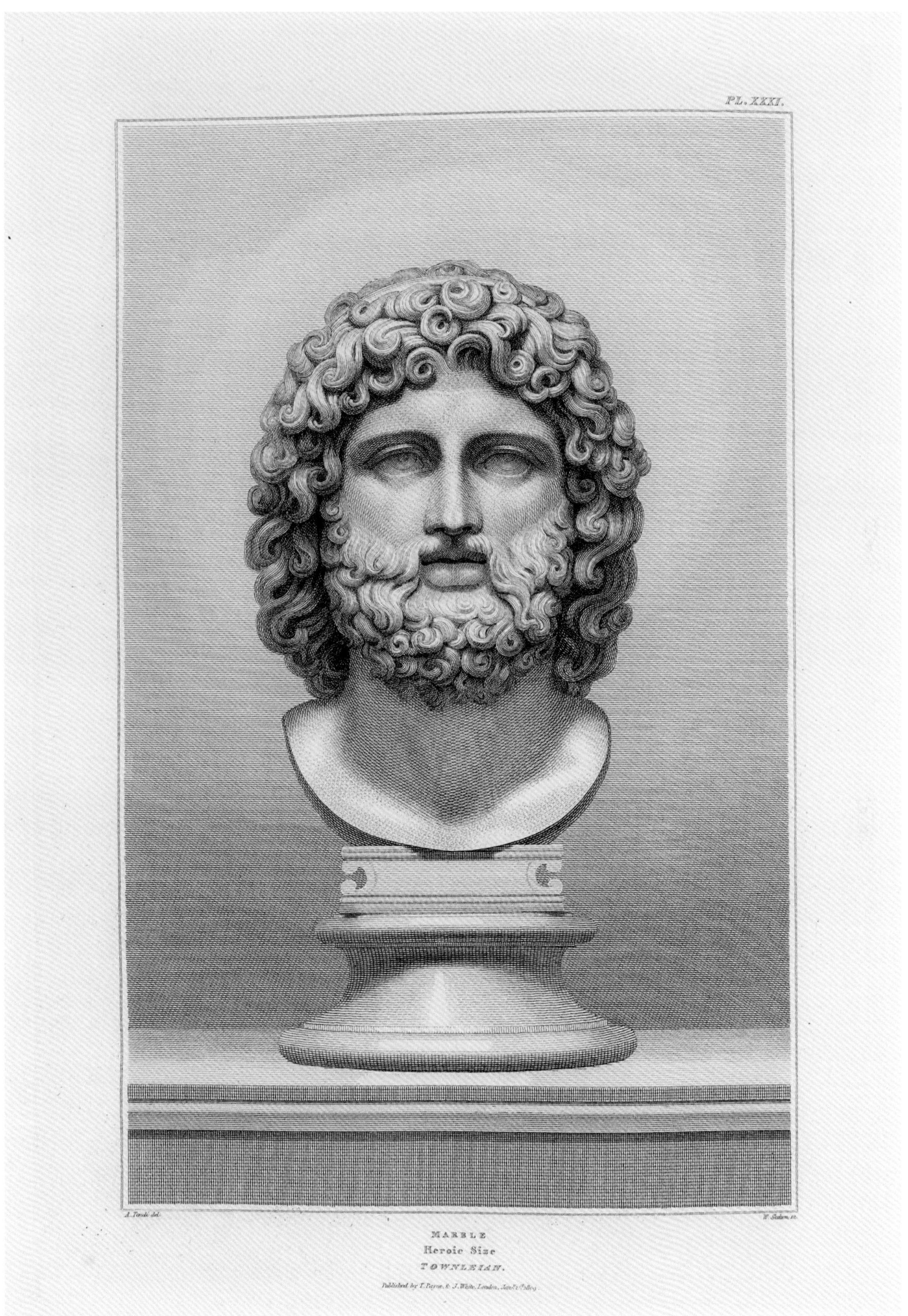

64. *'Head of Jupiter' (Parlour Catalogue: Library),*
engraved for Specimens of Antient Sculpture *(1809)*

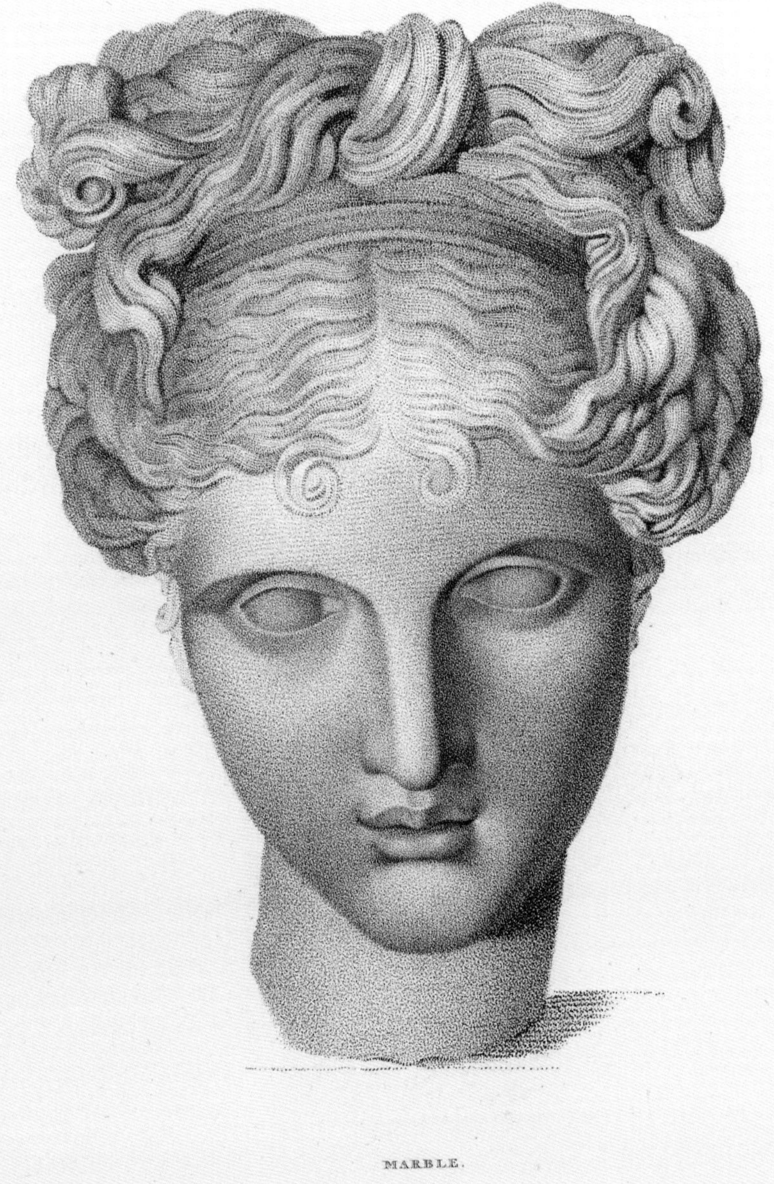

65. *'Head of Diana' (Parlour Catalogue: Library),*
engraved for Specimens of Antient Sculpture *(1809)*

Townley would have understood as an art form in its own right. The terracotta head was a model for a figure of Truth, an element in della Porta's elaborate monument to Pope Paul III in St Peter's, probably commissioned in 1547, and installed in 1575.[39] Such terracotta fragments are a valuable record of the complete design, which was soon deconstructed, and others survive in Rome. The present location of Townley's, however, is unknown.

The third unusual feature of the Street Drawing Room was Townley's collection of Indian art, which was on display by 1794. The British Museum owned some Indian objects, but the only comparable public display, the Oriental Repository at East India House, would open in 1801. Townley was a pioneer in Europe in collecting Indian art: formal study had only begun in 1771, with the discussion of art and architecture in Abraham Hyacinthe Anquetil-Duperron's study of Zoroastrianism. Townley was fascinated with the religions of India, particularly Hinduism, believing that they preserved the earliest principles of theology in human civilization. This idea of a 'primitive' system of worship was also the basis for his fascination with mystery cults.

Townley was particularly interested in a cave-temple on an island in Mumbai harbour known as Elephanta or Gharapuri. He probably first discovered it through d'Hancarville, who included in the first volume of the *Recherches* many references to '*la Pagode d'Eléphanta*', specifically the bi-gender figures in its sculpture. In 1784, while d'Hancarville was finishing the book at his house, Townley copied by hand a description of the Elephanta caves taken from a paper given by the Professor of Anatomy at the Royal Academy.

In the same year, Alexander Allan, a cartographer in the East India Company, removed a bas-relief from the Elephanta caves showing groups having sex, known as 'symplegmata'. Allan brought the sculpture by sea to England, where it

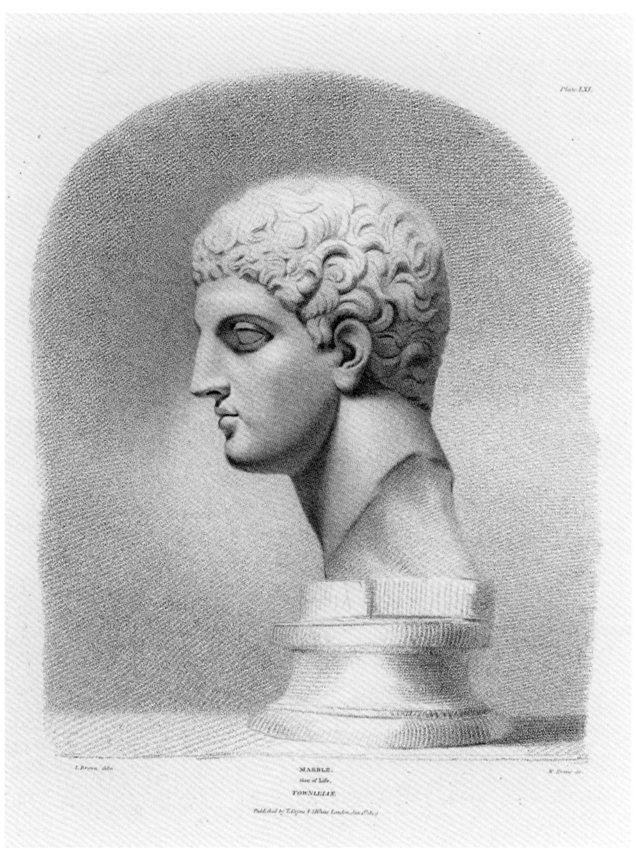

66. *'Head of a Dioscurus' (Parlour Catalogue: Library), engraved for* Specimens of Antient Sculpture *(1809)*

was bought by Townley's friend Thomas Astle and put on display at the Society of Antiquaries, before joining the Townley collection at Park Street.[40] D'Hancarville described it rapturously in the supplement to the *Recherches* in 1785.[41] Townley continued to be fascinated by the Elephanta caves, and in 1798 was given drawings of them made on site.

Townley's symplegmata, such as the Elephanta relief or a marble figure of a satyr copulating with a goat [68], were not on public display, or in the catalogue. However, they had a reputation, and visitors not in Townley's immediate circle could still apply for a viewing. The son of another collector hoping to see one such group wrote:

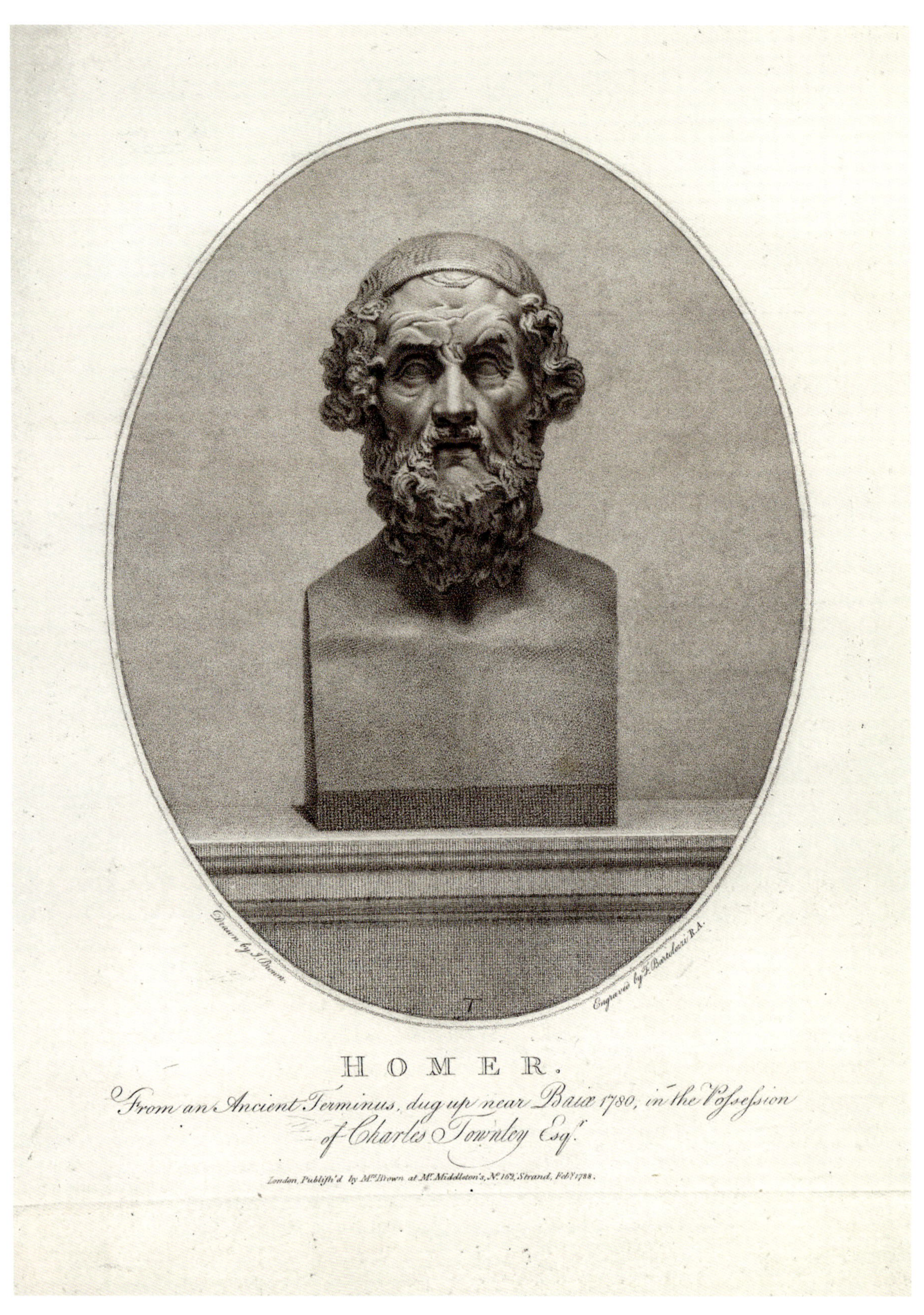

67. 'Head of Homer' (Parlour Catalogue: Library),
engraved by Francesco Bartolozzi from a drawing
by John Brown, published in 1788

'I fancy it is only for such amateurs whose passion for virtu will make them over look the subject'.[42]

The display at No. 7 Park Street was a unique feature in London. The city was developing its own early museum culture at the same time, but there was no institution displaying ancient art. Rather, displays were of contemporary art, European Old Masters and historical curiosities. The most prominent for the visiting tourist would probably have been the Holophusikon in Leicester Square, which opened in 1775, and later moved to a rotunda on Blackfriars Road. The collection was that of Sir Ashton Lever, who collected unsystematically, with an eye to public entertainment. It was a vast cabinet of curiosities rather than a museum in the modern sense.

The British Museum had opened in 1759, showing the collection of Sir Hans Sloane, who had bequeathed it to the nation on his death six years earlier. Sloane was a physician who in his 93 years had amassed over 71,000 objects, most of which were specimens of natural history. By the 1770s, the trustees of the British Museum were considering their project in opposition to the Holophusikon: they were displaying objects that 'will conduce to the improvement of Natural History as a branch of Philosophy'.[43] There was still no aesthetic dimension to compare to the display at Park Street.

The only comparable displays were those of collectors in their private homes. The Marquess of Rockingham had some marbles at his house in Grosvenor Square, while the Earl of Shelburne had his at Lansdowne House, just off Berkeley Square. Lansdowne House was built in 1762–68 by Robert Adam, but the projected gallery of antique sculptures was not completed. The collection was ultimately installed by Shelburne's son in a picture gallery to a design by Robert Smirke in 1816–19. Visitors in the late eighteenth century would have had to be invited if they wanted to see such works

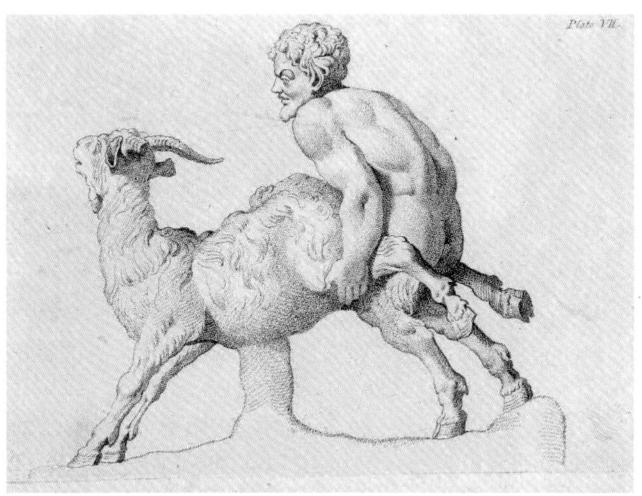

68. *D'Hancarville wrote that at Park Street* 'ce marbre singulier est gardé secrettement', *just as it is now at the British Museum: d'Hancarville [1784a], p. 328.*

as the famous *Hercules*, placed as they were in the Adam dining room. Thomas Hope had galleries in the Adams' Portland Place development: from 1804 these were opened for special viewings.[44] Townley's house, then, was unusual for making an aesthetic display of ancient artworks. Where then did Townley conceive of the idea?

On 21 February 1772, during his second trip to Italy, Townley met Pope Clement XIV in a formal audience. Apart from Townley's Catholicism, he would also have had antiquities to discuss, as Clement was an enthusiast who had made major additions to the papacy's collection. At the time of the meeting, work was underway on the Museum Clementinum, a transformation of part of the Villa Belvedere at the Vatican into a gallery for classical sculpture. It was here that, two and half centuries earlier, Pope Julius II had placed his sculpture collection, including the *Apollo* Belvedere and the *Laocoön* group.

Pope Clement's museum was one of the first formal displays of classical sculpture in the world, and it must have been what Townley had in mind when he returned to London, looking to house his

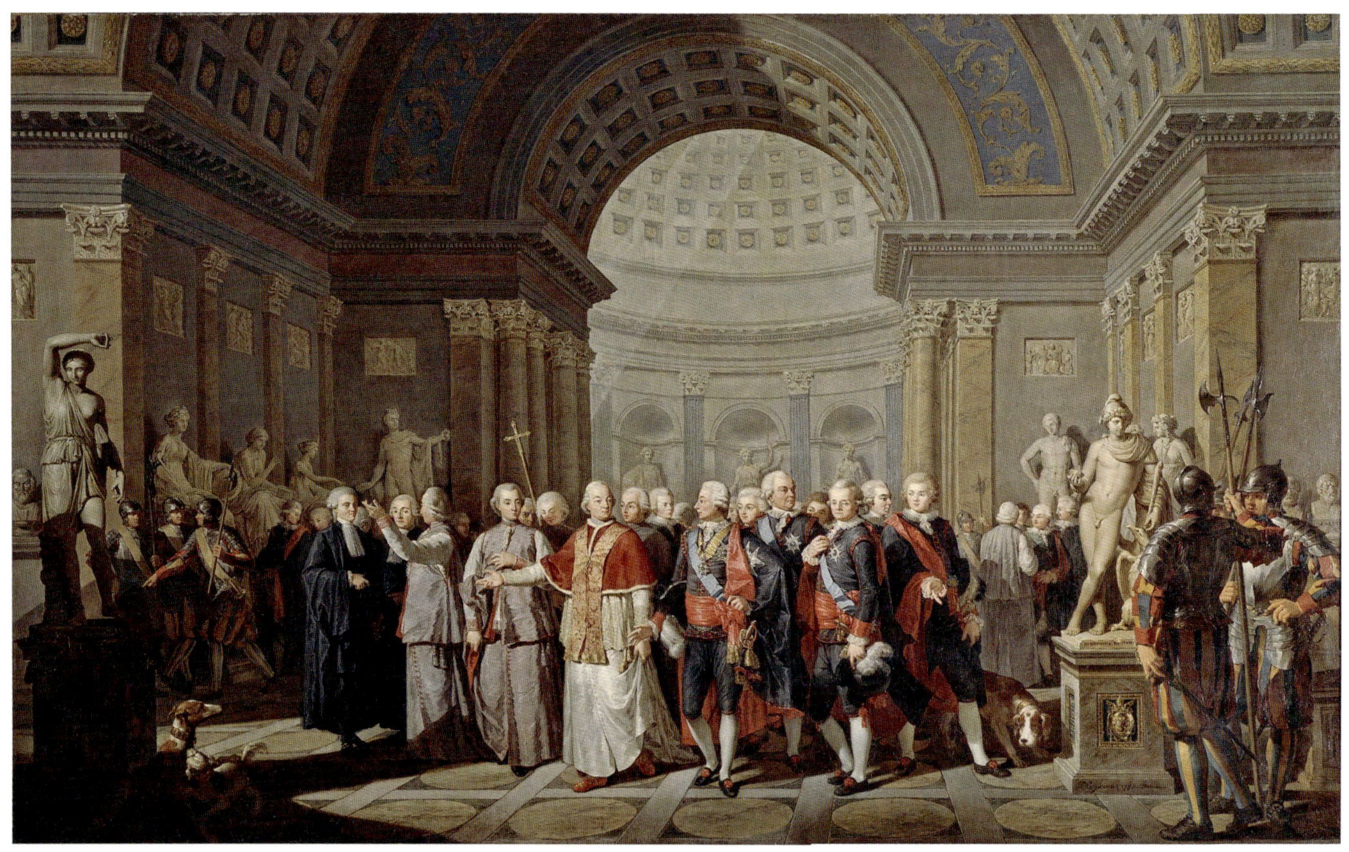

69. Pope Pius VI showing King Gustav III the Vatican
Galleries, *by Bénigne Gagneraux, 1785. The Museo Pio-
Clementino was opened on the first day of 1784, when
Gustav III was given a tour of the collection by Pope Pius VI
himself. On the far left are the curators, the Visconti brothers,
dressed in black cassocks. The Lutheran king was in Rome
to negotiate terms of toleration for Swedish Catholics. He
commissioned this painting to commemorate the tour, with
a copy also made for Pius. Shortly before his assassination in
1792, Gustav would found a similar museum in Stockholm.*

own collection. During the next few years
the construction of the new museum at the
Vatican continued to be one of the major cultural
projects of Europe. Clement died in 1774, and his
successor Pope Pius VI extended the museum with
even greater zeal, demolishing a chapel decorated
by Mantegna in the process, and building a new
wing to the Belvedere. The result was named
after both its founding popes – the Museo
Pio-Clementino [69].

Like Townley's display, the museum at the
Vatican was curated as a theatrical progression
through a suite of rooms. As Jeffrey Collins
writes, 'where the Pio-Clementino innovated
was in recasting the museum experience as
something transcendent or otherworldly, and
delivering a larger message ... that the popes were
the ultimate guardians of human culture'.[45] This

otherworldiness makes the Pio-Clementino a much closer analogue to Townley's display than anything in London.

Townley's programme of mystery cult ritual was of course quite different to anything at the Vatican. There were some superficial resemblances: at the eastern entrance to the Museo Pio-Clementino was a massive coffin, but Townley created a full programme of *katabasis*. There was a Stanza degli Animali, similar to the Street Parlour, but it did not have the presiding deity of Ceres to give the animals a mystical meaning.

Townley's display seems to have made for a popular attraction, and when records begin, in 1796, they show around five to six hundred visits annually, often consisting of a large party of people.[46]

In most cases Townley was present to show the visitor around. In James Boswell's biography of Samuel Johnson, Townley was given as a model for others to follow in opening up their collections to the public. The *Allgemeine Zeitung* wrote that it was by his public orientation that Townley favourably distinguished himself from his countrymen.[47]

When he was not around to give a tour, there was a two-volume guidebook, which listed the objects room by room. This was discreet: for example Priapus was referred to as 'the god of Lampsacus'. Nor did the guidebook discuss the symbolism of the groupings of objects on the ground floor: for this, Townley evidently had to be present himself, as the initiation priest (*telestes*).

It was at a relatively late stage that Townley decided to make the ground floor of No. 7 Park Street into a display space, and one of the non-architectural manifestations of this decision was that he discarded all the plinths he owned. No longer would antiquities be displayed on modern creations; instead, they were to be displayed on altars and pedestals of similar date to the

artworks themselves. With this approach Townley introduced the new Continental museum style, promoted by Piranesi and implemented at the Museo Pio-Clementino. The arrangement of sculpture was itself to be in an 'antique' style.[48] The unofficial curator after the departure of d'Hancarville was Joseph Nollekens, the leading portrait sculptor in London. Surprisingly, his reputation was not one of classical erudition. Nollekens used his practical knowledge of sculpture to supervise restorations and the installation of works in the house. He was also probably responsible for Townley's copy of one of the most notorious works of ancient erotic art. The symplegma of a satyr copulating with a goat had been discovered at Herculaneum, and was a quite different composition to the marble on the same subject owned by Townley [68]. Because drawing implements were prohibited in the Gabinetto Segreto at the Palazzo Portici, the group had to be recreated in terracotta from the artist's memory.[49]

Townley seems to have opened the house to the public by 1780.[50] By 1785 it was referred to as the 'Wilton House of London', referring to the manor house of the Earls of Pembroke near Salisbury where part of the Arundel collection was displayed.[51] In terms of international visitors, European nobility made regular appearances, as did any foreign ambassador stationed in London. Artists were frequent visitors, and it attracted influential ones such as James Barry and John Flaxman.[52] The latter said that the collection was 'ranking next after 2 or 3 which are to be found in Rome'.[53] The French scholar Quatremère de Quincy visited in 1788, and the painter Louise Élisabeth Vigée Le Brun visited repeatedly in 1802.[54]

The house was also an unofficial wing of the Royal Academy, whose students were welcome to draw from the sculptures. Female students were not yet admitted to the Academy, so the

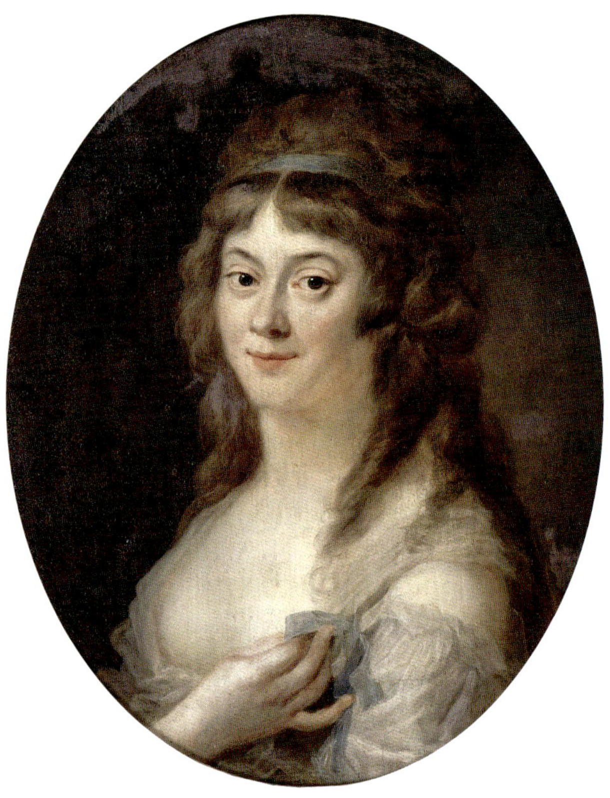

70. Manon Roland (1754–1793),
by Johann Julius Heinsius, 1792

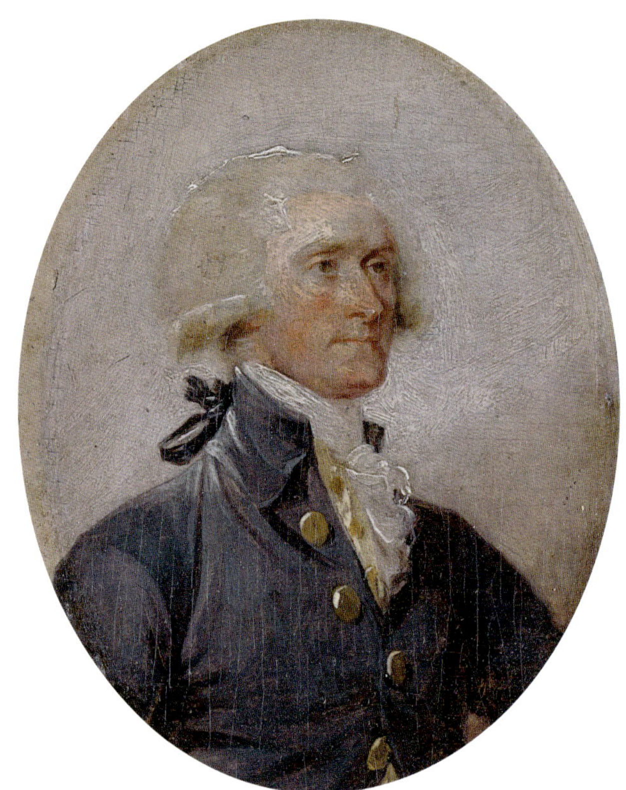

71. Thomas Jefferson (1743–1826),
by John Trumbull, 1788

woman drawing in the depiction of the Dining Room attributed to Chambers may have been an amateur [31, 43]. As records at the British Museum show, women represented a considerable number of the amateur students of the Antique.[55] This is despite the fact that there were concerns about the propriety of women drawing from the nude, concerns that increased later in the century.[56]

Perhaps more surprising is the interest of political figures, including four major revolutionaries. The first was French, Manon Roland [70], soon to be one of the most famous members, and ultimately martyrs, of the Girondin faction. She visited No. 7 Park Street in 1784, and in a letter to her daughter she described it as a striking contrast to the 'miserable' St James's Palace.[57] The Townley collection included works

that Roland had read about already in the writings of Winckelmann and in a survey of dress in antiquity.[58] She was particularly inspired by its sanctuary of creations by ancient Greek artists: 'every place is filled with their works snatched from the outrages of ignorance, or wrested from the scythe of time'.[59]

Thomas Jefferson [71] would have been famous as the principal author of the Declaration of Independence when he visited London in 1784 and 1786 to negotiate trade agreements for the new United States. Although his affair with Richard Cosway's wife Maria is generally thought to have taken place exclusively in Paris, other accounts have their first meeting beforehand, at 7 Park Street.[60] Another of Maria Cosway's reputed lovers was the revolutionary Pasquale Paoli [72], the leader of

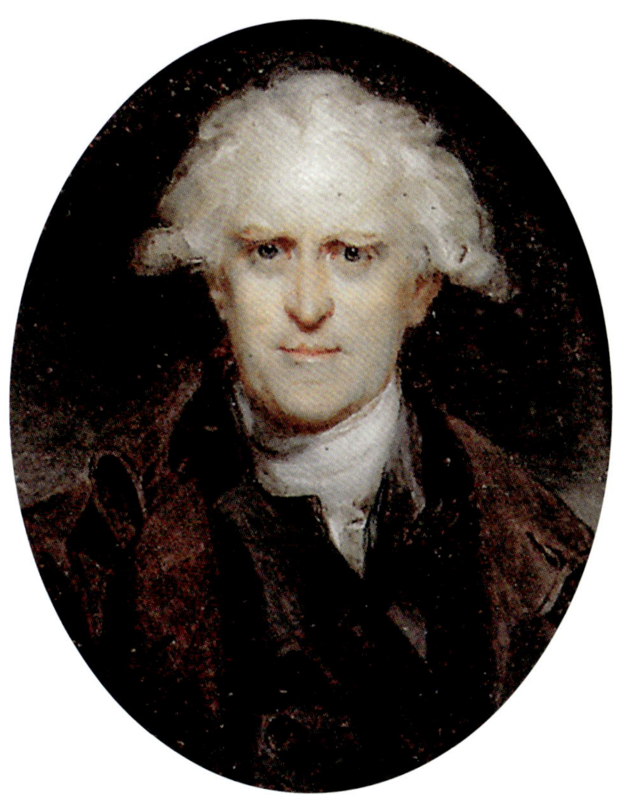

72. Pasquale Paoli (1725–1807),
by William Grimaldi, 1800

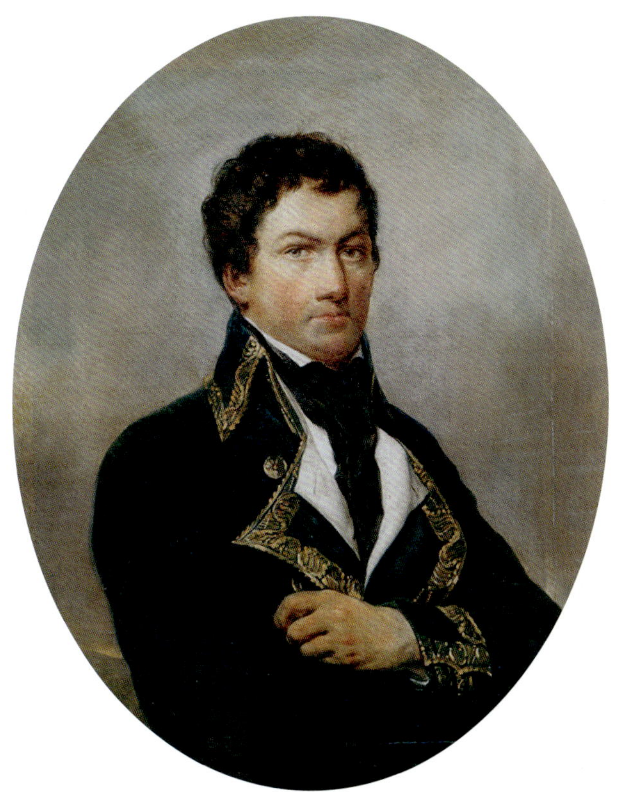

73. Francisco de Miranda (1750–1816),
by Georges Rouget, 1835 (detail)

the movement to free Corsica from French rule. He had been exiled to London in 1795 after the British decided to remove him as president of the 'Anglo-Corsican Kingdom', allowing the island to fall back into the hands of the French. Paoli visited No. 7 regularly in the company of Maria Cosway during his final years.[61]

In 1800, Townley's collection was visited by Francisco de Miranda [73], the Venezuelan revolutionary who sought to liberate all Hispanic America from Spanish rule. In his diary he noted that Townley was '*un hombre que ame, honre y respete las Bellas Artes*'.[62] At this time the Spanish empire, stretching from Alaska to Argentina, was administered from Madrid, to enormous economic profitability and increasing native discontent. At the time of his visit Miranda had just escaped from

France, where he had fought as a general in the Revolutionary Army before being imprisoned by the Jacobins and conspiring with monarchists to overthrow the Directoire.

One wonders what these four revolutionaries must have made of the collection at 7 Park Street, and whether they were aware of the dimension of Bacchic initiation. In Greece one of the god's titles was Dionysus Eleutherios, 'Bacchus the liberator'. In the eighth book of Plato's *Republic*, Socrates discussed the process of political revolution, from oligarchy to democracy, arguing that it was based on a liberation of desires in a citizen's soul (*psyche*). While he considered it harmful, Socrates compared this liberation, in an elaborate metaphor, to initiation into a Bacchic mystery cult.[63]

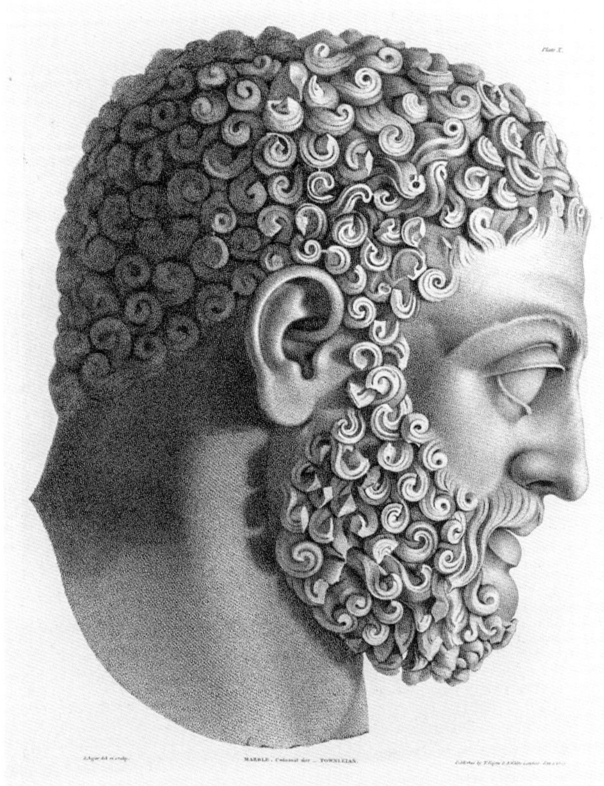

74a–b. *'Head of Hercules' (Parlour Catalogue: Park Drawing Room), engraved for* Specimens of Antient Sculpture *(1809) with the damage occasioned by religious bigotry (according to the text of* Specimens*) rectified*

Public accessibility had its costs. In 1780, anti-Catholic rioting spread through London, and Townley's house became a potential target. Popular feeling was always against the Catholics, with the much-mutilated statue on the wall separating Park Street from Queen Square a daily reminder of the undercurrent of hostility. Townley could have seen from his window the local children abusing it in the name of anti-Catholicism, and by the mid nineteenth century it had lost both its nose and right arm.[64]

Vividly evoked by Charles Dickens in his historical novel *Barnaby Rudge* (1841), the 'Gordon Riots' were named after their instigator, the Scottish Protestant Lord George Gordon.

In June, Gordon led a march of fifty thousand people to the Houses of Parliament in protest at a moderate extension of civil liberties to British Catholics. When the mob arrived in Westminster, a campaign of vandalism began that would last days. The government ordered four thousand troops to camp in St James's Park. Townley could have felt it foretold in his painting by Poussin of Titus attempting to restrain the Roman sack of Jerusalem [36].

Townley's name had been published as one of the signatories of an address that preceded the Roman Catholic Act, so he knew he would be a target. He appealed for royal protection through the physician to the Prince of Wales, Sir John Eliot. A dozen soldiers were dispatched to No. 7 Park Street for the house's protection, with two hand-grenades each, and a sign reading 'No Popery' was put up outside. Eliot wrote that this was 'for the honour of the nation, to which your genius and taste add so much lustre'.[65] Another friend offered her house to shelter the marbles.[66] Fortunately Park Street escaped the riots, and the vandalism to the statue of Queen Anne was not inflicted elsewhere. But religious bigotry emerges as a frequent source of anxiety in Townley's letters. Such a position was conventional for Enlightenment antiquarians, deriving in part from Lucretius's anti-religious comments in *De rerum natura*. Lucretius was quoted on the subject in Townley's letters, for whom these themes had a personal dimension.[67] In *Specimens*, the damage done to his colossal head of Hercules [74] was interpreted not as the work of Vandals and Goths, but of early Christians: 'the destruction here, as in other places, was not by the sudden impulse of barbarian fury, but by the deliberate operation of religious bigotry'.[68]

From 1794, there was a second great collection to be visited by the pilgrims to Park Street. William Smith's house at No. 6 Park Street

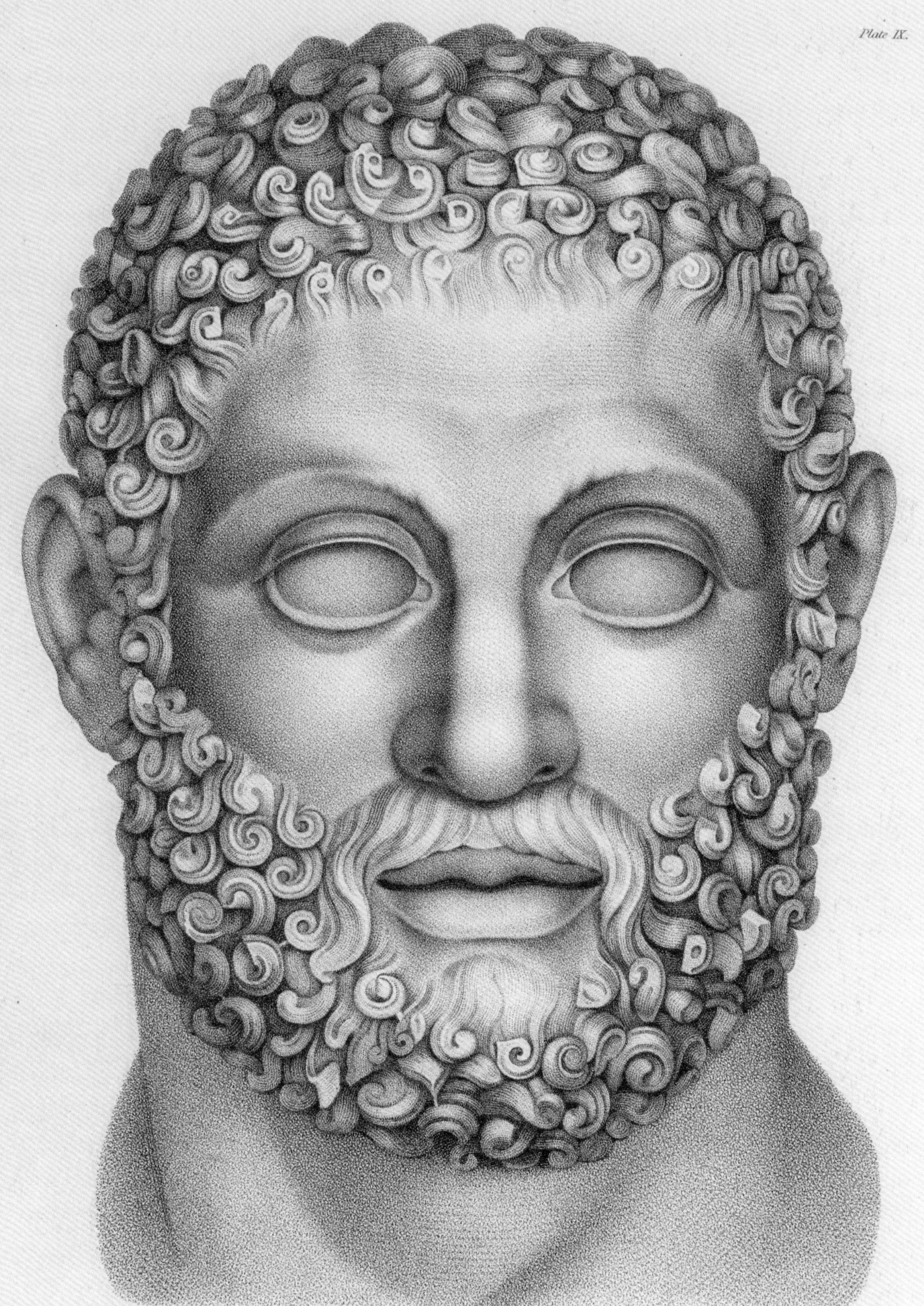

Plate IX.
J. Agar. del et sculp.
BRASS. Colossal-Size — TOWNLEIAN.
Published by T. Payne & J. White London Jan.1.1804.

(now 16 Queen Anne's Gate) displayed his paintings collection, and many of Townley's guests may have made a second stop there. In 1795 Smith purchased *Sarah Siddons as the Tragic Muse* (1784) by Joshua Reynolds, one of the masterpieces of British art. Smith's purchase, coming so soon after he moved in, may have been inspired by the memory of the late Reynolds's frequent visits to Townley's house, as well as by the antique Muses on display there. Smith's painting is now in the Huntington Art Gallery in San Marino, California.

The museum that is now best known as an analogue to Townley's is that of the architect John Soane. He created an unstructured ensemble of painting, sculpture and architectural fragments at his house at Lincoln's Inn Fields that survives intact to this day. Sir John Soane's Museum, however, was conceived well after Townley's death, during the expansion of the original house at No. 12 Lincoln's Inn Fields into the back of No. 13 (1808–09), the front of No. 13 (1812–13), and into No. 14 (1824).

Soane's name has not been found among those who applied to visit Townley's house, though he probably would have visited as part of a group. He must have drawn some inspiration from its memory, but in many ways the two displays were antithetical. While Townley's had been for members of the genteel public, Soane's was specifically for architecture students. Both took foreign models, but Townley's were Italian museums of antique sculpture, while Soane's were didactic French museums of architecture that had been formed after the Revolution.

Soane did not have anything like the systematic sensibility required to curate a didactic display of design. The patriotic project of his museum may also have caused a reaction against his French inspiration. The public pedagogy of the Musée des Monuments Français became at Lincoln's Inn Fields a picturesque domesticity, in line with British taste. The strangeness of Sir John Soane's Museum was the result of this contradictory mixture of museological modes, where the complete history of architecture was presented without any theoretical framework. There had been no such anxiety of influence at Park Street.

Townley nevertheless used his house for public service, for example for meetings of the trustees of the British Museum. In 1802–03 a committee was established to plan the new gallery of Egyptian antiquities. This comprised Townley, Joseph Banks and William Hamilton, with Thomas Astle replacing Hamilton after his death. Meeting at No. 7 Park Street afforded the committee 'abundant opportunities of studying the most approved methods of exhibiting works of Sculpture to advantage'.[69] This was worthwhile research, because Townley's sculptures arrived at the British Museum during the new gallery's construction, and it was decided that they should be displayed there instead.

Perhaps most revealing of the importance of the display at No. 7 Park Street was the decision of the painter Johan Zoffany to depict it in one of the key images of eighteenth-century Britain [75]. The painting, begun in 1781, is a 'conversation piece', a portrait group of close friends or family, engaged in a communal activity, located at home surrounded by their possessions. As such, the conversation was almost as much sociology as art. It was a form that emerged in continental Europe, arriving in Britain in the 1720s, and became a popular alternative to genre scenes, history painting and grand portraiture.

The painting is a *capriccio* of Townleiana, showing the Library fancifully filled with highlights from around the museum. Townley, seated in profile at the right, is shown with three friends, d'Hancarville, Charles Greville and Thomas Astle. Greville, shown with his arm

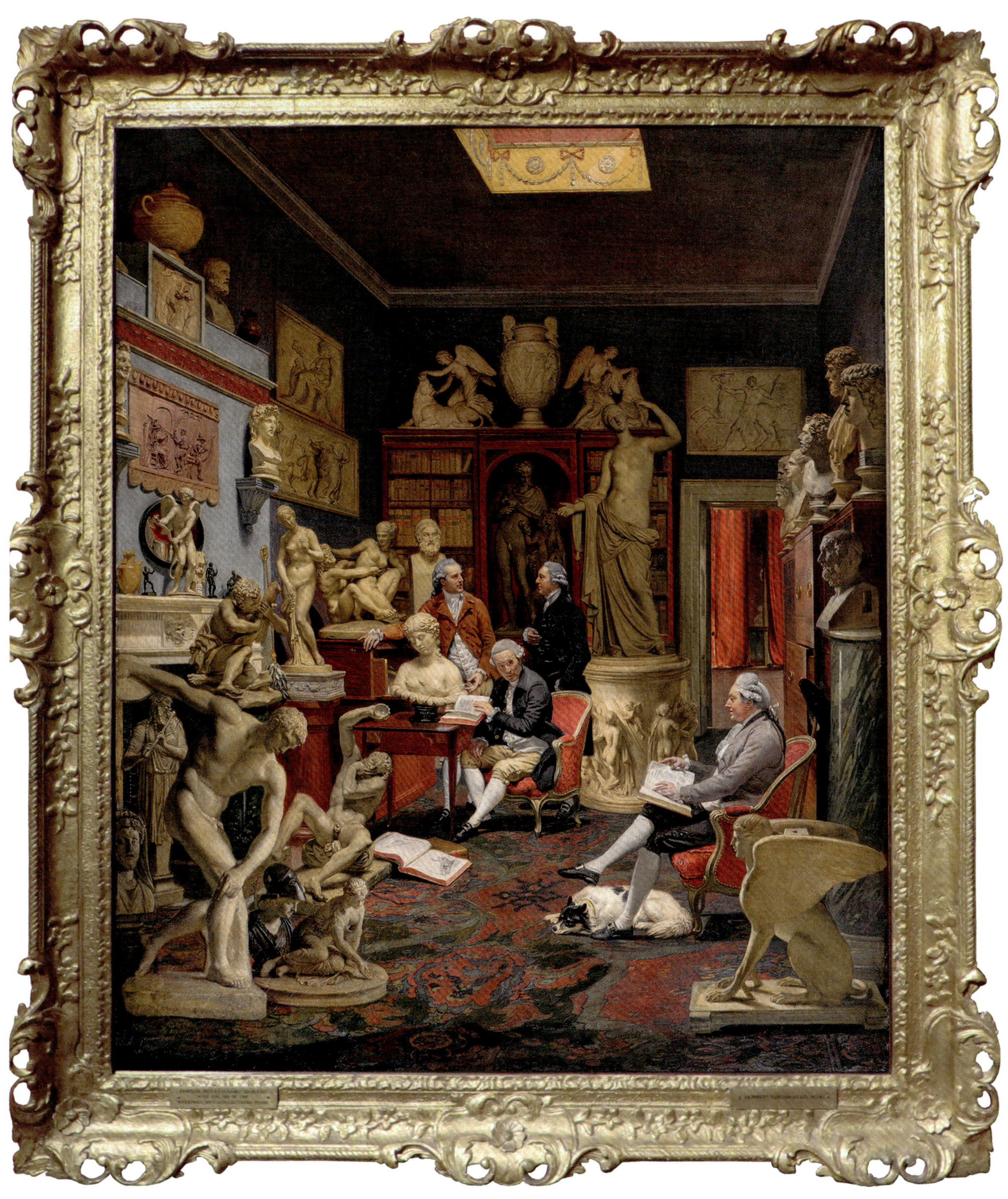

75. A Nobleman's Collection *by Johan Zoffany,
1781–83, exhibited 1790 and altered 1798*

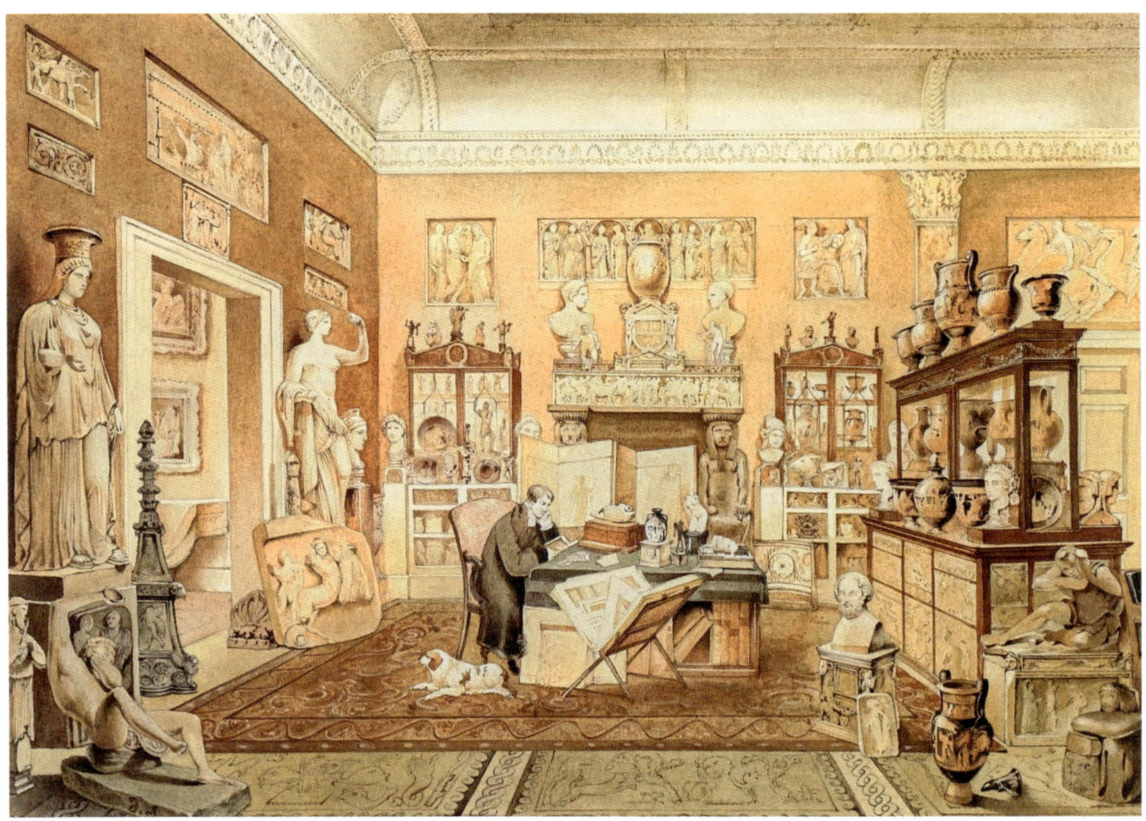

76. The Connoisseur, *by James Stephanoff, 1817*

around the bust of Isis, formed one of the world's finest collections of minerals, including gems and meteorites. Astle, shown in conversation with him, was a collector of books and manuscripts. His *Origin and Progress of Writing* was published in 1784, the same year as d'Hancarville's *Recherches*, and represented a closely analogous project. Baron d'Hancarville himself is shown in conversation with Townley: they both have books open, and are discussing the *Silenus recumbent* [58]. Next to the sculpture lies another book, open to a page showing a comparable example [59].

The concept for the painting was Zoffany's, probably inspired by the opening of Townley's house to the public the year before; he also shared the sitter's Catholicism. Zoffany did not finish the work for many years, having been interrupted by a long visit to India, and it was exhibited at the Royal Academy first in 1790. In 1798 he added the *Discobolus*, a new acquisition, and gave the painting to Townley, who wrote in his diary of his astonishment at receiving such a gift.[70]

The original intention may have been to produce a widely published mezzotint of the painting, and Townley even drafted a key to all the sculptures in the painting for general understanding.[71] Though a print was not realised in his lifetime, the painting has nevertheless become an endlessly reproduced image of the Enlightenment. A work of modern mythopoeia, it transformed Townley into the ideal *virtuoso*. When the print was finally produced in 1833, it bore the title '*The Townleian Museum*'.

In 1817, James Stephanoff exhibited the first in a series of watercolour drawings based on the antiquities collection of the British Museum. Titled *The Connoisseur* [76], it was clearly based on Zoffany's painting, which had since been exhibited at the British Institution. Stephanoff was probably also inspired by his own memories of Townley's house from his time in the Royal Academy Schools. Many of the sculptures reappear, and even a dog is present at his master's feet. But otherwise the connoisseur is alone, his robe suggesting that his studies are a break from a day job. His pose contrasts him with the sculpted figures, as is further emphasized by the placement of some objects behind glass. The word 'connoisseur' itself more narrowly emphasizes knowledge than does 'virtuoso'.

In contrast to Stephanoff's drawing, Zoffany's painting presents a sense of continuity with the ancient world. The poses of Townley and his friends explicitly mirror those of the sculptures that surround them. Rather than a solitary figure at the centre, scholars and sculptures are composed as part of a larger equilibrium. Such a sense of continuity was something that Townley's house embodied, epitomized in the tag 'knowing the old things, you will understand the new'. D'Hancarville put it this way, in a description of the ancient world:

Ces temps, si éloignés de nous, se lient avec celui où nous vivons; car c'est par la secrète influence qu'ils ont sur les Esprits, que les Siècles se touchent & se rapprochent, malgré l'intervalle de la Durée qui les sépare.[72]

This era, so distant from us, is bound with the one wherein we live; by its secret influence over the spirit, the centuries touch and reconcile, despite the division of time.

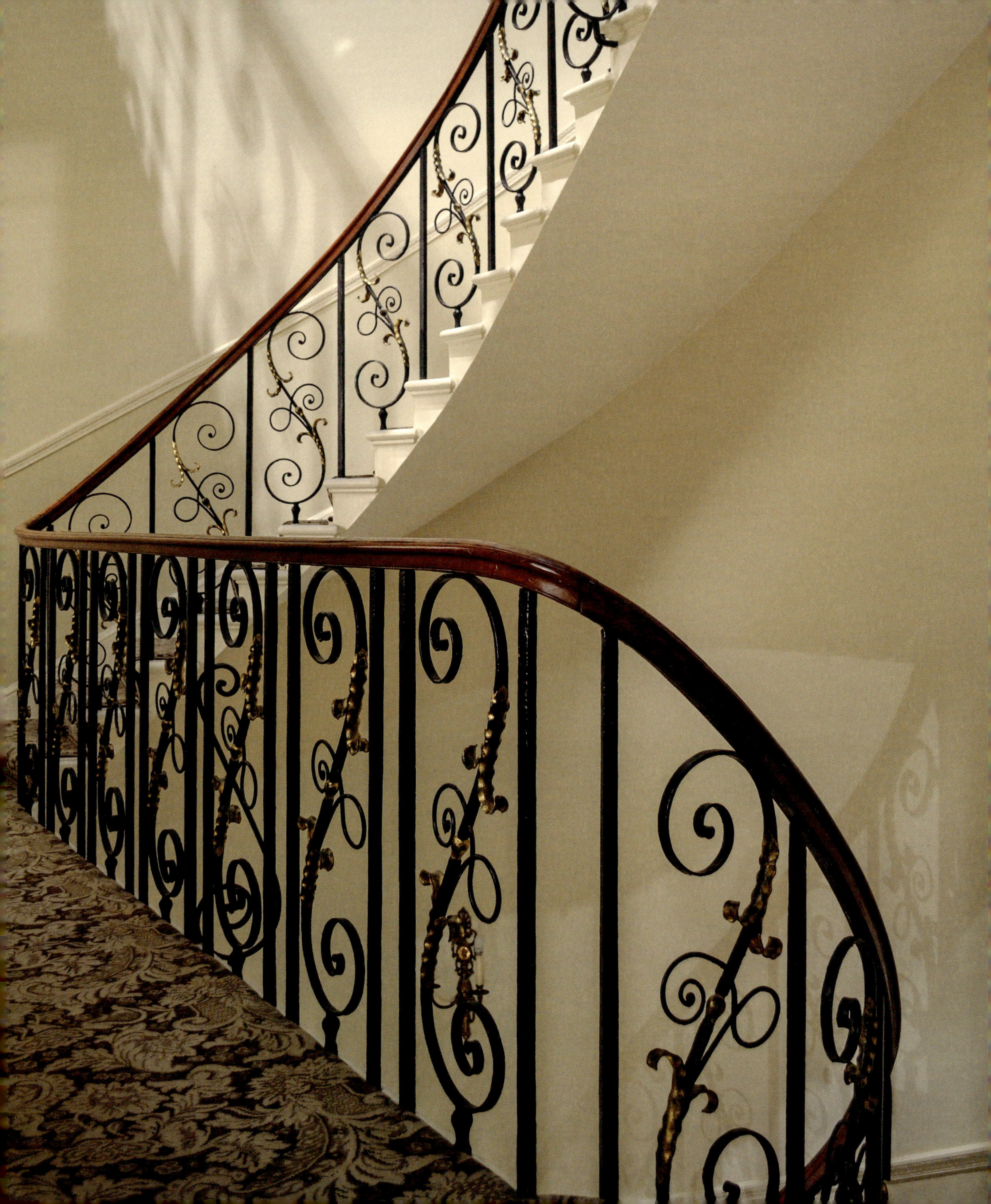

6. A HOUSE OF RESIDENCE

AT THE END OF THE EIGHTEENTH CENTURY, the neighbourhood of No. 7 Park Street developed a reputation for political radicalism. This was partly due to the presence of Jeremy Bentham, the giant of British philosophy who founded modern utilitarianism. From 1792 he lived at Queen Square Place, a cul-de-sac at the entrance to Queen Square [6]. The same year he used the house to display a model of his experimental prison, the 'panopticon', that persuaded the Prime Minister, William Pitt, to build the design. Somewhat appropriately, with Queen Square Place razed in the late nineteenth century, it became the present site of the looming Ministry of Justice.

Bentham also owned property in the environs of Queen Square Place, and used it to house refugees from Revolutionary France. He rented nearby houses to figures such as the social reformer Edwin Chadwick and the literary critic William Hazlitt. The latter was proud to live, from 1813 until 1819, at the house formerly owned by John Milton, known then as No. 19 York Street.

Another Bentham tenant was the dour Scottish political philosopher James Mill, who lived in Queen Square from 1814 until 1831 at the house now known as 40 Queen Anne's Gate. Thus it was also the childhood home of Mill's son, John Stuart Mill, and the site of his bizarre education, which involved learning ancient Greek at age three and reading most of its literature by age twelve. Public

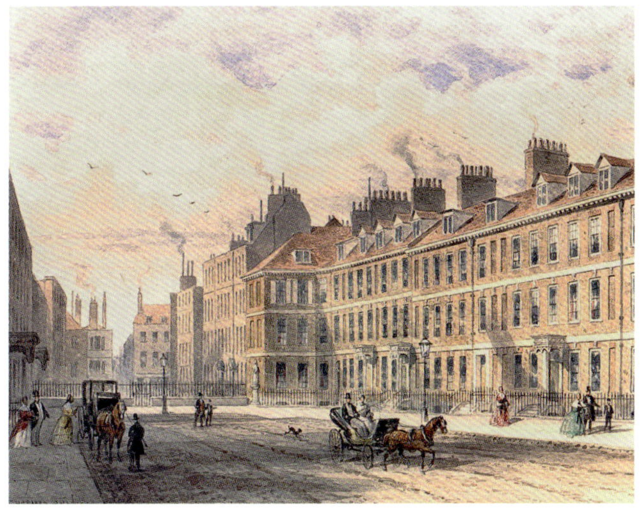

78. *Queen Square in 1851, in a watercolour drawing by Thomas Shepherd, showing the new arrangement of the barrier into Park Street*

FACING: 77. *The staircase of 14 Queen Anne's Gate, from the first-floor landing*

visits to No. 7 Park Street ended with Townley's death in 1805, so the Mill family missed out on its more sensual presentation of the classical world.

The sculptures that had been the dominant architectural feature of the house were removed to the British Museum. One exception is known: the relief of the mystical marriage over the entrance to the Dining Room was replaced, possibly in jest, with a relief of a large pig [79]. Long identified, erroneously, as a cast of the

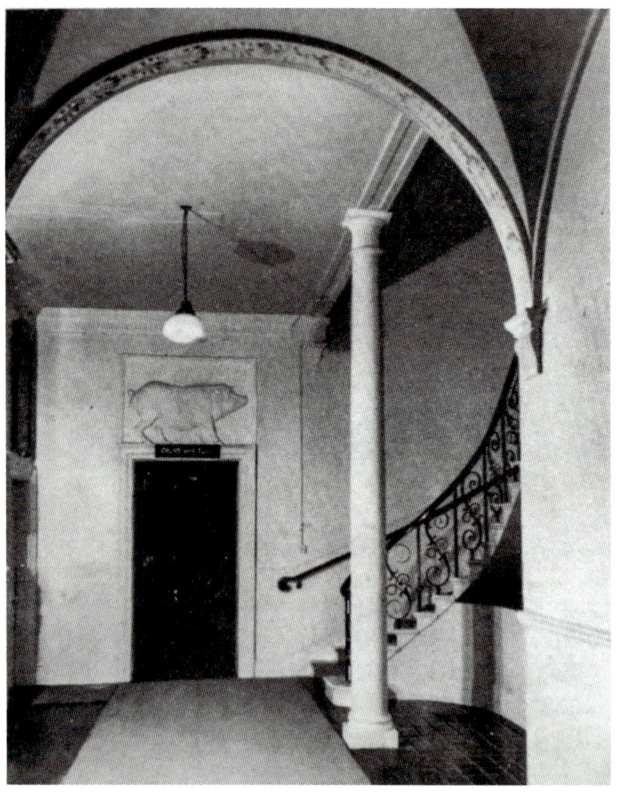

79. *The entrance to the Dining Room with the sculpture of a hog in situ, c.1952*

famous Florentine bronze *Porcellino*, it is likely to have been a contemporary work. A possible identification is the 'Berkshire hog' exhibited at the Royal Academy in 1799 by the sculptor George Garrard.[1] The pig remained over the door until renovations in the 1980s. Throughout the succession of august residents and businesses at 14 Queen Anne's Gate, the ground floor would be dominated by this somewhat absurdist feature.

Charles Townley's younger brother Ralph had died in 1766, so the house was first inherited by Edward, the youngest. Edward died in 1807, and like both his brothers had no children. While most of the estate then went to their sister, the house on Park Street was inherited by their uncle John, the younger brother of their father. This may have been because the size of the house was ideal for a

widower living alone, as John was, and as Edward had been.

John also shared Townley's scholarly interests, and was given a trusteeship at the British Museum in April 1807 to thank him for not obstructing the purchase of the marbles.[2] When John moved into the house on Park Street, he brought his library, reformatting the Dining Room and first-floor Drawing Room on the Park side to accommodate it. John died in 1813 in the second-floor bedroom overlooking the park, as his nephew had done.[3]

During all this time, the vast majority of Charles Townley's possessions were still at the house. When John's children sold most of the remainder, No. 7 Park Street must have become a much more conventionally habitable residence. It was at this time that John's widowed daughter Barbara [80] moved into the house, staying for

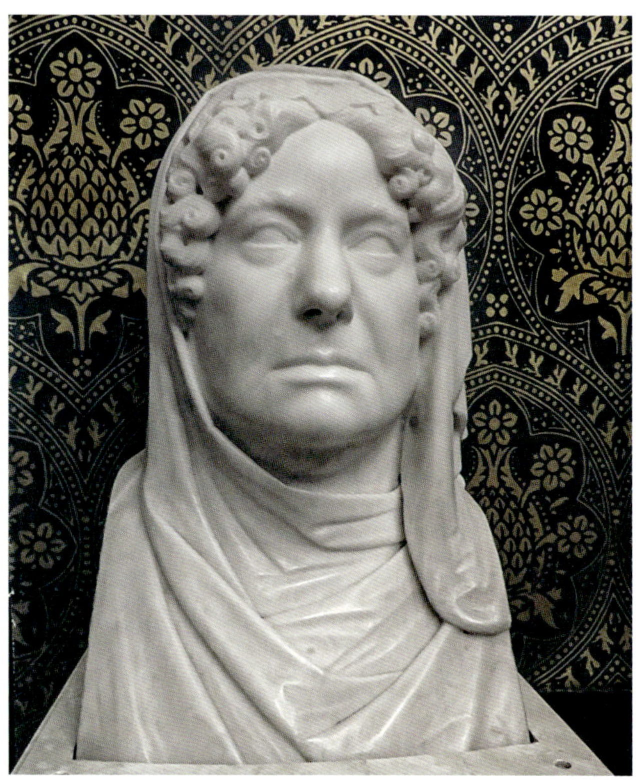

80. *Barbara Towneley (1758–1836) by William Griggs, c.1820*

four years from 1816. She was followed by her
brother Peregrine in 1821, and he is recorded as
a resident at the house until at least 1840.[4] He
also named his son Charles, which suggests that,
despite selling his cousin's collection, he had a
sense of his significance.

During these years the surrounding area
underwent a transformation. First, some time
before 1814, the statue of Queen Anne was moved
from the centre of the wall to its present position.
One large gate replaced the two smaller ones
flanked by the statue [78]. After its demolition in
1816, the lease for the Royal Cockpit remained
with the cockfighting company until 1824, when
Christ's Hospital refused to renew it on the
grounds of the sport's cruelty.[5] They probably also
had in mind the deleterious effect a new one would
have on the value of rents, as well as the greater
potential for residential space. The archway into
Dartmouth Street was taken down in 1829.

In 1836–38 a row of houses was built on the
site of the Cockpit, now Nos. 4, 6, 8, 10 and 12
Queen Anne's Gate. These were by James Elmes, a
rare executed project by a figure best known as an
architectural journalist. He was assisted by his son
Henry, who would go on to be one of the great
British architects of the Victorian era. No. 12 was
designed specifically for the Turkish ambassador,
and a grand Doric enfilade survives inside.

Peregrine Edward Towneley died in 1846, and,
although his children were still alive, they decided
to sell No. 7 Park Street. The first owner of No.
7 outside the Townley family was Thomas Spring
Rice [81]. Rice was Irish, but a fervent Unionist
who even proposed renaming his homeland 'West
Britain'.[6] In a sequence of events that would be
repeated for many subsequent owners of the
house, Rice's purchase of it followed a large
inheritance. His own income was nugatory, Irish
land having been devalued by the Great Famine
during the 1840s. His father-in-law, however, was

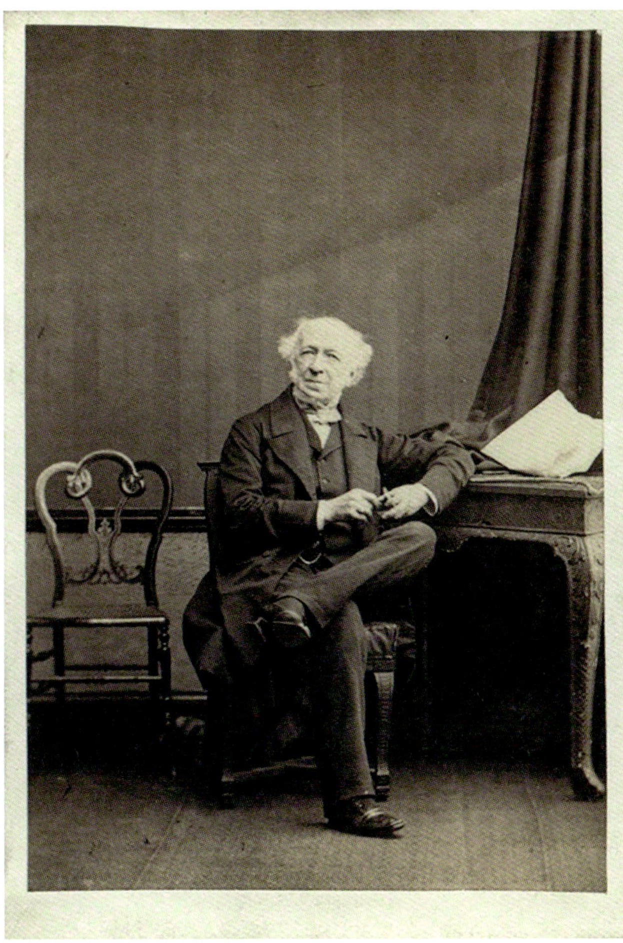

81. *Thomas Spring Rice (1790–1866). This portrait was
taken in the photographer's studio, not at Park Street.*

the wealthy Leeds industrialist John Marshall,
who died in 1845, leaving the estate that led to
Rice's purchase of the house in 1848.

During his time at the house, Rice was an
undistinguished member of the House of Lords,
a peerage having been awarded him after a brief
and unsuccessful period as Chancellor of the
Exchequer in 1835–39. Rice would charitably be
described as a journeyman politician, dependent
for his career on a patron. This patron was Henry
Petty-Fitzmaurice, Lord Lansdowne, the son of
Townley's collecting rival, and the builder of the
belated sculpture gallery at Lansdowne House.

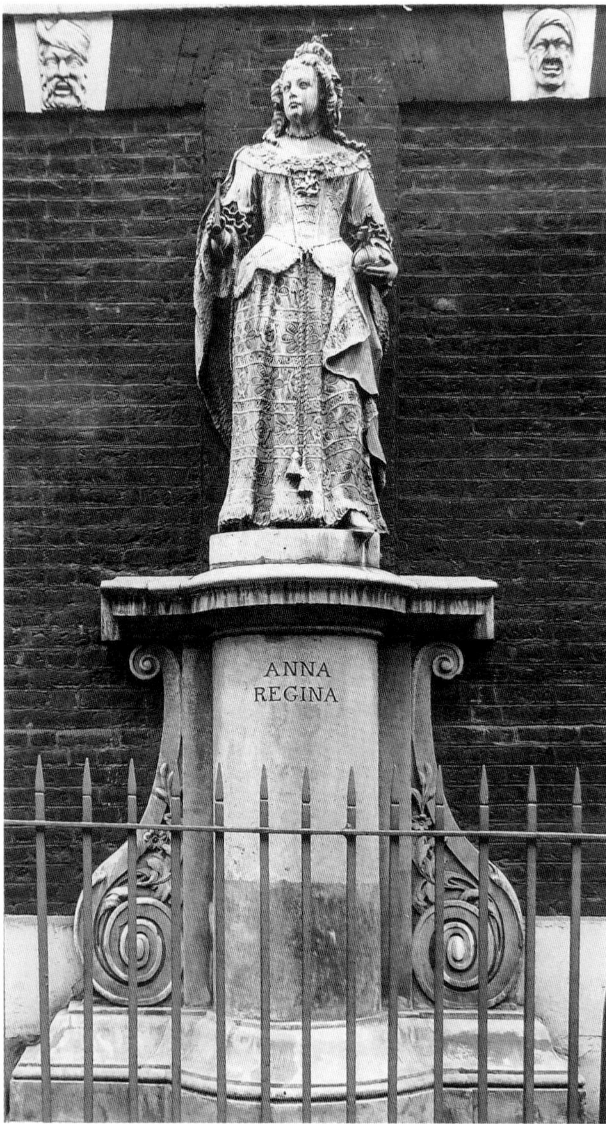

82. *Photograph taken in 1875 showing the statue of Queen Anne in its present location in Queen Anne's Gate. By an unknown sculptor, c.1705, the statue was restored by John Thomas in 1862.*

Rice retained the house as his London residence until his own death in 1866.

During this time action was finally taken regarding the traditional anti-Catholic vandalism of the statue of Queen Anne. Repairs would usually have been the responsibility of the Office of Works, but it was not listed as in their care, probably because since the first years of the century it had been attached to the wall of a private property. In November 1861 a group of local residents petitioned the Office to repair it, which assented and sought funds from the Treasury, arguing that no image of 'an illustrious sovereign should be left in a public place without a nose or a left arm'.[7] The repairs were made by John Thomas, notable as the artist in charge of the sculpture on the nearby Houses of Parliament. In May 1862 Thomas replaced the face, attached a left arm and added the inscription identifying the figure as Queen Anne, evidently in the hope that this would dissuade vandals [82]. The first report of continued vandalism arrived at the Office of Works in August.

The next occupier of No. 7 Park Street began a tradition of civil engineers in residence at the house, attracted by its proximity to the Institution of Civil Engineers on Great George Street. Joseph Cubitt [84] constructed great swathes of the railways that appeared across Britain in the middle decades of the nineteenth century. His most significant work while living at the house was building Blackfriars Bridge, connecting the City of London to Southwark on the south side of the Thames [83]. It is architecturally notable for its piers, with red granite columns and stone capitals carved by the sculptor John Birnie Philip. Completed in 1869, and subsequently widened, Cubitt's bridge is still in constant use by Londoners today.

Cubitt died at the house in December 1872. In 1873, while Cubitt's widow stayed on at the property, the railing and wall between Queen

Square and Park Street were removed. The whole
extent was renamed Queen Anne's Gate, and the
houses were renumbered.

The first owner of '14 Queen Anne's Gate',
rather than '7 Park Street', was the amateur
astronomer Frank McClean [85]. He bought the
house in 1874 with a recent large inheritance,
which he would also use to build a private
observatory at Tunbridge Wells. Two years later,
his son Francis was born, later to be a pioneer
in British aviation, establishing the Eastchurch

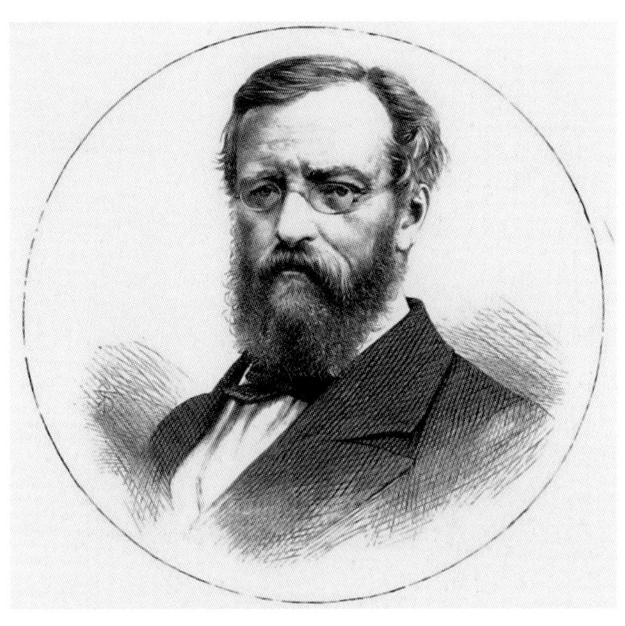

84. *Joseph Cubitt (1811–1872)*

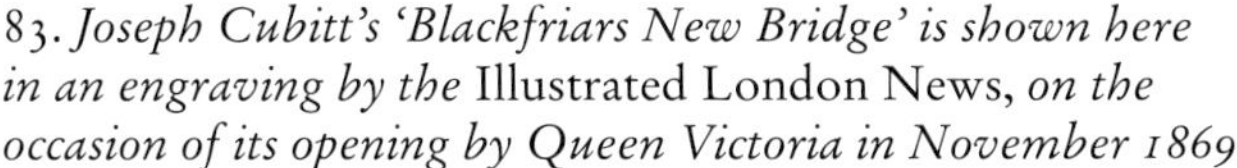

83. *Joseph Cubitt's 'Blackfriars New Bridge' is shown here
in an engraving by the* Illustrated London News, *on the
occasion of its opening by Queen Victoria in November 1869.*

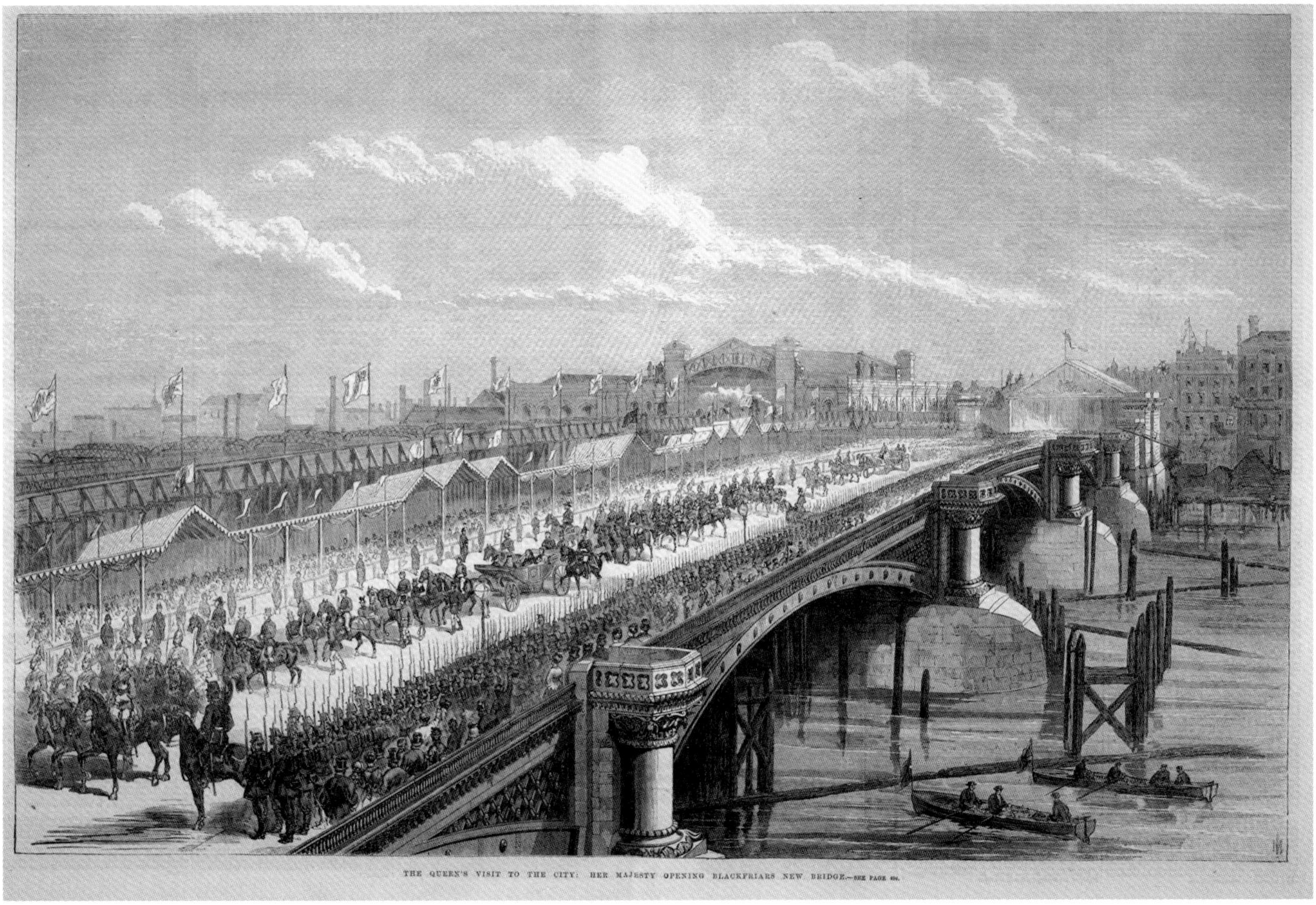

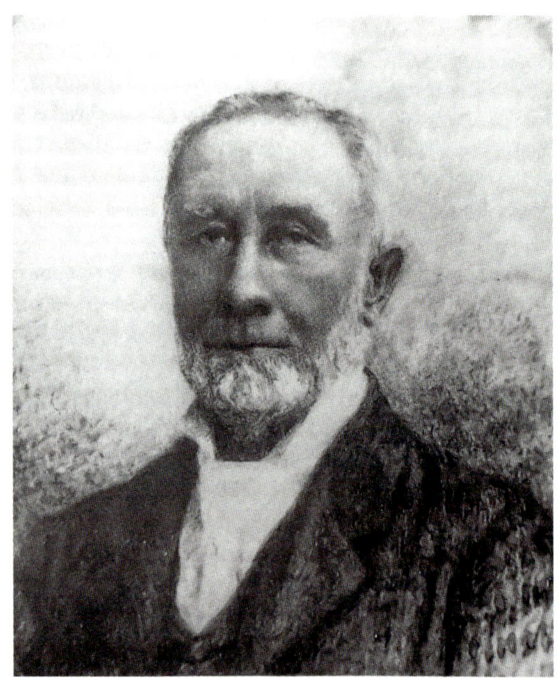

85. Frank McClean (1837–1904)

airfield in 1909 and testing aircraft built by the
Short Brothers. His only memories of Queen
Anne's Gate would have been childhood ones,
as his father sold it in 1883, having built a house
with a laboratory and heliostat elsewhere.

The next resident was the most aristocratic
in the whole history of the neighbourhood,
the eighth Duke of Marlborough [86]. George
Charles Spencer-Churchill was described by the
Prince of Wales, later Edward VII, as 'the greatest
blackguard alive'.[8] Now known as the uncle of
Winston Churchill, at the time he was notorious
for his womanizing, in particular his long-running
affair with the Countess of Aylesford. She gave
birth to his illegitimate child, precipitating divorce
proceedings, during which he inherited the
dukedom on the death of his father in 1883.

The duke was responsible for architectural
renovations to the house. The Entrance Hall was
given a new tessellated pavement with the Spencer-

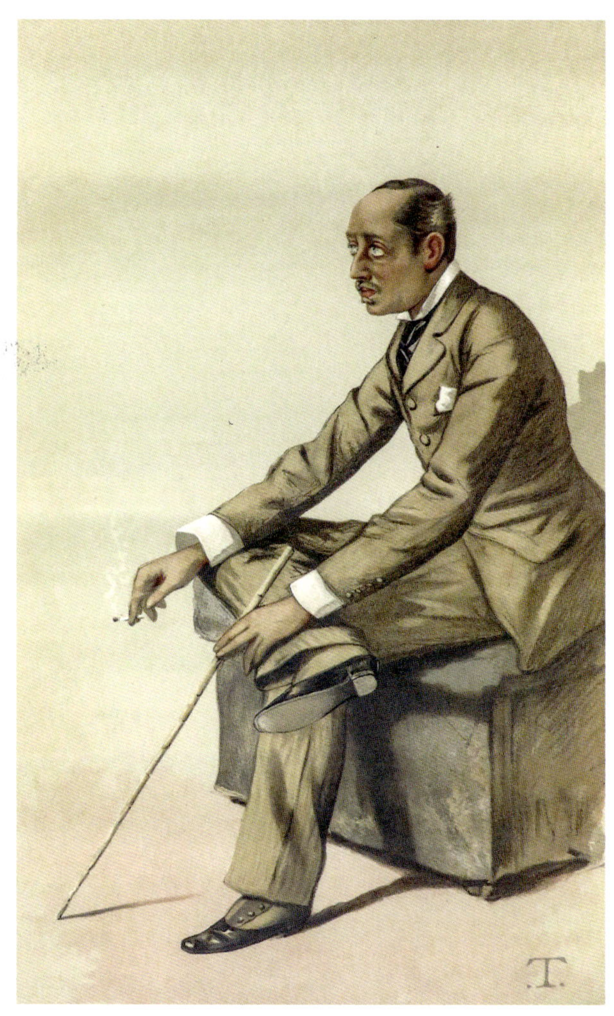

86. George Charles Spencer-Churchill,
8th Duke of Marlborough (1844–1892)

Churchill arms, a dense palimpsest of heraldry.
This suggests he was also responsible for the
closure of the lower flight of the main staircase,
leading from the ground floor to the basement.
Above it was floored over, and below bricked up,
so that its existence was forgotten for decades. It
was replaced with a new staircase, in the position
of the present secretary's office, leading from the
basement into an anteroom and then on into the
Dining Room through a new secondary door.
When the main flight was rediscovered in the
1950s, the wear on the stone steps showed it had
been in constant use prior to its closure.[9] Late
nineteenth-century manners evidently required the
clear segregation of traffic of master and servant.

Spencer-Churchill lived at Queen Anne's
Gate for the three years he spent as a bachelor,
from 1884 to 1887. He was on the lookout for a
lucrative marriage to fund his new responsibility,
Blenheim Palace, a masterpiece of Baroque
architecture that is also one of the largest buildings
in Britain. In 1888 he married an American
socialite, Lily Hamersley, née Price, the widow of
a real estate heir in New York. It was a Gilded Age
marriage straight from the pages of Henry James,
a transatlantic union of money and title. The duke
used the resulting influx of American cash to
restore Blenheim Palace, where he died four
years later.

The duke was followed in 1888 by Elliott Lees
[87], who had recently become a Conservative MP
and must have chosen the house for its proximity
to the Houses of Parliament. He was made a
Baronet in 1897, and in 1900–01 participated
as a captain in the Second Boer War. Britain's

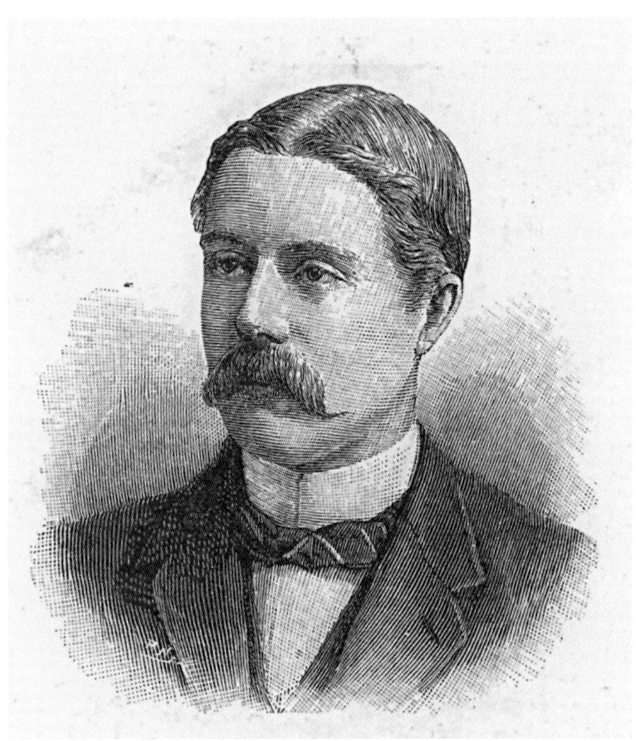

87. *Elliott Lees (1860–1908)*

victory over the independent Boer states in 1902
resulted in their annexation and the formation
of the present territory of South Africa. History
also remembers the war for the British invention
of concentration camps, when for the first time
civilians were systematically interned as a tactic of
warfare. The notoriety of the resulting mass death
partly led to the defeat of the Conservatives at
the next election in 1906, and Lees lost his seat to
a Liberal. He then departed Queen Anne's Gate,
leaving it to his son, who stayed there for a year
after his graduation from university.

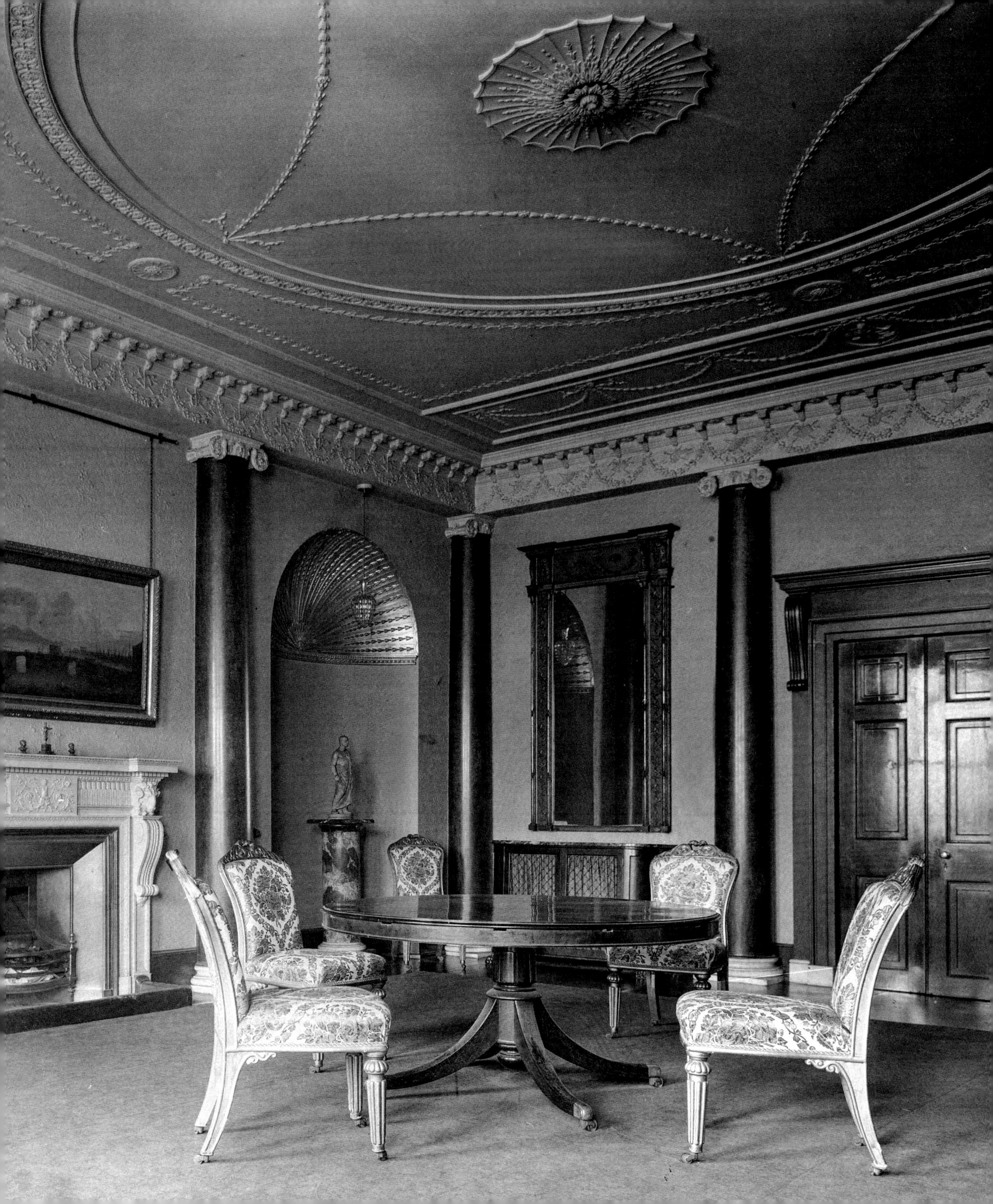

7. A HOUSE OF CAMPAIGN

AFTER A CENTURY OF RELATIVELY QUIET domesticity, the former No. 7 Park Street returned to national importance in the 1910s. John St Loe Strachey [89] arrived in 1909, and he made the house directly instrumental to the progress of the 'Great War'. Strachey was editor of the conservative weekly magazine *The Spectator*, the most widely read political periodical in the country. He was, and remains, the magazine's longest-serving editor, presiding over it for nearly four decades, from 1887 until 1925. Coincidentally, since 2007 the premises of *The Spectator* have been near the residence of its former editor, on Old Queen Street.

Strachey knew the history of No. 14 Queen Anne's Gate, if only from his daughter Amabel. Later a prominent poet and Communist, Amabel lived and was educated at the house, and as a teenager she published the first modern account of 'the Townley Museum'.[1] She also published a short play, imagining a debate at the house between Charles Townley and Horace Walpole, each icon of the eighteenth century defending his own taste. While impressively researched, Strachey could not avoid projecting the aesthetic assumptions of her own time, when 'Classicism' and 'the Gothic' had etiolated into a binary of rationality and irrationality. She had Townley declare that 'Restraint, Temperance, and Reticence must always be the three foundations of Art. They are the three

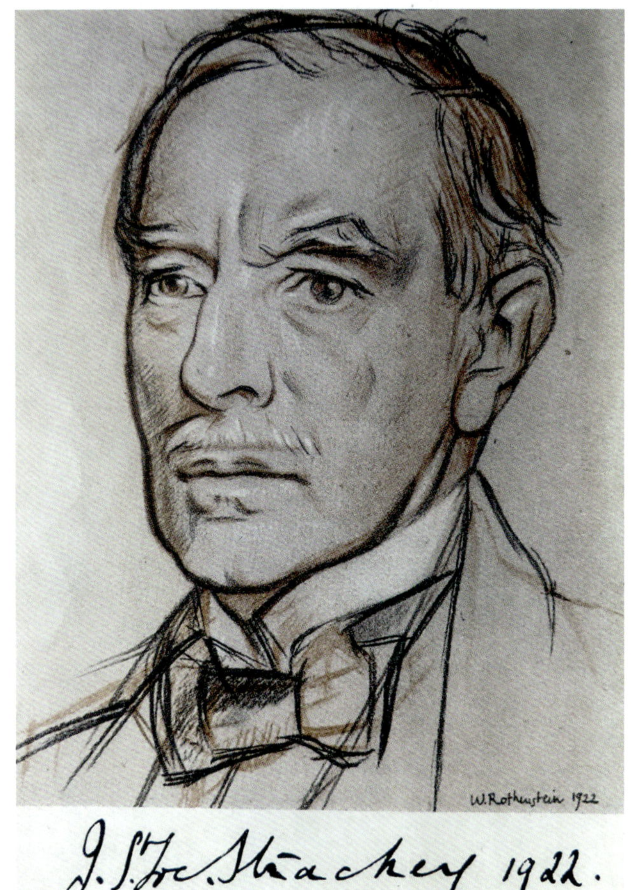

89. *John St Loe Strachey (1860–1927)*

FACING: 88. *The Dining Room in 1915, as Strachey's tea-party guests would have known it*

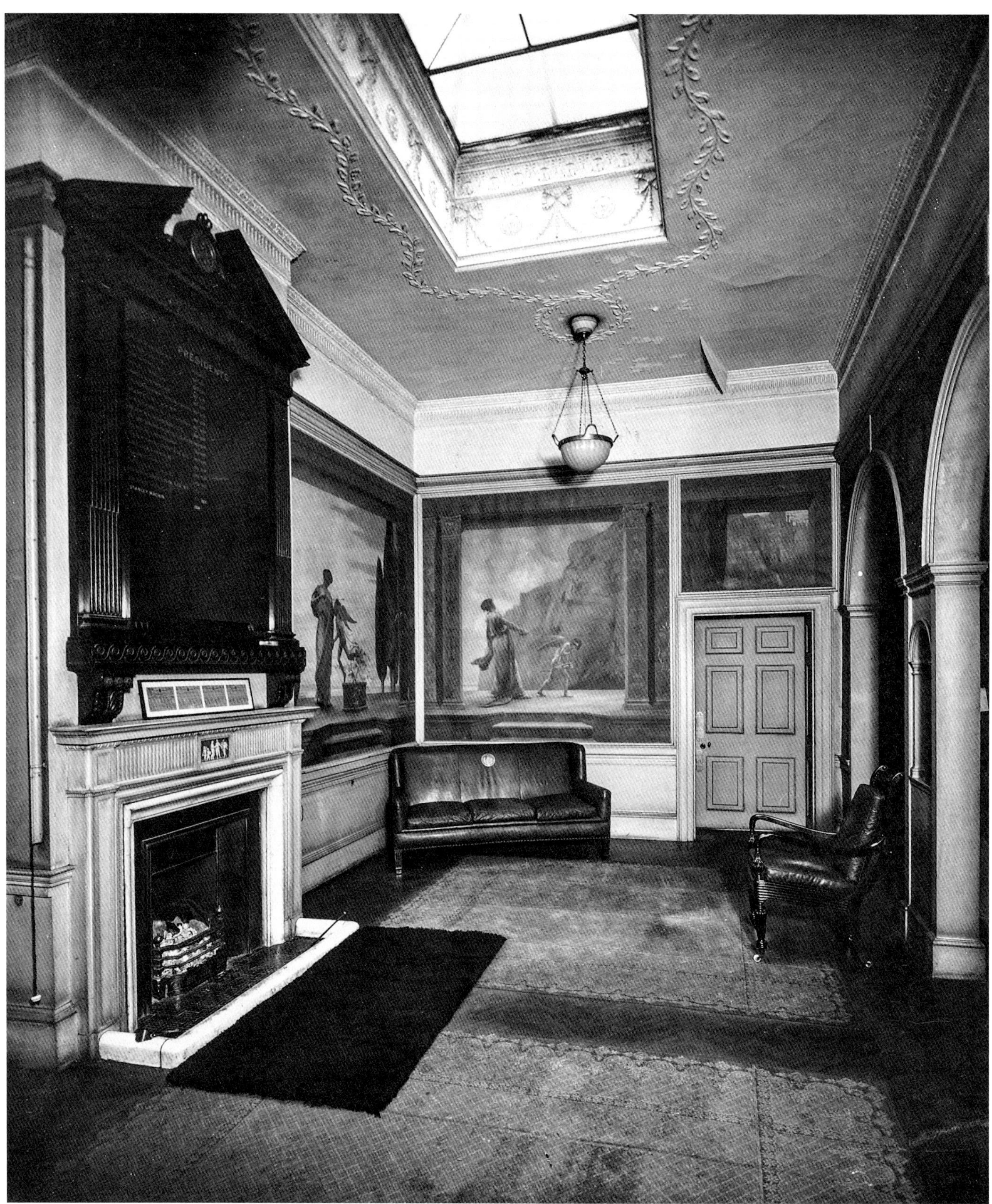

watchers by the gate, the three austere guardians of the temple. They are to Art what Self-denial, Charity and Humility are to Religion.'[2]

Around this time her father commissioned his younger brother to add murals to the library on a classical theme of Venus and Cupid [90]. Harry Strachey was also the art critic for *The Spectator,* and had been mounting a lukewarm defence of the new Continental painting of the Post-Impressionists. This work was being embraced without reservation by the Bloomsbury Group, but, though Strachey was in contact with its members, such as the painter Duncan Grant, he was a generation older than them. His own painting was in the academic mural tradition that was the antithesis of Bloomsbury, and it was in this mode that he decorated the library at No. 14 Queen Anne's Gate.

John St Loe Strachey seems to have displayed none of the bohemian rebelliousness of his more famous cousin, the biographer and Bloomsbury Group member Lytton Strachey. Indeed John seems to have fully embodied the hearty Victorian rectitude that Lytton set out to deconstruct in works like *Eminent Victorians* (1918). Two particular aspects of St Loe Strachey's moral endeavour were that he was a great enthusiast for war with the German Kaiser, and that he was a promoter of the 'special relationship' between Britain and America. These came together in a belief that America must aid Britain in the war effort, and in *The Spectator* he wrote that he considered President Wilson's policy of neutrality to be a moral failure.[3] On 4 August 1914, the same day that Britain joined the war, the United States declared its neutrality. The house in Queen Anne's Gate then became the centre of an unofficial campaign.

The Censor's Office had refused to give American journalists any briefings about developments in the war effort, for fear of crucial information being discovered by the Germans. As a result, the American journalists had threatened to move en masse to Berlin, and to get their information from the German government.[4] Strachey saw the damage this would do to any attempt to change American public opinion, which had been hostile to intervention in Europe. His proposed solution was for the Prime Minister to speak exclusively to American journalists 'off the record': they would know what was going on, but would not publish any of it. However, the government could not allow any such meeting to take place in an official capacity.

Strachey took action in early September 1914 by inviting the Prime Minister Herbert Henry Asquith to lunch at No. 14 Queen Anne's Gate. He also invited correspondents from *The Chicago Daily News, The United Press, The New York Times* and *The New York Press.* At the lunch, Asquith answered questions from the reporters for over two hours. Catering was provided by Gunter's Tea Shop in Berkeley Square, with a staff of old service men as waiters, to prevent any secrets from emerging.

The result was such a success that the meetings became a fixture, with Strachey's 'American tea-parties' held for two hours each Wednesday from 4.30 pm. Each afternoon there would be a new guest of honour, often cabinet ministers or military officials. The event was kept secret from foreign journalists who were not American. Nor did the journalists ever publish details of what they heard. Strachey wrote in his memoirs that 'every consideration of sound business and professional pride as well as of honour made it quite certain

90. This photograph is the only record of Harry Strachey's murals, which were painted over some time in the twentieth century. They depict the story of Cupid being stung by bees, and then mocked by Venus (Theocritus, Idyll 19).

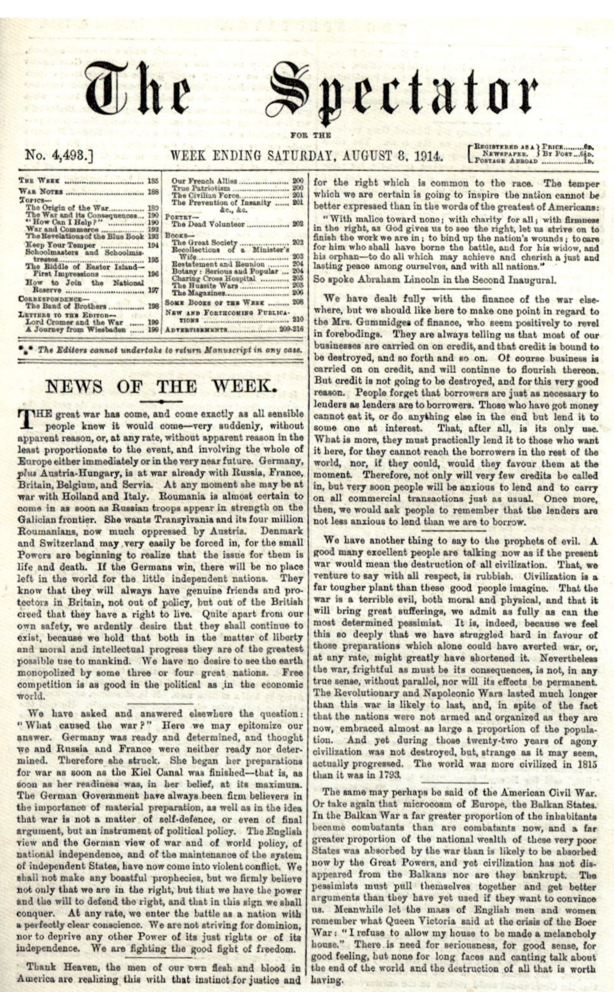

The Spectator

FOR THE

No. 4,498.]   WEEK ENDING SATURDAY, AUGUST 8, 1914.   [Registered as a Newspaper. Postage Abroad] Price......6d. By Post...6½d. ......1d.

*** *The Editors cannot undertake to return Manuscript in any case.*

NEWS OF THE WEEK.

THE great war has come, and come exactly as all sensible people knew it would come—very suddenly, without apparent reason, or, at any rate, without apparent reason in the least proportionate to the event, and involving the whole of Europe either immediately or in the very near future. Germany, *plus* Austria-Hungary, is at war already with Russia, France, Britain, Belgium, and Servia. At any moment she may be at war with Holland and Italy. Roumania is almost certain to come in as soon as Russian troops appear in strength on the Galician frontier. She wants Transylvania and its four million Roumanians, now much oppressed by Austria. Denmark and Switzerland may very easily be forced in, for the small Powers are beginning to realize that the issue for them is life and death. If the Germans win, there will be no place left in the world for the little independent nations. They know that they will always have genuine friends and protectors in Britain, not out of policy, but out of the British creed that they have a right to live. Quite apart from our own safety, we ardently desire that they shall continue to exist, because we hold that both in the matter of liberty and moral and intellectual progress they are of the greatest possible use to mankind. We have no desire to see the earth monopolized by some three or four great nations. Free competition is as good in the political as in the economic world.

We have asked and answered elsewhere the question: "What caused the war?" Here we may epitomize our answer. Germany was ready and determined, and thought we and Russia and France were neither ready nor determined. Therefore she struck. She began her preparations for war as soon as the Kiel Canal was finished—that is, as soon as her readiness was, in her belief, at its maximum. The German Government have always been firm believers in the importance of material preparation, as well as in the idea that war is not a matter of self-defence, or even of final argument, but an instrument of political policy. The English view and the German view of war and of world policy, of national independence, and of the maintenance of the system of independent States, have now come into violent conflict. We shall not make any boastful prophecies, but we firmly believe not only that we are in the right, but that we have the power and the will to defend the right, and that in this sign we shall conquer. At any rate, we enter the battle as a nation with a perfectly clear conscience. We are not striving for dominion, nor to deprive any other Power of its just rights or of its independence. We are fighting the good fight of freedom.

Thank Heaven, the men of our own flesh and blood in America are realizing this with that instinct for justice and for the right which is common to the race. The temper which we are certain is going to inspire the nation cannot be better expressed than in the words of the greatest of Americans:

"With malice toward none; with charity for all; with firmness in the right, as God gives us to see the right, let us strive on to finish the work we are in; to bind up the nation's wounds; to care for him who shall have borne the battle, and for his widow, and his orphan—to do all which may achieve and cherish a just and lasting peace among ourselves, and with all nations."

So spoke Abraham Lincoln in the Second Inaugural.

We have dealt fully with the finance of the war elsewhere, but we should like here to make one point in regard to the Mrs. Gummidges of finance, who seem positively to revel in forebodings. They are always telling us that most of our businesses are carried on on credit, and that credit is bound to be destroyed, and so forth and so on. Of course business is carried on on credit, and will continue to flourish thereon. But credit is not going to be destroyed, and for this very good reason. People forget that borrowers are just as necessary to lenders as lenders are to borrowers. Those who have got money cannot eat it, or do anything else in the end but lend it to some one at interest. That, after all, is its only use. What is more, they must practically lend it to those who want it here, for they cannot reach the borrowers in the rest of the world, nor, if they could, would they favour them at the moment. Therefore, not only will very few credits be called in, but very soon people will be anxious to lend and to carry on all commercial transactions just as usual. Once more, then, we should ask people to remember that the lenders are not less anxious to lend than we are to borrow.

We have asked what is to say to the prophets of evil. A good many excellent people are talking now as if the present war would mean the destruction of all civilization. That, we venture to say with all respect, is rubbish. Civilization is a far tougher plant than these good people imagine. The fact that war is a terrible evil, both moral and physical, and that it will bring great sufferings, we admit as fully as can the most determined pessimist. It is, indeed, because we feel this so deeply that we have struggled hard in favour of those preparations which alone could have averted war, or, at any rate, might greatly have shortened it. Nevertheless the war, frightful as must be its consequences, is not, in any true sense, without parallel, nor will its effects be permanent. The Revolutionary and Napoleonic Wars lasted much longer than this war is likely to last, and, in spite of the fact that the nations were not armed and organized as they are now, embraced almost as large a proportion of the population. And yet during those twenty-two years of agony civilization was not destroyed, but, strange as it may seem, actually progressed. The world was more civilized in 1815 than it was in 1793.

The same may perhaps be said of the American Civil War. Or take again that microcosm of Europe, the Balkan States. In the Balkan War a far greater proportion of the inhabitants became combatants than are combatants now, and a far greater proportion of the national wealth of these very poor States was absorbed by the war than is likely to be absorbed now by the Great Powers, and yet civilization has not disappeared from the Balkans nor are they bankrupt. The pessimists must pull themselves together and get better arguments than they have yet used if they want to convince us. Meanwhile let the mass of English men and women remember what Queen Victoria said at the crisis of the Boer War: "I refuse to allow my house to be made a melancholy house." There is need for seriousness, for good sense, for good feeling, but none for long faces and canting talk about the end of the world and the destruction of all that is worth having.

91. *The front page of* The Spectator *following Britain's declaration of war in 1914*

that there would be no betrayal'.[5] The event was soon put on a more official footing when Strachey was directly ordered by the Prime Minister's private secretary to continue the events exactly in the same pattern.[6]

Many cabinet ministers appeared as guests of honour, including former Prime Minister Arthur James Balfour, Chancellor of the Exchequer Reginald McKenna, and successive Lord Chancellors Richard Haldane and Stanley Buckmaster. The last of these, the very day he was appointed, came straight to Queen Anne's Gate to answer questions, indicating the significance of the forum.[7] Strachey also would have known the First Sea Lord, Jackie Fisher, who had been his neighbour at 16 Queen Anne's Gate for a year after he moved in. Fisher had left the house, but was recalled in 1915 on the orders of Winston Churchill to lead the Navy, in which capacity he tried to prevent the disastrous Gallipoli Campaign.

One of the first guests of honour was Sir Edward Grey, the Foreign Secretary. Conveniently, he lived opposite, at Nos. 1–3 Queen Anne's Gate. Before the war there had been considerable uncertainty whether it was possible to prevent conflict, and whether Britain ought to declare war on Germany. On 3 August 1914, Grey made his decision, giving a speech in the House of Commons that forcefully argued that Britain was duty-bound to attack Germany if Belgium was invaded. An ultimatum was sent and, on its expiry the next day, Asquith declared war.

Subsequent responsibilities were left to the War Office, and Grey played little active role before his resignation in December 1916. But in later years he would have great doubts as to whether he was right to have steered Britain out of its carefully cultivated neutrality. He encapsulated the popular feeling about the war when he recalled that evening of 3 August, writing that its arrival had made him feel as if the 'lamps are going out all over Europe; we shall not see them lit again in our life-time'.[8] A friend recalled the scene: 'We were standing together at the window looking out into the sunset across St James's Park, and the appearance of the first lights along the Mall suggested the thought'.[9]

Richard Burdon Haldane, a Liberal of the same generation as Grey, was another local guest: he lived at No. 28 Queen Anne's Gate. Haldane moved to the house in 1905, upon his appointment to lead the nearby War Office in the new government. The next year he began the work of building up an army for war with Germany, and, even though he was no longer in the post in August 1914, it was he that Asquith asked to begin mobilization. However, Haldane was disliked in his party for his support for Irish Home Rule, and, following a campaign against him, Asquith dropped Haldane from government in May 1915. Nevertheless, a biographer has written that 'no minister bore greater responsibility for Britain's capacity to engage Germany'.[10]

Strachey's plan was a complete success, and the American journalists remained in London, feeling that they were finally receiving the respect that had been denied them by the Censor's Office. In November, they rewarded Strachey with a lavish dinner at Claridge's. By the spring of 1915, they were privately voicing their disapproval of Wilson's policy of neutrality.[11] The tea parties lasted for nearly three years, the last taking place soon after the United States joined the war in April 1917.[12]

In his memoirs, Strachey does not claim to have been attempting to influence American neutrality with his tea parties. With self-conscious implausibility he even claims that the only reason they ended in April 1917 was because of his own poor health.[13] Published in 1922, it would perhaps have been premature for the memoir to have revealed the role of a journalist in government diplomacy, especially one who was still working at *The Spectator*. However, the self-regard revealed throughout the book evidently prevented its author from keeping completely silent.

During the war, Arthur Bolton wrote the first architectural history of the house for *Country Life*; Bolton would later become the curator of Sir John Soane's Museum.[14] There was another coincidental connection with the Townley era: during a visit to the front late in 1915, Strachey let out the house to Lord Elgin's great-granddaughter.[15] Strachey certainly knew enough about the history of his house to realise that his 'tea parties' revived the idea of the house as an intellectual salon that had been dormant for a century. Then the subject for discussion had been the mystery cults of Continental pagans; in the twentieth century the secrets were military ones.

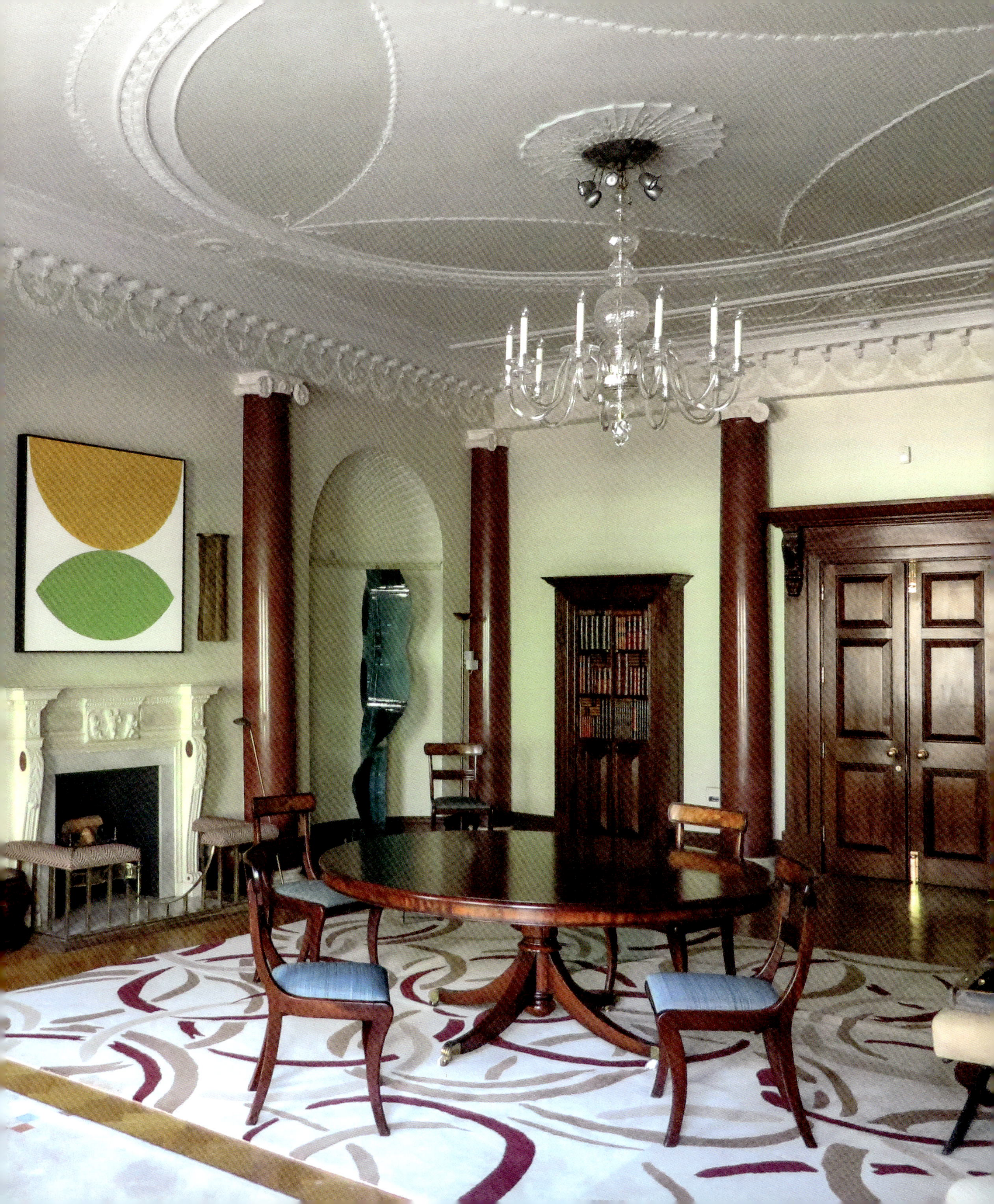

8. A HOUSE OF COMMERCE

IN THE TWENTIETH CENTURY, QUEEN Anne's Gate became a creative hub in British architecture. Throughout the 1910s and 1920s, the two biggest names in the architectural establishment had their offices on the street, next door to each other at Nos. 17 and 19 [93] – Edwin Lutyens and Aston Webb. During this period, Webb designed and executed the present façade to Buckingham Palace (1913) and became President of the Royal Academy (1919–24). Lutyens, meanwhile, designed the palace of the British Raj, the Viceroy's House in New Delhi (1912–29). In these two small terraced houses on Queen Anne's Gate, the public face of empire was forged.

The first important architectural figure to arrive had been Edward Hudson, editor of *Country Life*, who lived in the L-shaped house at No. 15 Queen Anne's Gate from 1908. Before moving in, Hudson had the interiors remodelled by Lutyens. Around the same time, the architect also remodelled interiors at No. 28 for Lord Haldane and No. 32 for Lady Allendale. Evidently enamoured of the street, he moved his office to No. 17 in 1910. Around this time, Webb was constructing the Admiralty Arch at the end of the Mall, and he moved his office to No. 19 in the same year.

John St Loe Strachey let No. 14 in 1917, selling it in 1919, making him the house's final private

92. The Dining Room at No. 14 Queen Anne's Gate, 2017

resident. He was followed by a four-decade occupancy by the Association of British Chambers of Commerce [94]. The Association shared some of the previous era's status as a political salon: the house was used for meetings by business delegates from each local chamber of commerce to determine their policy in terms of lobbying the government. Resolutions would be passed, an annual presidential address was given, and the house was used as a venue to host politicians to convince them in person. This had been the motive for the move to Queen Anne's Gate: the former premises in Parliament Mansions, Victoria Street, had been inadequate for hospitality. The Association funded this extravagance by raising the rates paid by individual chambers to become members.

The Association was not the only such lobbying group: the Federation of British Industries had been founded in 1916 to meet the demands of more manufacturing and industrial businesses. However, the Association was more powerful during these decades. The Association's change of locations coincided with an expansion of duties whereby four committees would have distinct prerogatives: one would focus on postal services and transport, another on taxation, another on foreign affairs; finally there was a general advisory committee.

The Association's lobbying consistently followed two main lines, which embodied the

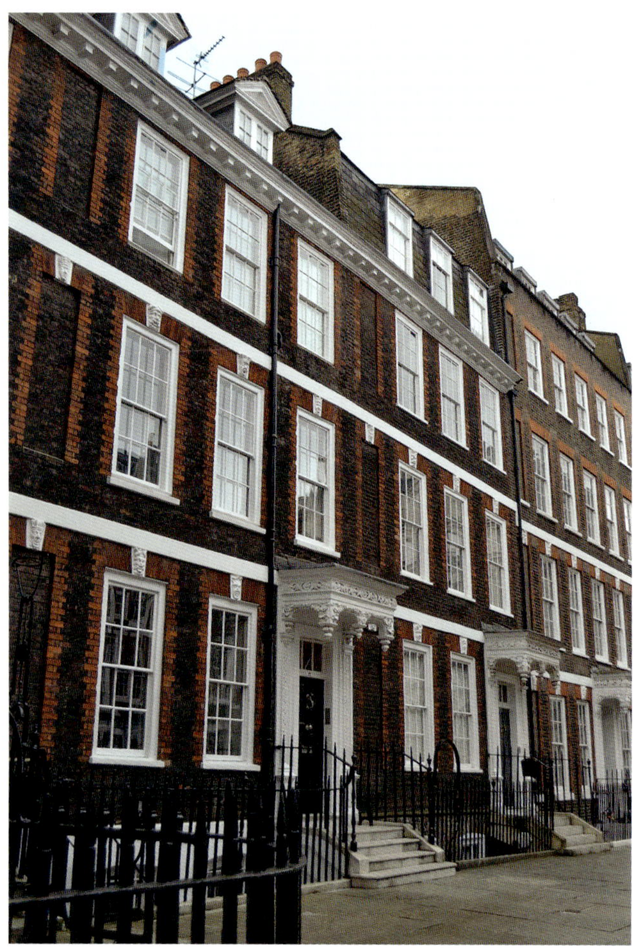

93. *Nos. 17 and 19 Queen Anne's Gate, the former offices of the architects Edwin Lutyens and Aston Webb, respectively*

mainstream of economic thought in the 1920s. One was to fight for lower taxes for business, the other to reduce public spending by local authorities that would drive up industrial wages of skilled workers. The Association's policy was characteristic of what is now known as 'neoclassical' economics, whereby full employment could be achieved as long as the government reduced its intervention to a bare minimum. The rise in taxation following the First World War had come as a shock to businessmen who had amassed their fortunes in a completely different economic era. When the stock market crashed in 1929, they felt vindicated, and

the Association blamed high taxation and public spending.

The real causes of Britain's woes, including the return to the gold standard in 1925, were completely overlooked by the Association. Nor did they recognize their mistakes in retrospect. Instead they redoubled their efforts to lobby the government for a policy of what we would now call 'austerity'. They were successful, and the new Labour Prime Minister, Ramsay MacDonald, pursued the policy to such an extent that he was expelled from his own party. High levels of unemployment were the result throughout Britain in the 1930s. Even the official account of the history of the British Chambers of Commerce states that 'the plain fact of the matter was that the Association was not equipped to understand or resolve the problems of the post-war international and financial scene'.[1]

Aston Webb died in 1930, and Edwin Lutyens evidently did not want to stay on without his neighbour of two decades, departing the street in 1931. Edward Hudson stayed for a few more years, dying at his home in 1936. The eight-month Blitz during the Second World War destroyed huge swathes of historic London. Though two bombs hit the street, Queen Anne's Gate survived to the end of the Blitz in May 1941.

The Keynesian revolution had little impact at the Association of British Chambers of Commerce. When the Labour Party was elected after the Second World War on a programme of nationalization, the Association was shocked and unprepared. Ironically, the result was probably the highlight of their years at the house. The hostility of the political climate was good for membership, and many new chambers joined in the hope that the Association could protect their interests. Furthermore the vastly increased economic responsibility that the government had taken upon itself meant it had to cooperate

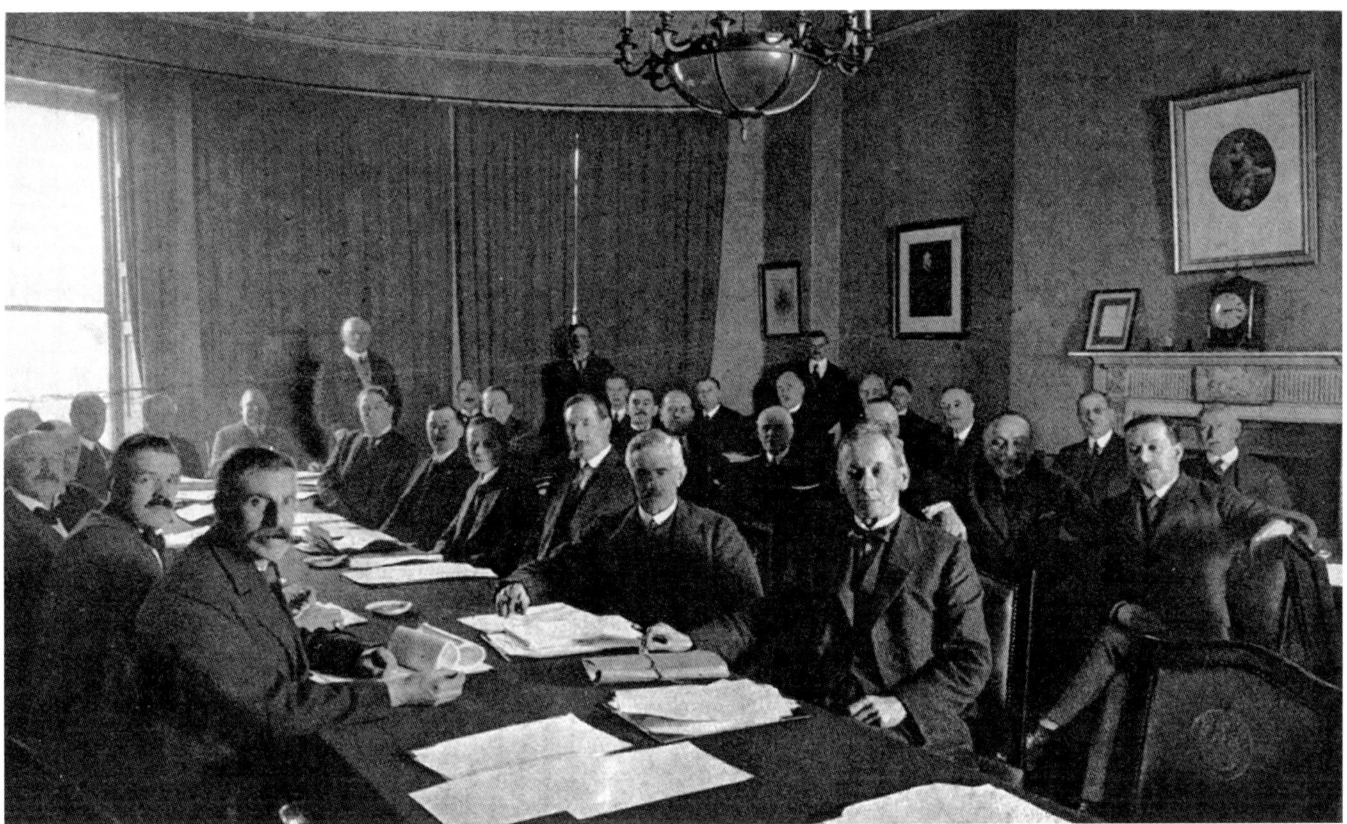

94. *The Park Drawing Room in 1923, when it was known as 'The Firth Room'. The Executive Council of the Association of British Chambers of Commerce is shown here at a meeting on 7 February.*

much more with industry, so, despite the extreme difference of interests, it frequently had recourse to the Association for comments on its proposals. These preliminary private debates were usually much more important to the shape of bills than the public debates on them in Parliament.

The Association had further important duties during its years at No. 14 Queen Anne's Gate. For example it had sole responsibility for issuing Certificates of Origin, which the government had delegated to it in 1923. That it had an effective monopoly had not been intentional, because other bodies delegated the same responsibility had dropped out of the scheme. Until 1966, other chambers or organizations could not become

designated issuers of Certificates of Origin, and chambers could not withdraw from the Association without losing their empowerment to issue certificates.

After the war, the centre of British architecture returned to the street. First, the National Trust moved to Nos. 40, 42 and 44 Queen Anne's Gate in 1945. Then, two years later, Nos. 9–13, diagonally across from No. 14, became the offices of the Architectural Press. From 1947 until 1991, this was where the weekly *Architects Journal* and the monthly *Architectural Review* were created. Icons of British architectural history were constant visitors, such as Nikolaus Pevsner, John Summerson and Ian Nairn.

On its arrival, the Press created a pub in the basement, the 'Bride of Denmark', for the use of its staff. The warren-like interior was created over many years from ornamental features salvaged from Victorian pubs damaged during the Blitz, and it hosted international architecture celebrities such as Frank Lloyd Wright and Le Corbusier.

In 1950, the Association began the first of the two major twentieth-century alterations to No. 14. This one consisted in an extension of the third floor and an addition of a fourth floor on the Park side. The work was done relatively sensitively, with the new staircases approximating the original Wyatt ironwork. The spiral staircase was replaced with a lift, which continued to the top floor. The flight of the main staircase from the ground floor to the basement was rediscovered and opened up for use.

However, despite this gesture of confidence in the Association's future at the building, the levels of energy there soon dropped. The cause was the arrival of a Conservative government in 1951, which prioritized business interests to the extent that complex negotiations were no longer necessary. Individual chambers all basically agreed about policy, and did not engage with broader issues to the extent that a forum for debate was required. In 1953, the Association stopped publishing the results of their annual general meeting, and the annual dinner was cancelled. Instead, work was devolved to smaller committees and sub-committees. With the structure of the institution so transformed from four decades before, the Association departed Queen Anne's Gate in 1959.

The offices were transferred to the use of the consulting engineering firm founded by Terence Patrick O'Sullivan. O'Sullivan was an expert on reinforced concrete who had been involved in the construction of Battersea Power Station. During his company's time at the house, the office was used for consulting on transport projects abroad, becoming enormously successful and establishing satellite offices in Bangkok in 1964 and Nairobi in 1968. O'Sullivan died in 1970, and his company was followed by the Laing Investment Company, a branch of the infrastructure developers John Laing plc, who remained at the house until 1984.

In 1983, the National Trust moved across the lane to the vast Edwardian Baroque tower at Nos. 36 and 38. In 1991, the Architectural Press was bought and asset-stripped by the infamous media proprietor Robert Maxwell, shortly before his death. As a result, it was forced to leave Queen Anne's Gate, and the 'Bride of Denmark' was dismantled and sold. By contrast the National Trust left the street at the volition of its own management, which in 2003 controversially moved most of the charity's staff to Swindon. This ended nearly six decades of residence at Queen Anne's Gate, during which it had transformed British heritage as much as the Architectural Press had influenced contemporary design.

AXEL JOHNSON IN LONDON

The next tenant at No. 14 has remained until the present day – the Swedish family-owned Axel Johnson Group. The Group's trading interests had begun from a small base in Sweden in 1873; by the end of the century a network of contacts, agents and customers had been established and extended in the main trading nations of Europe. Great Britain came into focus very early on, but some early attempts to establish offices there were only partially successful.

The main trading activities of the Group at the time were exports from Sweden to Britain of iron and steel products and imports in the other direction of coal and coke. Its expanding shipping interests also contributed to the need to establish a permanent presence in Britain, and particularly in London. This became imperative by the beginning of the First World War, which disrupted shipping activities.

The Group's first London office was at No. 15 Saint Mary Axe, and opened in December 1915. The location was chosen for its proximity to the Baltic Exchange, the centre of maritime transportation markets until its destruction by the IRA in 1992. The location was also close to the Liverpool Street railway terminus, as well as its new Underground station. This had been opened in 1912 to extend the 'Central London Railway' (now the Central Line), and was the first to be built with escalators.

Records show that the first local employee was a Mr L.T. Freeman, who joined on 1 November 1915 and retired after fifty years' service in 1965. His widow was paid a pension by the company until she died in March 2008. Longevity and continuity have always been strong features in the Group's activities.

When the war ended, the question arose as to the need to continue with an office in London, as shipping activities were more or less back to normal. It was decided to carry on, using the London office as a base for expanding international trading activities. The office was moved to Gracechurch Street; a few years later, in 1922, it was moved to 101 Leadenhall Street, around the corner from the Baltic Exchange.

The next move was outside the City of London to Africa House in Kingsway, a colossal classical monolith built in the 1920s. In the 1950s, the move west continued, to Villiers House in the Strand, a modernist building built earlier in the decade. Despite its more recent construction relative to the other properties, it was evidently not very well built, because it was severely damaged by a large fire in January 1979.[2] As a result, most of the archive of the Group's London office was lost.

By the end of the year, the office was moved to Aldwych House. This was an elegant Parisian-style building of 1906–07 originally housing the offices of the *Morning Post*, but extended to become general offices in 1927–28. It has since been converted into a hotel. The company did not intend to remain here for long: it had received a large insurance payout after the fire, and wanted to have its own property, instead of being a tenant alongside many others. The result was the purchase of a lease at No. 14 Queen Anne's Gate, to last from 1984 until 2106. 'Qaggie', as it became known, represented for the first time an immediate identification between the company in London and its architectural location.

In 1984 a large building project was begun to refurbish the house as a modern office. On the ground floor, the flight of the staircase to the basement was connected up with the main stairs to the upper storeys, creating a spacious atrium. The third floor was rebuilt, with a new staircase up from the second floor. The fourth floor was also

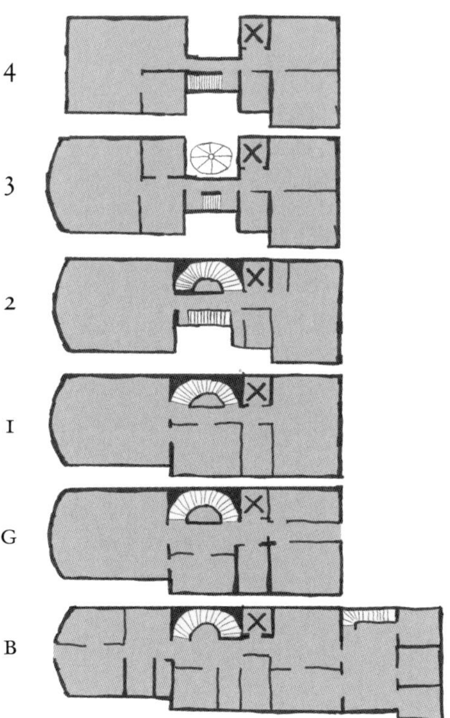

95. Plans of 14 Queen Anne's Gate, 2017

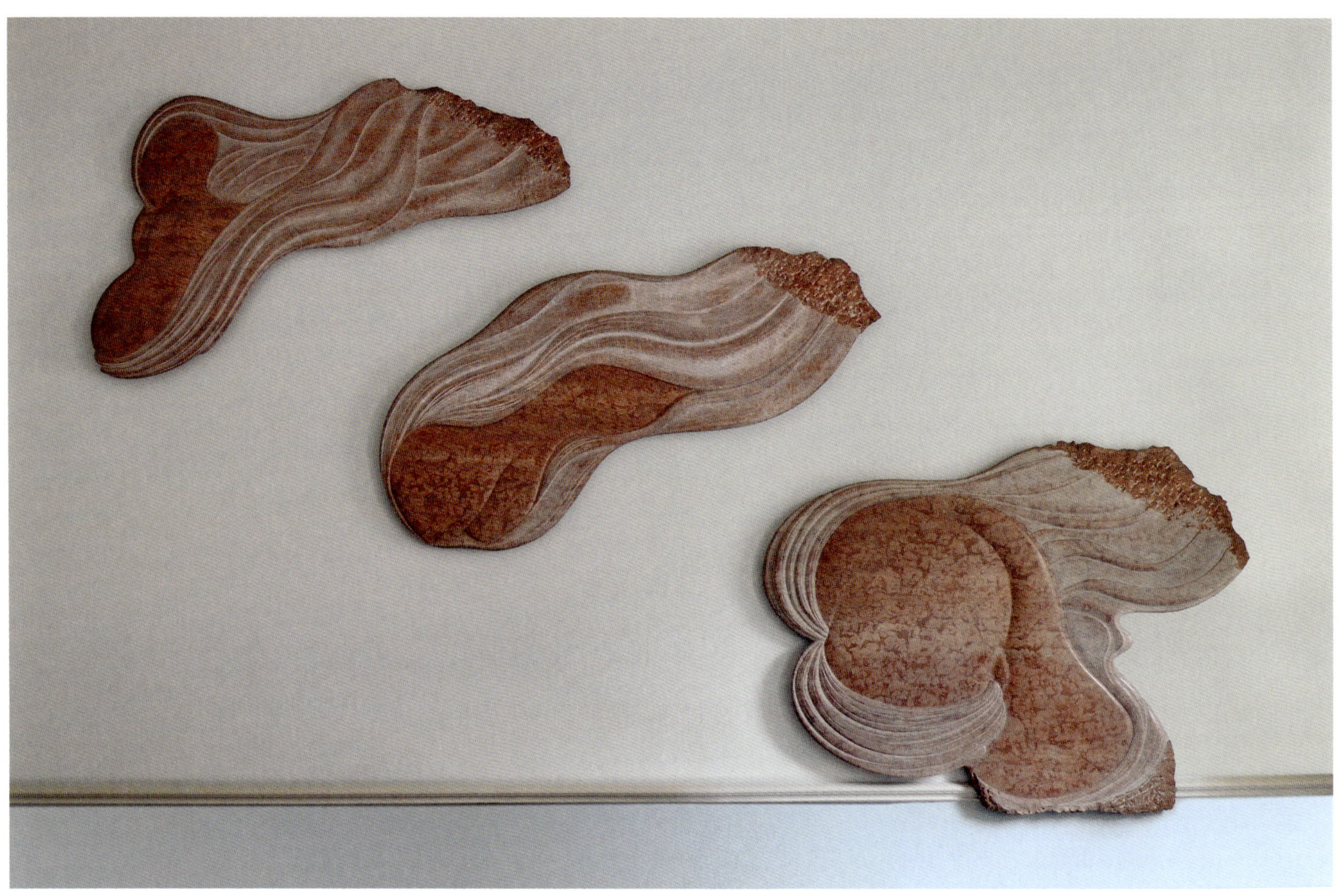

96. Ecstasy: St Agatha, *by Stephen Cox, 1983*

rebuilt and extended to the street side of the house, creating a flat for family members and company visitors, until it was transformed into office space in the 1990s.[3] The new additions were made sensitively: the house was by now a Grade I Listed building. As in the 1950s, the builders recreated Wyatt's ironwork on the new flights of stairs, and only close examination reveals the superior craftsmanship of the original. A fire escape was added, leading from the top floor to the second.

The Axel Johnson Group soon revived the house's historical use as a venue for the display of sculpture. The largest is by the contemporary British sculptor Stephen Cox. *Ecstasy: St Agatha* (1983) [96], a wall-mounted piece in the Street Drawing Room, abstracts the Sicilian saint's martyrdom into three forms of red Verona marble. Its mystical eroticism is entirely in the tradition of Charles Townley: the art historian Stephen Bann wrote that the 'severing of the saint's body prompts Cox, paradoxically and almost perversely, to relish the headlong erotic allure of shoulders, buttocks and breasts'.[4] Bann compares its drapery to Bernini, and its eroticism with Indian art. It could not be more appropriate, then, for the room that originally displayed both a giant terracotta head by della Porta and a collection of Indian 'idols'. At No. 14 Queen Anne's Gate, as d'Hancarville wrote, 'the centuries touch and reconcile, despite the division of time'.

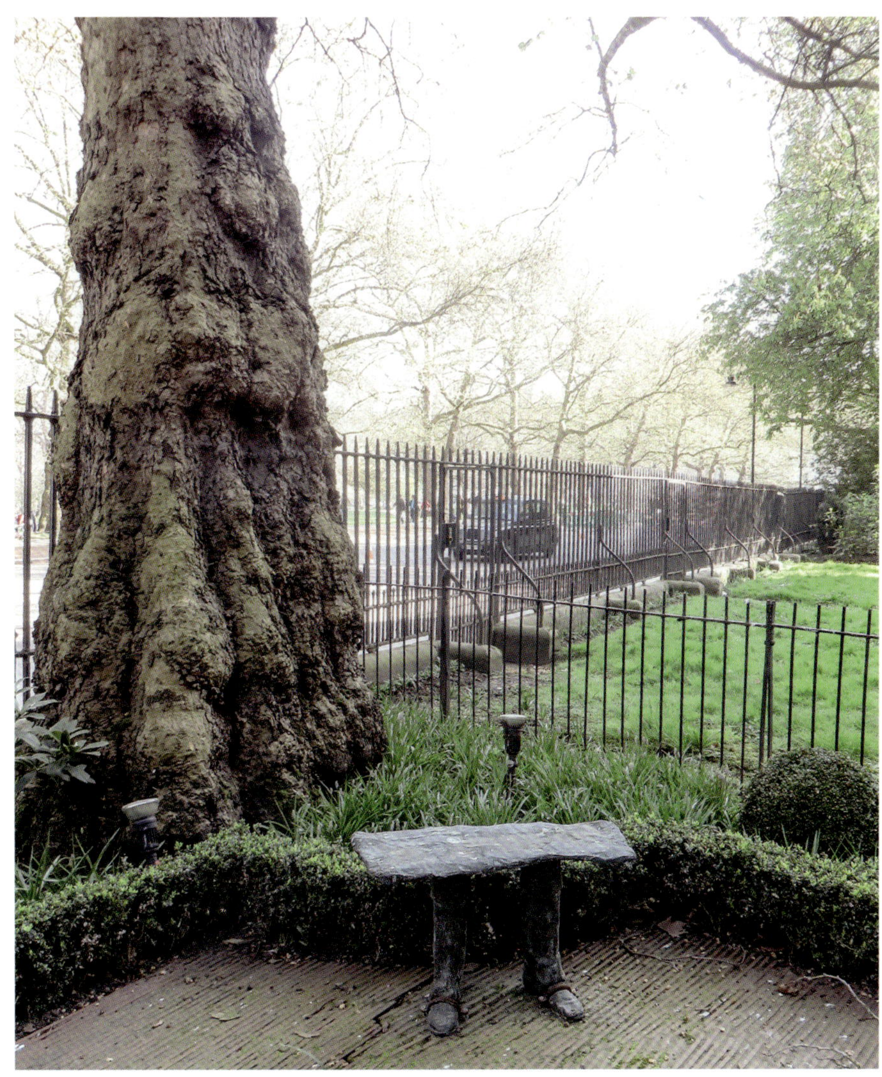

97. *The garden at 14 Queen Anne's Gate, with* Carolus Rex *(2007) by the sculptor Annika MasOlle Skarendahl. The work is a humorous homage to Charles XII (1682–1718), the great warrior king of Sweden who claimed only to remove his jackboots when he went to sleep.*

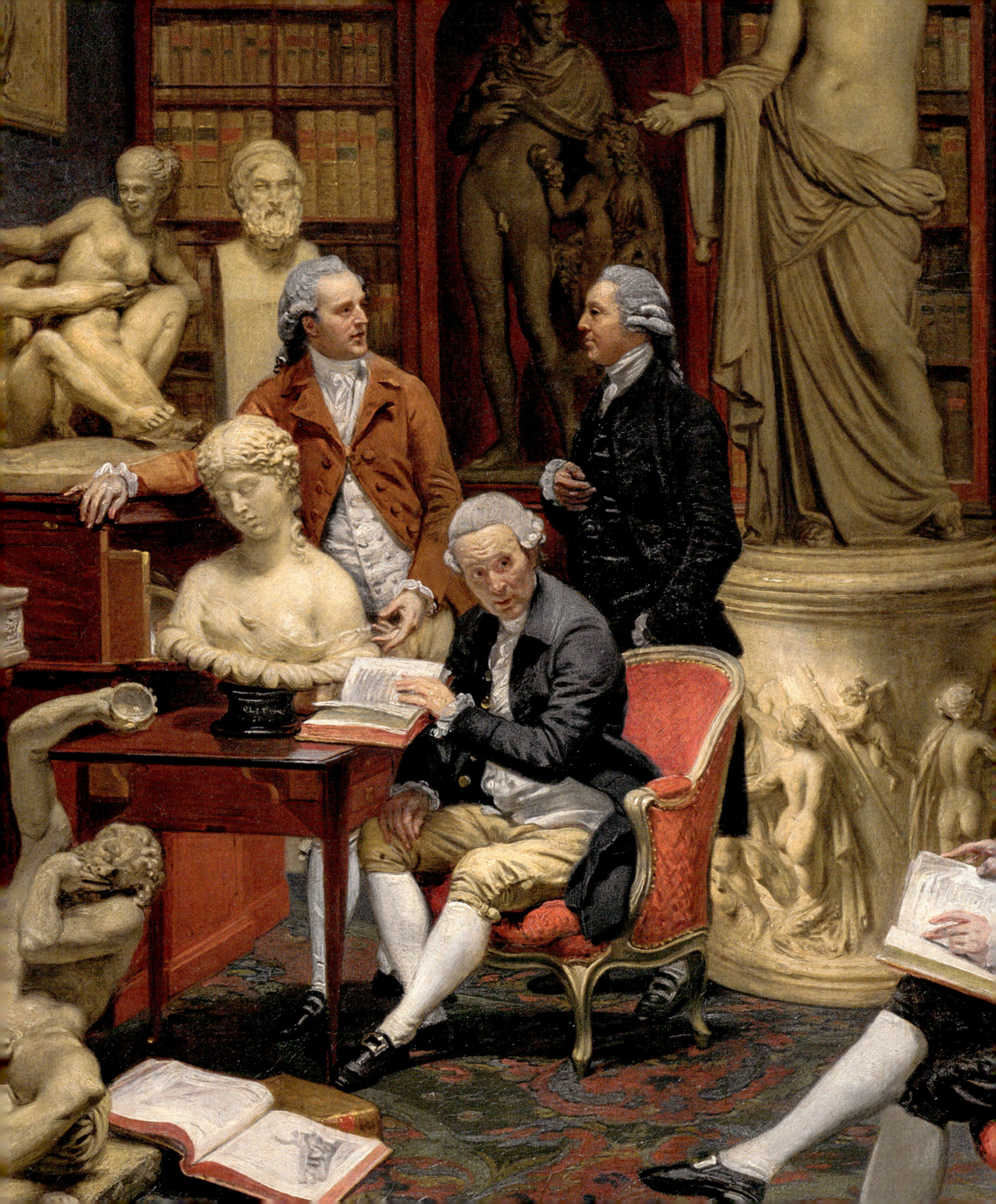

The *Recherches*

It may be argued that, with the distribution of Townley's collection across the British Museum, the most vital legacy of No. 7 Park Street is instead the enormous work of scholarship that was written there, a three-volume treatise on ancient art. The author called himself the 'Baron d'Hancarville' [98], and the work was titled *Recherches sur l'origine, l'esprit et les progrès des arts de la Grèce* (1784–85) [99]. One of the greatest and strangest monuments of Enlightenment thought, it presented an origin story for the theology and visual culture of human civilization, while challenging the authority of Christianity, and pioneering the study of erotic art.

While d'Hancarville's other publications have been explored by modern scholars, the *Recherches* has not been given an extended discussion.[1] Since the Victorian era, d'Hancarville has had an extremely negative reputation in Britain, no doubt due to his interest in ancient erotica. Portrayed as a pornographer and a thief, he is often made to embody everything that modern art historians and classicists perceive as decadent and superficial about eighteenth-century antiquarianism. This has included accusing him of forgery, when in fact his erudition sometimes exceeded that of his modern critics.[2] In the last decade, however, d'Hancarville's work has begun to be rehabilitated by scholars.[3]

Pierre-François Hugues had styled himself the 'Baron d'Hancarville' somewhere during his picaresque progress from family bankruptcy in Nancy to captaincy in the army of Mecklenburg-Schwerin to publishing a treatise on the collection of William Hamilton in Naples. The title is probably an invented conflation of Baron d'Holbach and Madame d'Arconville, two influential Parisian *salonniers*. D'Hancarville may not have been born into the

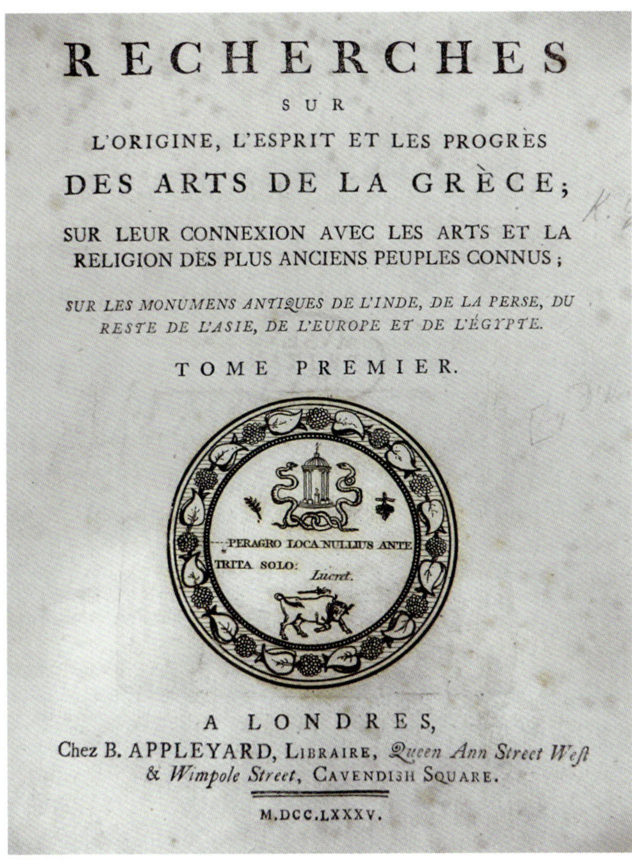

99. *The quotation on the invented coin is from Lucretius, and translates as 'I travel where no foot has trod before' (De rerum natura, IV, 1–2.). Though the title page dates the book to 1785, it was published and had appeared in libraries by the end of 1784.*

FACING: 98. *Baron d'Hancarville, seated, detail of* A Nobleman's Collection *by Johan Zoffany* [75]

intellectual establishment, but he read voluminously, and talked his way into studying many of the major private collections of Europe. One of these was 7 Park Street, and it was here, probably in the Library, that the *Recherches* was written.

The project of the book was to trace the origins of ancient Greek art in the designs and religion of older societies across all Europe and Asia. In the perspective of Townley and d'Hancarville, one could only understand the motives of artists by understanding their theology, of which mystery cults preserved the most ancient principles. Every detail of a work like the Portland Vase had to be deciphered with reference to a symbolic code.[4] The major innovation of the *Recherches* was to propose a single universal religious system that underlay all antique myth and symbolism.

Conventional Christian interpretation of the pagan world had once been that ancient art was an expression of polytheistic idolatry, but since the Renaissance this account had been questioned. Revivers of Neoplatonism like Marsilio Ficino argued that in fact the doctrine of the ancients was monotheistic, and that Christianity had no special claim to the concept. The first to apply this idea to visual art was Johann Joachim Winckelmann, who interpreted antique sculptural works not as idols but as allegories. Scholars of the Enlightenment like the comte de Caylus attempted to make the Renaissance project more scientific by focusing not on texts but datable objects. In the pre-Revolutionary era, rationality had a radical edge, because it subverted the premises of divinely ordained power structures.

Charles Townley's sympathy for the brand of scholarship in the *Recherches* can be traced to the man who tutored him in Paris as a teenager, John Turberville Needham. When Townley met him he was already an eminent scientist: indeed a part of the reproductive organ of the squid bears his name to this day. In 1761, after Townley departed his stewardship, Needham published a tract proposing a common ancestry for the Chinese alphabet and Egyptian hieroglyphics. He also courted accusations of atheistic materialism from no less a radical than Voltaire, with whom he conducted a pamphlet war in 1769.

D'Hancarville's early heroes had been Winckelmann and Caylus, but he later became influenced by another, more esoteric strain in Enlightenment thought. Before arriving in London in 1776, he spent time at the Bibliothèque Mazarine in Paris, where he worked with the librarian, the Abbé Leblond.[5] The Abbé's milieu was one of hermetic, occult scholarship: it was here, for example, that the modern study of the tarot began. That work was initiated in 1781 by Antoine Court de Gébelin, in the eighth volume of his study of primitive religion.[6] Another adept was Charles-Francois Dupuis, who published his first article on primitive religion in 1779.

The *Recherches,* published late in 1784, was one of the first major works to come out of this milieu. The influence is manifest in the study of esoteric religious ritual, mysterious either for its practice in times before theology was codified, or because it was a 'mystery cult' whose authority was based on secrecy. We are used to thinking of such work in opposition to that of the *philosophes* and *Aufklärer,* but this categorical distinction is an anachronistic one, and d'Hancarville would have considered the ancient occult to be a perfectly rational object of study.

Nevertheless, to modern readers, the methodology of the *Recherches* can seem closer to alchemy than science. Unlike Winckelmann, d'Hancarville was a euhemerist, freely conflating myth and history, and treating characters like Hercules, Janus and Shiva as real historical figures. Objects and designs were brought together across thousands of miles and centuries of history with little more than the associative structure of symbolism.

The first volume of the book was devoted to the iconography of human civilization's primordial religion, with at its centre a universal creator of being, '*l'Être Générateur*'. This bi-gender creative power was worshipped in different aspects that were repeated across different societies: Bacchus in Ancient Greece corresponded to Brahma in India, for example. Religion in the *Recherches* was influenced by deism, defined against Revelation or an active divine presence in the world. As such, the '*Être Générateur*' represented a doctrinal antithesis to the '*Être suprême*'

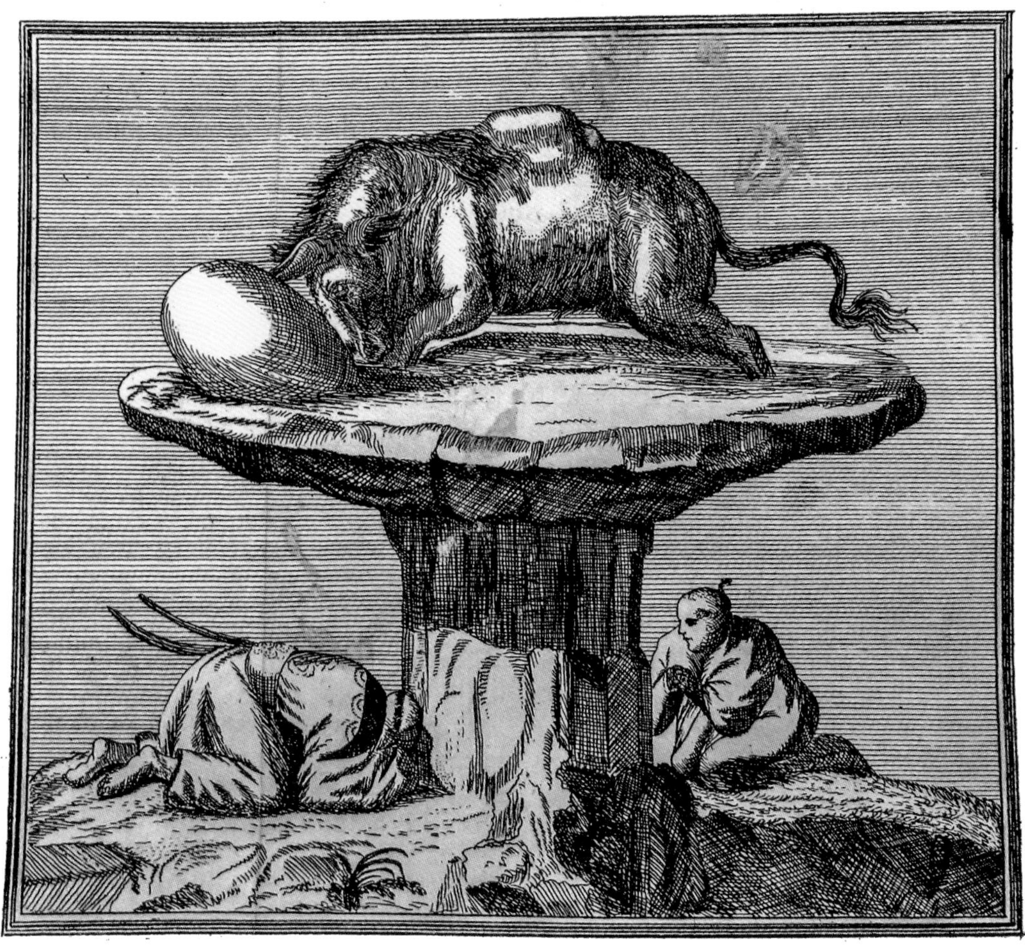

100. *This illustration, from the first volume of the* Recherches, *shows an idol from a Japanese 'temple du Bœuf' in Kyoto (Méaco). The image is derived from one first published in 1669 in a popular book about Japan, based on dubious accounts by Dutch travellers in the East India Company. D'Hancarville interpreted the bull charging the egg as a symbol for the creation of the world, connecting it with the eggs consecrated in Bacchic mystery cults (D'Hancarville [1784a], pp. 65–66).*

that would soon be formulated by Maximilien Robespierre.

Common motifs had already been noted across early civilizations, with patent Abrahamic debts to paganism being neutralized in various ways. Some mythographers argued that the motifs were adopted by different early civilizations independently: the similarity was due to the motifs' common source in nature.[7] Others traced them back to a primordial civilization with authority in Scripture, such as the descendants of Noah's son Ham – a theory proposed by Jacob Bryant a decade before the *Recherches*.[8] Either way, Christian authority over paganism could be reasserted.

D'Hancarville argued for a primordial civilization completely independent of Abrahamic Scripture. Its religious practices were adopted by every subsequent culture, including that of the Israelites, meaning that long before Christian Scripture was written its religion existed and was practised among the pagans. D'Hancarville claimed he was proving the great antiquity of Christianity: it was, '*avant la loi même*', the religion of the earliest human culture.[9] The devout may have found this an ambiguous consolation, but there is no reason to doubt its sincerity.

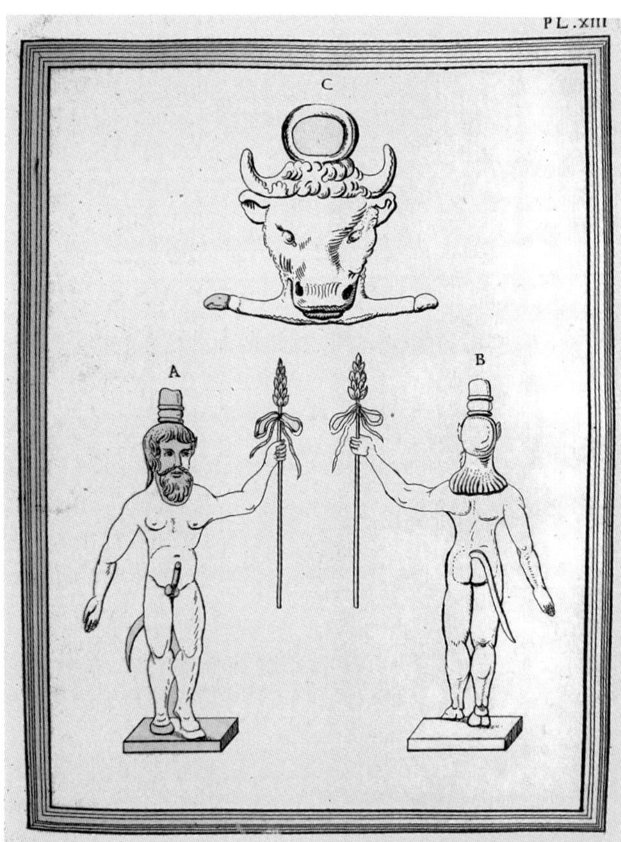

101. *In this plate from the* Recherches, *d'Hancarville illustrates a bronze ornament in Townley's collection, interpreting the ox as a representation of Bacchus and the double phallus as life, equivalent to the serpent. Together they are 'la puissance Génératrice' (I, p. 144). Below is a bronze figure from the collection of Townley's friend, the MP Roger Wilbraham.*

The primordial civilization that he proposed as the origin of all religious practice was that of the Scythians, a Greek term still used to refer to the nomadic tribes who originated in southern Siberia and came to dominate all of Central Asia. Formidable warriors and pioneers of horse breeding, they are now estimated to have flourished from 900 BC until 200 BC, though d'Hancarville believed they were much more ancient. The French astronomer and revolutionary Jean Sylvain Bailly had a similar theory about the influence of the Scythians, but he evidently considered it too subversive, and it went unpublished until 1798, after his death.

D'Hancarville also proposed that the Scythians had invented coinage, by which the diffusion of their religion could be traced through motifs. This is what made the theory useful for the understanding of visual art, because different aspects of the '*Être Générateur*' were embodied in different symbols. These symbols were combined in idols, their meanings being carried through even when the artists themselves were not consciously aware of it.

The creation of 'being' was separated into the creation of the material world and the creation of life: the first was represented by the ox (*bœuf*), the second by the snake (*serpent*) [101]. The primordial chaos from which they both derived was represented by the egg (*l'œuf de Cahos*) [100]. The creator itself was bi-gender, embodying 'active' and 'passive' powers of generation, represented through the male and female sexual organs. A third distinction was between the sun in the upper and lower hemispheres, represented by a star or a crescent respectively. The latter was the nocturnal sun (*le soleil nocturne*), and connected back to the ox through the shape of its horns.

The interpretation of these symbols was derived from the mystery cults that were so important to Townley, and this led to discussion of the erotic art that featured in Bacchic orgies. D'Hancarville was one of the first scholars to discuss priapic imagery in detail, showing its diffusion across all cultures. The connection with Indian art had first been made in 1780, when Sylvain Maréchal made a passing reference to Anquetil's discussion of *linga* in his commentary on the depictions of Priapus found at Herculaneum.[10] D'Hancarville seized on this connection, developing it at length, and it was probably the most influential idea in his book.

The second volume moved from esoteric iconography to more conventional history. The first chapter showed how coins were used as part of funerary rites, themselves based on a conception of the underworld common to all world religions. The second was on the dating of coins using letter-forms, including a defence of Michel Fourmont's account of Greek inscriptions. Ironically it was Richard Payne Knight, another protégé of Charles Townley, who ultimately revealed Fourmont to have indeed forged the inscriptions discussed here.[11] The final chapter was the most focused in the entire book, presenting a chronological development of mass-produced coin designs. Moving out of a mythical past and into recorded history made this chapter the book's most conventional piece of scholarship.

Townley was addressed at the very beginning of the *Recherches* in the 'Discours préliminaire à Mr. Charles Townley' [102]. In it d'Hancarville explained the importance of understanding the symbolism of antiquity for the appreciation of the Townley marbles. He also thanked Townley for sharing his enthusiasm with '*les amateurs & les curieux*', and for furnishing d'Hancarville himself with '*réflexions*' that he had incorporated into the book.[12]

Charles Townley first met d'Hancarville in March 1768, during his brief but transformative first visit to Naples. The Frenchman soon found himself expelled from the city for reasons that remain unknown, though they may relate to a volume of erotic art that was published there.[13] In 1776 d'Hancarville came to London to do further work on Hamilton's vases, which had been acquired by the British Museum. He reconnected with Townley, becoming a regular at his house, and began to plan out the major work that would occupy them both for the next five years.

The *Recherches* started out as an account of the Townley collection, but soon evolved into a survey of all British collections, with Townley and d'Hancarville travelling around the major houses of the country

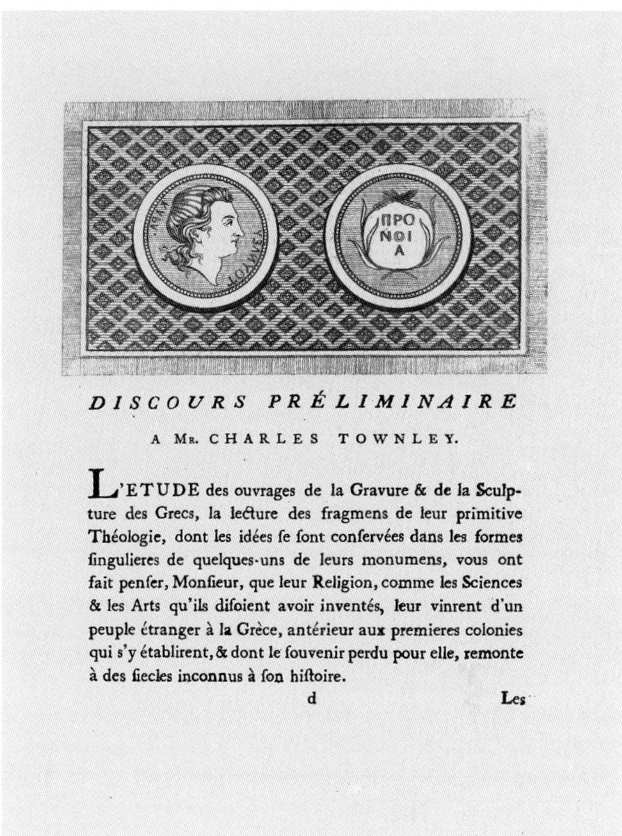

102. *The heading to the 'Discours préliminaire' of the* Recherches *depicts an imaginary coin with on one side Townley's head and name and on the other the inscription 'πρόνοια', meaning 'prudence' or 'prescience'.*

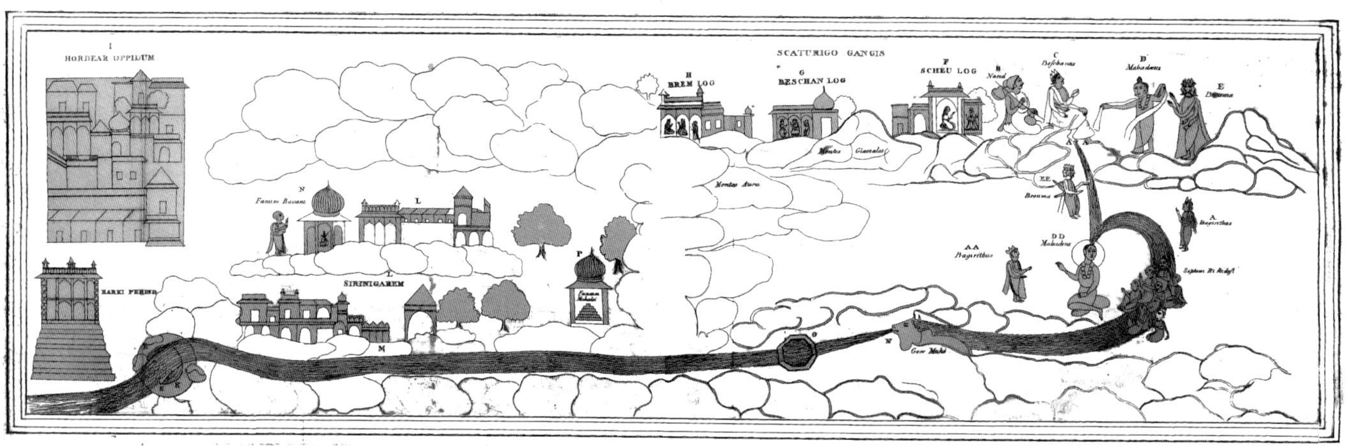

104. *This illustration, from the third volume of the* Recherches, *may be based on a drawing by d'Hancarville himself. It depicts the Hindu creation myth through the descent of the Ganges from heaven, at the top right, to the cities of Srinagar ('Sirinigarem') and Haridwar ('Hordéar'), on the far left. In between is the river's traditional source, Gomukh ('Gow-Muki'), a Hindu pilgrimage site in the Himalayas. Its name translates as 'cow's mouth', associating it by animal symbolism with the primordial creative power that in Greece d'Hancarville found manifested in Bacchus.*

in 1779. The next year, d'Hancarville included his theories on the sexual cults of the ancients in two more volumes of erotica that were published under his name in France.[14] By the time the *Recherches* was proposed to a London publisher in July 1783, it had been reconceived as an attempt to provide the first principles for understanding the symbolism of antique sculpture. D'Hancarville must have worked diligently to have the book finished quickly: the two volumes were published in November 1784, their authorship anonymous.

John Gillies, a Scottish historian of ancient Greece, wrote a rave review.[15] However, the *Recherches* found a critic in Paul Henry Maty, a librarian in the department of natural history and antiquities at the British Museum, the department at which Townley's antiquities would soon be arriving.[16] Maty published a periodical summarizing foreign publications, employing a ferocity that was noted by Edward Gibbon and Horace Walpole. His negative review remains the longest discussion of the *Recherches*

in English, and it is unfortunate that the book's Anglophone authority should remain the dyspeptic Maty.

To d'Hancarville's credit, he responded with a supplementary volume in May 1785, reprinting the bad review in full. In libraries, the two volumes of 1784 are usually catalogued together with this one. Aside from addressing criticisms, the supplementary volume consisted of two new chapters, the first dealt with the Ganges and the related Hindu gods [104], the second with Persian art and the worship of Mithras. But, whether because of Maty's review or the book's own obscurity, the *Recherches* was not the publishing phenomenon that d'Hancarville seems to have believed it would be. 313 copies were printed, and by March 1787, 200 had been sold.[17] He left for Paris in November, and after the Revolution he went on to Rome and Venice [105]. He died a few months after Townley in 1805, in Padua.

If not a commercial success, the *Recherches* was still influential. British scholars Richard Payne Knight and James Christie published major works dependent on it. Despite being defiantly anti-intellectual, Henry Blundell referenced the ideas of the *Recherches* throughout his catalogue of his collection.[18] Thomas Hope designed furniture using its ideas of symbolic ornament, and John Soane's notes record his desperate struggle to apply d'Hancarville's ideas to architecture.[19]

On the Continent, Charles-Francois Dupuis eventually published his theories in full in 1795,

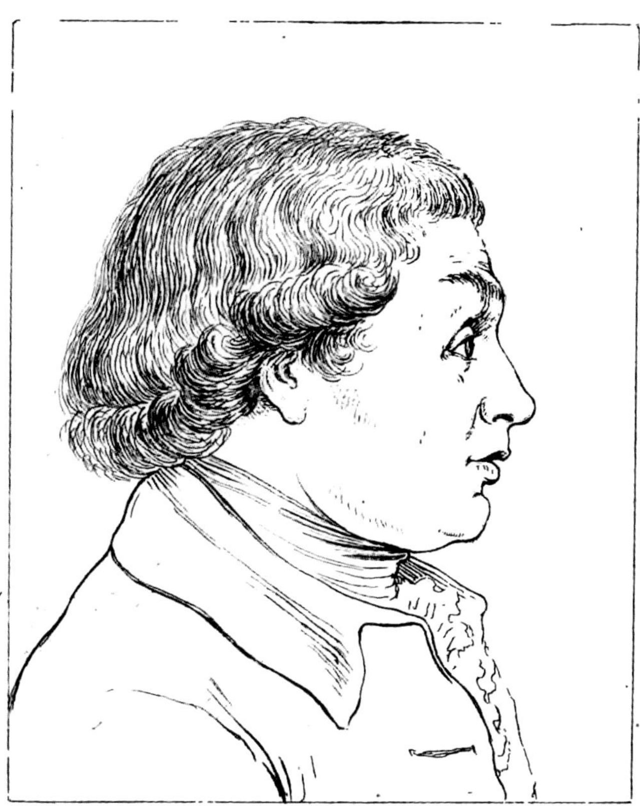

105. *In Venice, d'Hancarville joined the salon of the Greek countess Isabella Albrizzi, where he would have met Byron and Canova. This portrait was made during that period, and was published with Albrizzi's recollections of him.*

creating an entire industry of radical French mythographers, and finding an international readership in multiple languages.[20] But it has recently been shown that Dupuis was himself deeply indebted to the *Recherches* and its use of symbolism to discover the earliest forms of religion. [21] This would make the *Recherches* as extensively and covertly influential over culture as the mystery cults it described. However, for d'Hancarville there seems to have been none of the sense, pervading Dupuis and his followers, that the sexual dimension to religion was inherently subversive.

Accounts of Townley often deny his subscription to the theories of the *Recherches*, as if he was temporarily deceived by them, or merely used d'Hancarville for his own intellectual prestige. The evidence, however, suggests that, while Townley had a sense of the limitations of the *Recherches*, he fully agreed with its broad argument. In a letter he described it as essential for an understanding of ancient art, and he sent copies to all his friends around Europe.[22] Certainly, he was aware that the book was highly imaginative, but this was not necessarily to its disadvantage. In later years he developed his own differing opinions, but these were, if anything, even more speculative. The first account of his marbles at the British Museum quoted Townley briefly on the subject, giving a text that refers to symbolism based on the 'Supreme Triade' of Earth, Water and Æther (the 'fifth element' that was thought to fill outer space).[23]

Modern scholarship was established during the nineteenth century in opposition to the kind of speculative esotericism characterizing the *Recherches*. Adolf Michaelis, a pioneer in the *kunstwissenschaftlich* study of ancient sculpture, referred to the book as 'a fantastic farrago of mystico-symbolical revelations and groundless hypotheses'.[24] But with its androgynous divinities and interdependent civilizations, the *Recherches* can also be read as an epic counternarrative against essentialism of race, doctrine and gender. In the twenty-first century we may respond with d'Hancarville's own defence: that it is all, at least, a beautiful idea ('*convenite almeno, che se la cosa non è vera, è bene immaginata*').[25]

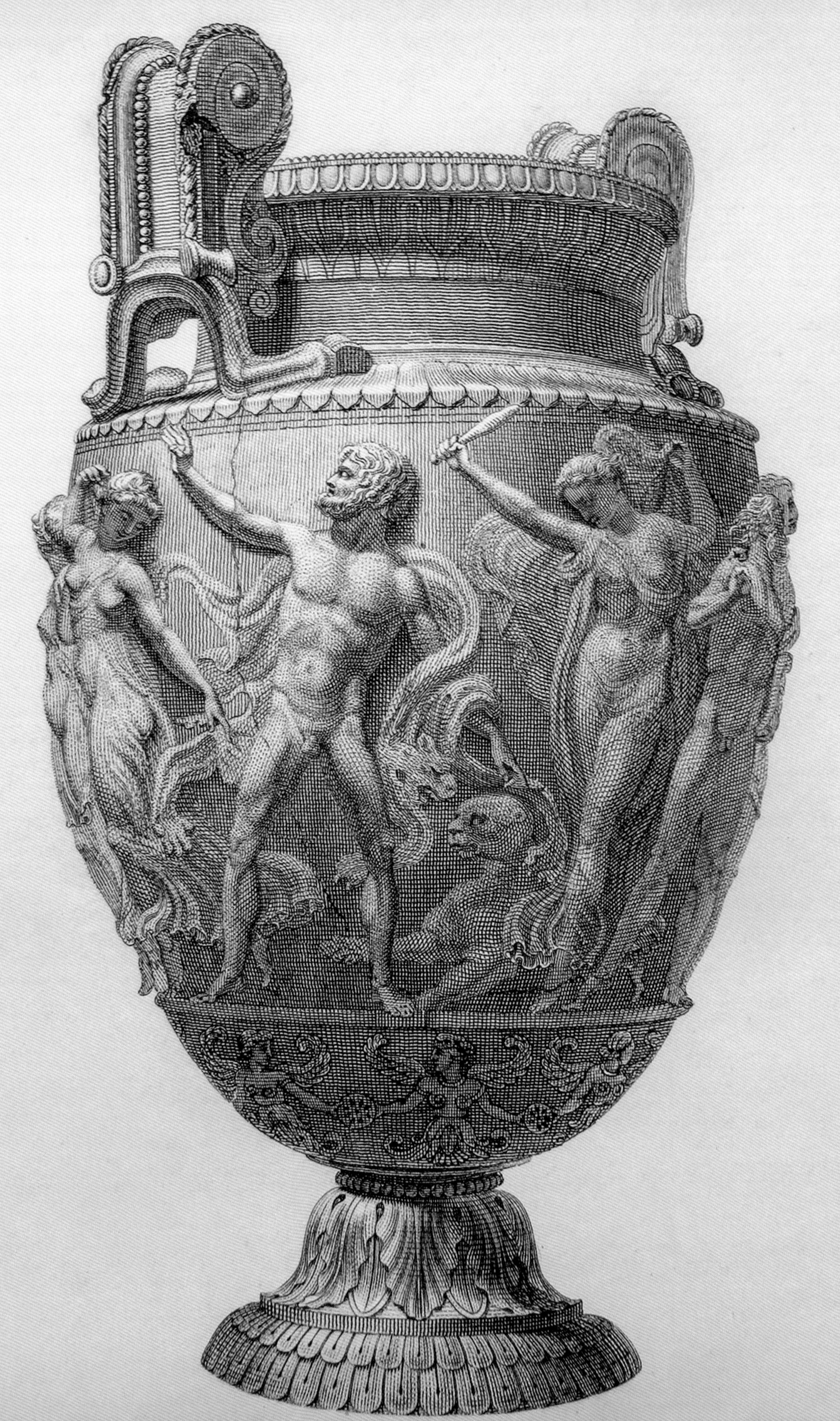

Charles Townley on the Townley Vase

In 2008, two reduced copies of the Townley Vase in bronze were acquired for No. 14 Queen Anne's Gate. They are displayed in the Dining Room, the site of the original in the house. Created by the Art Union of London in 1871, the copies evince the continued relevance of the Townley collection throughout the Victorian period. They also offer an opportunity to see the form of the composition, as the original is in storage at the British Museum.

In 1789, Townley commissioned an illustration of the vase from the eminent engraver Conrad Martin Metz. He also wrote an extended discussion of the work to accompany the image, although he ultimately decided not to include it. Nor was Townley's interpretation included in the commentary when the British Museum printed an adapted version of the engraving in its catalogue of the marbles in 1812. The manuscript, however, survives, and is transcribed in full below for the first time.[1]

The main concern of the text is to show how the vase embodies aspects of mystery cult practice, in particular its veneration of the 'generative spirit'. He gives the ordinary reader a sense of what these primitive systems of worship involved, and connects them to those of the 'Hindoos'. While the ideas are based on material in the third chapter of the *Recherches*, they are mostly Townley's own interpretations, including the premise that the figures shown are Bacchus and Ariadne.[2]

The discussion of 'revolution' would have been particularly resonant in 1789, as the French king was dethroned and the Jacobins took power. Townley's

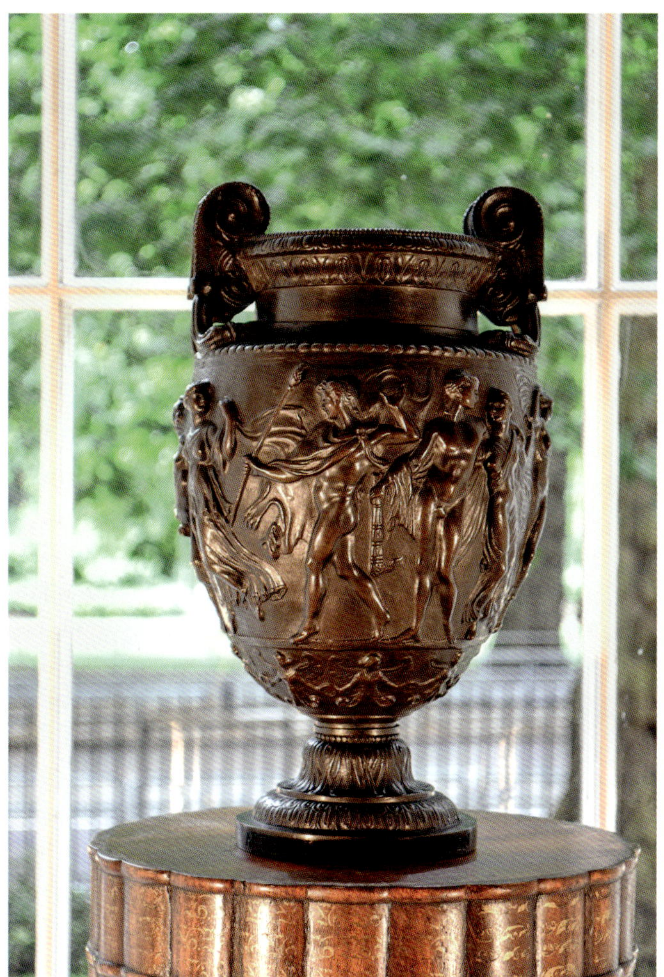

107. A reduced copy of the Townley Vase in the Dining Room at 14 Queen Anne's Gate

FACING: 106. Detail of an engraving of the Townley Vase, 1812

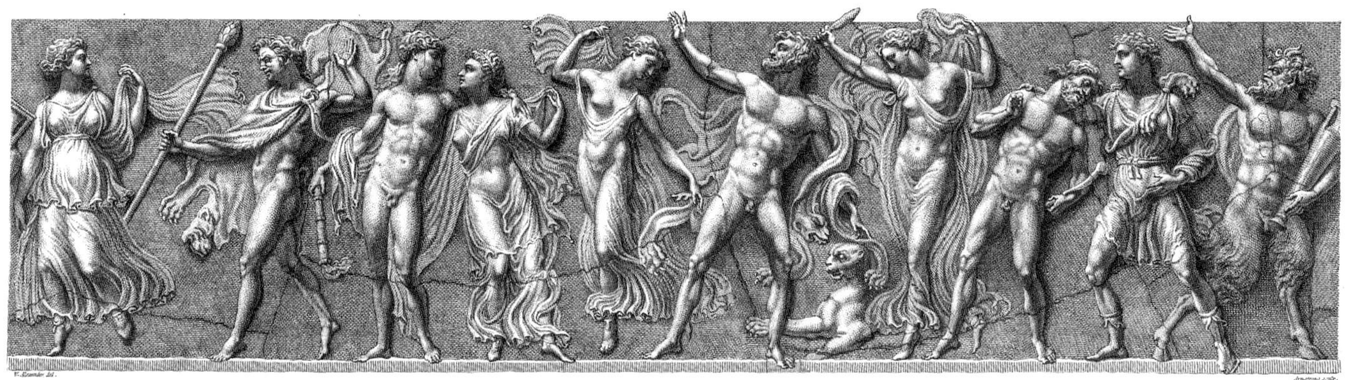

108. Panoramic view of the relief on the Townley Vase, 1812

text suggests that revolution was an essential aspect of nature, necessary for the preservation of harmony in the universe, with destruction as important as generation. This was antithetical to the way that revolution was portrayed at the time. In his pamphlet *Reflections on the Revolution in France* (1790), Edmund Burke, a Whig politician and the father of British conservatism, described revolution as contrary to nature, representing a war or usurpation against it.

The other notable motif of Townley's interpretation is androgyny, recalling the bi-gender '*Être Générateur*' of the *Recherches*, and anticipating the same theme in literary Romanticism. Samuel Taylor Coleridge, best known as the poet of the 'Rime of the Ancient Mariner' (1798), is often quoted for saying that 'a great mind must be androgynous', referring to the necessity for overcoming reductive theoretical binaries.[3] This idea

was embodied in Percy Bysshe Shelley's poem 'The Witch of Atlas' (1820), where the title character creates an ideal hermaphrodite to accompany her on her journeys.

Perhaps the greatest lyric poem of British Romanticism is John Keats's 'Ode on a Grecian Urn' (1819). Keats did not identify a specific vase as his inspiration, but, in terms of what he could have seen at the British Museum, the decoration of the Townley Vase best fits his description of 'mad pursuit' and 'wild ecstasy'. The urn of the poem is inspiring in its hermetic mystery, which 'dost tease us out of thought/ As doth eternity'. Keats asks, 'What leaf-fring'd legend haunts about thy shape/Of deities or mortals, or of both,/In Tempe or the dales of Arcady?' Townley's text can be read as an attempt to answer that question.

Vase

A vase of white marble, of excellent workmanship, three feet high, in the collection of C.T. Esq. in London. It was found in the excavations made by Mr Gavin Hamilton amongst the ruins of the magnificent Villa of Antoninus Pius, situated near Civita Lavinia, ancient Lanuvium, in the spot now called Monte Cagnolo, where many valuable marbles have at various times been discovered, and now adorn the Vatican, the Villa Albani, and other great collections.

The figures upon this vase relate to the Mysteries of Bacchus, which were instituted to record the animation of the universe, and the harmony with which it is continued by the various revolutions performed by nature. The principal group in this composition seems to be that of Bacchus embracing Ariadne, under which personages the union of male and female germs of production are personified. Fire being the original symbol of the deity in his creative, as well as his destroying capacity, and Bacchus being held in the ancient theology as the emanation of the deity and delegated by him with the powers of animating and harmonizing the universe, he is therefore here represented with the sacred fire under the form of a torch in his hand, and embracing Ariadne, who is the Ceres or the magna rerum parens, *by which union animation and action is given to all things.*

Bacchus however comprises in his nature the generative qualities of both sexes; on which account, when he is represented singly and young, his form participates of the female character. This female division of Bacchus, according to the different operations over which she is made to preside, or to the qualities which are attributed to her, is distinguished under the various appellations of Ariadne, Venus, Diana, Lucina, Hecate, Leda, Ceres, Proserpine, Minerva, and in fine that of Isis, who in fact comprehends all those personages.

This group is attended as usual by fauns, sileni, satyrs, nymphs, and the panther, expressing by their various motions, and by their encircling this vase, the activity and rotations of matter by which the constant renewal and harmony of the universe is preserved: it is in conformity to these mythological ideas that the representations of Bacchus and of the generative spirit are generally accompanied, as upon this vase, with the symbols of destruction, such as the pointed amphora carried by the satyr[+], the dagger in the hand of a bacchant, the destroying animal the panther, and the skins of the goat, of the lion or of some of the animals, which are used as the symbols of the actual means of production, and are worn by Bacchus or by his above mentioned agents, because the spoils of those symbolical animals denote their previous destruction.

Vases were employed as sacred symbols because their form was analogous to that of the cup of the lotus flower, which represents the waters, or the passive means of production, personified under the denomination of Isis. Representations therefore of the generative power and of the form of Bacchus and his agents are usually placed as ornaments upon the vases in allusion to that primitive theological idea adopted by all ancient people, namely that the creative spirit moved or acted upon the waters, meaning thereby the junction of the active and passive mediums by which all production is effected.

Hence the innumerable compositions in which the deity in his various capacities and divisions is thus symbolically placed upon boats, shells, birds, plants and animals of the aquatic kind, and other objects used upon ancient monuments to represent the waters; hence the androginous unions of bodies, belonging to the different elements, fire, air, earth & water, which being the apparent means of production, employed by the supreme motion-giver, were judged to be the most proper emblems of his creative power. These emblems are still used for this purpose amongst the Hindoos who have the least varied from this primitive mode or system of religious worship.

This will account for the androginous figures which ornament the lower division of this vase, without minutely explaining the parts of their composition; it may be proper however to observe that the upper part of these figures unite the male and female sexes of the human species. The lower parts are composed of the aquatic plant, the lotus, which as before observed is the symbol of the waters, so that in the composition of these figures, which also have wings, the idea of the generative spirit acting upon that element is again ingeniously repeated, as it is again by the patera or bason held in their hands; for the protuberance, usually seen in the center of this sort of patera, represents the Phallus or the generative power, which is surrounded by the waters, contained in the hollow of the patera. The lingum of the Hindoos is formed on the same principle, as are the patera which appear upon the most ancient and modern sacred monuments of those people: it is therefore to recall the animating powers of the supreme ruler of all things that the heathen representations of him are so generally seen bearing this instrument.

+ *This pointed amphora on account of its being used to keep wine buried in the ground became the emblem of the productive germ in its inactive state, and on various monuments allusive to this subject it is carried to the* inferi *by fauns, satyrs and emaciated figures of Mercury as a representation of Bacchus, Mercury being the conductor of the* manes *to those regions of repose.*

NOTES

INTRODUCTION

1 Anonymous (1804), p. 484.
2 Thucydides (2014), 22.4.
3 Townley, Knight (1809).

CHAPTER 1

1 Quoted in Cox, ed. (1926), pp. 78–81.
2 Hatton (1708), I, p. 62.
3 Scott (1957), p. 9.
4 Smith (1828), p. 267.
5 Scott (1957), p. 58
6 British Museum, Townley Papers (hereafter BM TY) 3/13.
7 BM TY 3/16 ('Particulars of the state of a house in Park Street, Westminster, belonging to Cha. Townley Esq. taken Dec 24th 1777').

CHAPTER 2

1 Whitaker (1876), II, p. 543.
2 Clarke, Penny (1982); Jenkins, Sloan (1996).
3 Goethe (1994), p. 442.
4 Huntington Library, San Marino, MS HM 1.
5 BM TY 7/1376 (letter from General Whyte to Charles Townley, 25 October 1768).
6 BM TY10/3, p. 4, 'A general account of objects and expenditures relative to Virtù from January 1768'.
7 BM 1805,0703.451.
8 BM TY 7/2028 (letter from Richard Cosway in London to Charles Townley in Rome, 24 February 1772).
9 BM TY 7/2028.
10 Jones (1801), XII, p. 376.
11 BM TY 7/796–851 (letters from John Towneley to Charles Townley, 1773–74).
12 Cox, ed. (1926), 10, pp. 130–31.
13 BM TY 10/25 (priced list of intaglio rings).
14 Anonymous (1729), p. 43.
15 BM TY 7/1257 (letter from Ann Russell to Charles Townley, 4 February 1787).
16 BM TY 7/1642 (letter from Thomas Hervey to Charles Townley, 11 August 1772).
17 Ellis (1836), I, p. 9.
18 BM TY 7/1052 (letter from Charles Greville to Charles Townley, November 1790).
19 BM TY 7/1593 (letter from Samuel Solly to Charles Townley, 31 October 1791).
20 Williams (1933), p. 220.
21 Ibid.; BM 1805,0703.100.
22 TY/7/477 (letter from Thomas Jenkins in Rome to Charles Townley in London, 3 December 1788).
23 Vaughan (1988), p. 376.
24 Smith (1828), p. 241.
25 Ibid., p. 266.
26 Dio Cassius (1927), pp. 4–5 (from the epitome of Book 71 by Xiphilinus).

CHAPTER 3

1 Towneley (c.1804).
2 Livy (1936), 39.8.
3 Letter from Robert Adam to James Adam, 24 July 1760, quoted in Fleming (1961), p. 368.
4 BM TY 3/14 (draft particulars for building and finishing a house in Park Street).
5 Guilding (1996), p. 28.
6 BM TY 3/14.
7 Bentley, ed. (1978), I, p. 318.
8 Robinson (1979), p. 28.
9 BM TY 3/16, 'Particulars of the state of the house in Park Street'.
10 Robinson (1979), p. 31.
11 Towneley (c.1804).
12 Ibid.
13 Cook (2004).
14 BM TY/8/51 (accounts of commissioning designs of sculpture galleries from Vicenzo Brenna and James Byres).
15 BM TY 7/376 (letter from Thomas Jenkins to Charles Townley, 29 October 1777).
16 BM TY 7/625 (letter from Gavin Hamilton to Charles Townley, 5 December 1777).
17 BM TY 3/14.
18 BM TY 6/626 (letter from Gavin Hamilton to Charles Townley, 20 February 1778).
19 BM TY/7 (letter from Thomas Jenkins in Rome to Charles Townley in London, 15 July 1779).
20 Vaughan (1988), p. 363.
21 BM TY 8/15, 'Chambers by my uncle drawing of the Hall' (21 October 1795).

22 Roland (1800), p. 199.

CHAPTER 4

1 Mitter (1977), p. 91.
2 Penny (1984), p. 55.
3 Quoted in Coltman (2009), p. 271.
4 Roland (1800), p. 199.
5 Ingamells (1997), p. 946.
6 Ibid., pp. 946–47.
7 BM TY 7/611 (letter from Gavin Hamilton in Rome to Charles Townley in London, 12 June 1776).
8 Ingamells (1997), p. 947.
9 Ellis (1836), I, p. 10.
10 BM TY 7/1080 (draft letter from Charles Townley to Lord Lansdowne, Earl of Shelburne, 3 May 1792).
11 BM TY 10/2, p. 7, 'An account of Books bought at Naples'.
12 BM TY 8/2, April 1768 (Receipts and payments in France and Italy). See also Vaughan (1988), p. 65.
13 Walker (1988), p. 320.
14 Leslie, Taylor (1865), II, p. 633.
15 BM 1805,0703.43.
16 BM TY 7/523 (letter from Thomas Jenkins to Charles Townley).
17 BM TY 7/534 (letter from Thomas Jenkins to Charles Townley, 3 July 1794).
18 Anonymous (1816); [Knight] (1816).
19 Coltman (2006), p. 265.
20 Townley (1799).
21 Quoted Vaughan (1988), p. 431.
22 Taylor (1832), I, p. 174.
23 Burnage (2017), pp. 28–29.
24 BM TY 2/1–2 (Abstract of the will of Charles Townley).
25 Smith (1828) p. 359.
26 Abbott (1805).
27 Smith (1828), I, p. 260.
28 Ellis (1836, 1846).
29 Waagen (1854), I, p. 18.
30 Cole, ed. (2009), p. 528.
31 Ibid., p. 525.
32 *Architects' Journal*, 18 February 1987.
33 De Ricci (1930), pp. 88–89.
34 Bailey (1886), pp. 187–92.
35 Editorial, *Burlington Magazine* (June 2017).

CHAPTER 5

1 Anonymous (1802), p. 216; Anonymous (1804), p. 484.
2 Wilson, ed. (2013), p. 524.
3 Bowden (2010), passim.
4 BM 1805,0703.155.
5 BM 1805,0703.211.
6 BM 1805,0703.123
7 Townley (1804), I, p. 25.
8 BM 1805,0703.136.
9 The basin is BM 1805,0703.228; the bath is BM 1805,0703.233.
10 Parlour Catalogue 1804, I, p. 16.
11 BM 1805,0703.227.
12 The terminus of Ceres is BM 1805,0703.18, the Pan is BM 1805,0703.25, the acrobat is BM 1805,0703.6, and the sacrificed bulls are BM 1805,0703.4, 5.
13 D'Hancarville (1784a), pp. 368–69.
14 Smith (1828), I, p. 262.
15 BM 1805,0703.68.
16 BM 1805,0703.143.
17 Plato (1925), 250b-e.
18 Thalia is BM 1805,0703.33; the Diana is 1805,0703.12.
19 The caryatid is BM 1805,0703.44; the Venus is BM 1805,0703.15.
20 Townley (1804), I, pp. 20, 23.
21 Webster (2011), p. 436.
22 BM 1805,0703.183.
23 D'Hancarville (1784a), I, pp. 326–29.
24 BM 1805,0703.7.
25 BM 1805,0703.28, 29.
26 D'Hancarville (1784a), I, pp. 340–41.
27 Ibid., p. 367.
28 Smith (1828), I, p. 218, 264.
29 BM 1805,0703.114.
30 Smith (1828), I, p. 264.
31 Haynes (1975), p. 11; Walker (2004), pp. 23–25.
32 BM 1805,0703.16.
33 D'Hancarville (1784b), II, pp. 299–300.
34 BM 1805,0703.30, 1805,0703.2.
35 D'Hancarville (1784a), I, pp. 339–40.
36 The Jupiter is BM 1805,0703.50, the Diana is BM 1805,0703.61, the Homer is BM 1805,0703.85, the Dioscurus is BM 1805,0703.70.
37 BM 1805,0703.87. Townley (1804), II, p. 32.
38 British Library, Burney MS 86.
39 Townley (1804), II, p. 13.
40 BM 1805,0703.264.
41 D'Hancarville (1785), p. 104.
42 BM TY 7/1361 (letter from Charles Blundell to Charles Townley, 9 October 1791).
43 Blagden (1777).
44 Waywell (1986), p. 43.
45 Collins (2012), p. 115, 140.

46 Vaughan (1988), p. 374.
47 Boswell (1826), III, pp. 103–04; Anonymous (1804), p. 484.
48 BM TY 7/288 (letter from d'Hancarville in Naples to Townley in Rome, dated 12 July 1768).
49 BM M.550.
50 BM TY 7/1204 (letter from William Sandys to Charles Townley, 16 October 1780).
51 Public Advertiser, 7 June 1785.
52 BM TY 1/11 (diary entry for Saturday 26 January 1799).
53 Vaughan (1988), p. 375.
54 Ibid., p. 374.
55 Myrone (2017).
56 Whitley (1928), p. 263.
57 Roland (1800), p. 199.
58 Lens (1776).
59 Roland (1800), p. 199.
60 Williamson (1905), p. 16.
61 Vaughan (1988), p. 375.
62 Miranda (1930), pp. 323–4.
63 Plato (1969), 560.d-e.
64 Blackwood (1989) p. 34.
65 BM TY 7/1562–3 (letters from Sir John Eliot MP to Charles Townley).
66 BM TY 7/1552 (letter from Lady Elizabeth Craven to Charles Townley, 22 June 1780).
67 BM TY 7/644 (letter from Gavin Hamilton to Charles Townley, 1780).
68 Townley, Knight (1809), I, pp. 15–16.
69 Records of the British Museum, hereafter BM CE, 4/2 768.
70 BM TY 1/10 (diary of Charles Townley). Fully quoted in Webster (2011), pp. 441–3.
71 Clarke and Penny (1982), p. 189.
72 D'Hancarville (1776a), pp. 32–33.

CHAPTER 6

1 Roscoe (2009), p. 504.
2 BM CE 1/5 1017.
3 Smith (1828), I, p. 266.
4 Cox, ed. (1926), pp. 94–96.
5 Scott (1957), p. 150.
6 Rice (1834), p. 29.
7 Blackwood (1989), p. 34.
8 Quoted in Magnus (1964), p. 141.
9 Knowles (1952), p. 4.

CHAPTER 7

1 Strachey (1913), pp. 233–34.
2 [Strachey] (1914), p. 1082.
3 Strachey (1922), p. 339.
4 Ibid., p. 325.
5 Ibid., p. 329.

6 Ibid., p. 337.
7 Ibid., p. 335.
8 Grey (1925), p. 20.
9 Spender (1927), pp. 14–15.
10 Matthew (2004).
11 Strachey (1922), p. 339.
12 Ibid., p. 335.
13 Ibid., p. 335.
14 Bolton (1915), pp. 14–19.
15 Ibid., p. 14.

CHAPTER 8

1 Ilersic, Liddle (1960), p. 188.
2 Interview with a fireman, 18 January 1979. Audio recording in the LBC/IRN Digitisation Archive.
3 Richard Ellis Chartered Surveyors (1984).
4 Bann (1997), p. 12.

APPENDIX A

1 Jenkins, Sloan (1996), pp. 146–55.
2 Haskell (1987a), p. 40.
3 Moore (2008); Pop (2015), pp. 180–191.
4 D'Hancarville, (1784b), II, p. 155.
5 Godwin (1994), p. 5.
6 Gébelin (1773–1782).
7 Knight (1818), section 230.
8 Bryant (1774).
9 D'Hancarville (1784a), p. 189.
10 Maréchal (1780), III, p. 111.
11 Knight (1791), pp. 111–30.
12 D'Hancarville, (1784a), I, p. xxviii.
13 D'Hancarville (1770b).
14 D'Hancarville (1780a, 1780b).
15 Gillies (1785), p. 321.
16 Maty (1785), pp. 17–25.
17 Moore (2008), p. 157.
18 Knight (1787); Christie (1825); Blundell (1803).
19 Watkin (1996), Chapter 4, passim.
20 Dupuis (1795). See also, for example, Dulaure (1805).
21 Moore (2008), pp. 162–3.
22 BM TY7/413 (letter from Charles Townley to Thomas Jenkins, 20 April 1782).
23 Ellis (1836), I, p. 6.
24 Michaelis (1882), p. 99.
25 Albrizzi (1807), p. 57.

BIBLIOGRAPHY

Abbott, C. 1805. Letter to Joseph Banks, 30 June. Natural History Museum Library and Archives, Kew. BC 2.313–14

Ackermann, R. 1808–10. *The Microcosm of London,* I–III. London

Albrizzi, I.T. 1807. *Ritratti.* Brescia

Anonymous 1729. *Hell Upon Earth, or the Town in an Uproar.* London

— — — 1771. *Antichità di Ercolano esposte.* Naples

— — — 1802. *The Picture of London for 1802; Being a Correct Guide to All the Curiosities, Amusements, Exhibitions… in and Near London.* London

— — — 1804. 'Sir William Hamilton. (Beschluß.)', in *Kaiserlich- und Kurpfalzbairisch Privilegirte Allgemeine Zeitung,* 121 (30 April), pp. 483–84

— — — 1816. *Report from the Select Committee on the Earl of Elgin's Sculptured Marbles.* London

— — — 2017. 'Changing the British Museum'. Editorial, *Burlington Magazine,* 159

Bailey, J.E. 1886. 'The Towneley Library', *Palatine Notebook 3,* pp. 187–92

Bann, S. 1997. *Stephen Cox: Dulwich Picture Gallery.* London

Bentley, G.E., ed. 1798. *William Blake's Writings.* Oxford

Birch, S. 1861. *Description of the Collection of the Ancient Marbles in the British Museum with Engravings,* XI. London

Blackwood, J. 1989. *London's Immortals: the complete outdoor commemorative statues.* London

Blagden, C. 1777. Letter to Joseph Banks, 28 October. Natural History Museum, BL D.T.C. I 148–51

Blundell, H. 1803. *An Account of the Statues, Busts, Bass Relieves, Cinerary Urns, and other ancient marbles, and paintings at Ince.* Liverpool

Bolton, A.T. 1915. 'A London House of the Eighteenth Century', *Country Life,* 4 December (supplementary edition), pp. 14–19

Boswell, J. 1826. *The Life of Samuel Johnson,* III. Oxford

Bowden, H. 2010. *Mystery Cults in the Ancient World.* London.

Bryant, J. 1774. *A New System, or an Analysis of Ancient Mythology.* London

Burnage, S. 2017. 'The British School of Sculpture – A Case Study', in Edwards, Burnage eds. (2017), pp. 21–33

Cavaceppi, B. 1768. *Raccolta d'Antiche Statue Busti Bassirilievi Ed Altre Sculture Restaurate.* Rome

Cicero. 1923. *On Old Age, On Friendship, On Divination.* Cambridge, MA.

Christie, J. 1825. *Disquisitions upon the painted Greek vases, and their probable connection with the shows of the Eleusinian and other mysteries.* London

Clarke, M., Penny, N. 1982. *The Arrogant Connoisseur: Richard Payne Knight 1751–1824.* Manchester

Cole, E., ed. 2009. *Lived in London: Blue Plaques and the Stories Behind Them.* London

Coleridge, S.T. 1835. *Table Talk.* London

Collins, J. 2012. 'Museo Pio-Clementino, Vatican City: Ideology and Aesthetics in the Age of the Grand Tour', in Paul, ed. (2012), pp. 113–14

Coltman, V. 2006. *Fabricating the Antique: Neoclassicism in Britain, 1760–1800.* Chicago and London

Combe, T. 1812, 1815, 1818. *Description of the Collection of the Ancient Marbles in the British Museum with Engravings,* I–III. London

Cook, B.F. 1985. *The Townley Marbles.* London

— — — 2004. 'Charles Townley', *Oxford Dictionary of National Biography.* Oxford

Cox, M.H., ed. 1926. *Survey of London: St Margaret, Westminster, Part I.* London

d'Hancarville, P.F.H. 1766, 1770a, 1776a, 1776b. *Antiquités etrusques, grecques et romaines tirées du Cabinet de M. Hamilton.* Naples

— — — 1770b *Veneres et Priapi uti observatur in gemmis antiquis.* Possibly Naples

— — — 1780a. *Monumens de la vie privée des douze Césars.* Nancy

d'Hancarville, P.F.H. 1780b, *Monumens du culte secret des dames romaines*. Nancy

— — — 1784a, 1784b, 1785. *Recherches sur l'origine, l'esprit et les progrès des arts de la Grèce*. London

Daniell, T. 1800. *Antiquities of India*. London

Dio Cassius 1927. *Roman History, Volume IX: Books 71–80*. Translated by Earnest Cary, Herbert B. Foster. Cambridge, MA

Dulaure, J.-A. 1805. *Des Divinités Génératrices, ou du Culte de Phallus*. Paris

Dupuis, C.F. 1795. *L'origine de tous les cultes*. Paris

Edwards, J., Burnage, S. eds. 2017. *The British School of Sculpture c.1760–1832*. London

Ellis, H. 1836, 1846. *The Townley Gallery of Classical Sculpture at the British Museum*. London

Fleming, J. 1961. *Robert Adam and his Circle*. London

Gébelin, A.C. de 1773–82. *Le Monde primitif analysé et comparé avec le monde modern*. Paris

Gillies, J. 1785. Review, *The Monthly Review*, November

Godwin, J. 1994. *The Theosophical Enlightenment*. Albany

Grey, E. 1925. *Twenty-Five Years 1892–1916*. New York

Goethe, J.W. von 1994. *The Collected Works Volume 6: Italian Journey*. Princeton

Guilding, R. 1996. 'Robert Adam and Charles Townley'. *Apollo*, 143, no. 409, pp. 27–32

Haskell, F. 1987a. 'The Baron d'Hancarville: An Adventurer and Art Historian in Eighteenth-Century Europe', in Haskell (1987b), pp. 30–45

— — — 1987b. *Past and Present in Art and Taste: Selected Essays*. New Haven and London

Hatton, E. 1708. *A New View of London*. London

Hawkins, E. 1830, 1835, 1842, 1845. *Description of the Collection of the Ancient Marbles in the British Museum with Engravings V, VII, IX, X*. London

Haynes, D.E.L. 1975. *The Portland Vase*. London

Ilersic, A.R., Liddle, P.F.B. 1960. *Parliament of Commerce: The Story of the Association of British Chambers of Commerce 1860–1960*. London

Ingamells, J. 1997. *A Dictionary of British and Irish Travellers in Italy (1701–1800)*. New Haven

Jenkins, I., Sloan, K. 1996. *Vases and Volcanoes: Sir William Hamilton and his collection*. London

Jones, W. 1801. *The Theological, Philosophical and Miscellaneous works of the Rev. William Jones*. London

Kip, J. 1710. *A Prospect of the City of London, Westminster and St. James' Park*. London

Knight, R.P. 1787. *An Account of the Remains of the Worship of Priapus lately existing at Isernia, in the Kingdom of Naples: in two letters … to which is added A Discourse on the worship of Priapus and its connexion with the Mystic Theology of the Antients by R.P. Knight*. London

— — — 1791. *Analytical Essay on the Greek Alphabet*. London

[— — —] 1816. *Explanation of Part of the Evidence of Richard Payne Knight Concerning the Elgin Marbles*. London

— — — 1818. *An Inquiry into the Symbolical Language of Antiquity*. London

Knowles, A.R. 1952. *Number Fourteen, the Home of the A.B.C.C.* London

Lens, A.C. 1776. *Le Costume, Essai sur les habillements et les usages de plusieurs peuples de l'antiquité prouvés par les monuments*. Liège

Leslie, C.R., Taylor, T. 1865. *Life and Times of Joshua Reynolds*. London

Livy 1936. *Books XXXVIII-XXXIX with an English Translation*. Cambridge

Magnus, R. 1964. *Kind Edward the Seventh*. New York

Maréchal, S. 1780. *Les Antiquités d'Herculanum*, III. Paris

Matthew, H.C.G. 2004. 'Richard Burton Haldane', *Oxford Dictionary of National Biography*. Oxford

Maty, P.H. 1785. Review, *The New Review*, January

Michaelis, A. 1882. *Ancient Marbles in Great Britain*. Cambridge

Miranda, F. de. 1930. *Archivo del General Miranda*, 4. Caracas

Mirri, L. Carloni, M. 1776. *Vestigia delle terme di Tito*. Rome

Mitter, P. 1977. *Much Maligned Monsters: History of European Reactions to Indian Art*. Oxford

Moore, J. 2008. 'History as Theoretical Reconstruction? Baron d'Hancarville and the Exploration of Ancient Mythology in the Eighteenth Century', in Moore, Morris, Bayliss, eds. (2008), 137–67

Moore, J., Morris, I.M., Bayliss, A.J., eds. 2008. *Reinventing History. The Enlightenment Origins of Ancient History*. London.

Myrone, M. 2017. 'Drawing after the Antique at the British Museum, 1809–1817: 'Free' Art Education and the Advent of the Liberal State', *British Art Studies*, 5

Nichols, J. 1818. *Illustrations of the literary history of the eighteenth century*, III. London

Niebuhr, C. 1780. *Voyage en Arabie & en d'autres Pays circonvoisins*, II. Amsterdam and Utrecht

Paul, C., ed. 2012. *The First Modern Museums of Art*. Los Angeles

Penny, N. 1984. 'Townley at the B.M. and Cavaceppi at the Clarendon Gallery', *Burlington Magazine*, 126, pp. 55–56

Piranesi, G.B. 1778. *Differentes vues de quelques restes de trois grands édifices qui subsistent encore dans le milieu de l'ancienne ville de Pesto autrement Possidonia, et qui est située dans la Lucanie*. Rome

Plato 1925. Plato in Twelve Volumes, Vol. 9. Cambridge, MA

— — — 1969. Plato in Twelve Volumes, Vols. 5 & 6. Cambridge, MA

Pop, A. 2015. *Antiquity, Theatre, and the Painting of Henry Fuseli*. Oxford

Pyne, W.H. 1819. *The History of the Royal Residences*, II. London

Records of the British Museum. British Museum, Central Archive. BM CE

Ricci, S. de 1930. *English Collectors of Books & Manuscripts (1530–1930)*. Cambridge

Rice, T.S. 1834. *Speech on the Repeal of the Union with Ireland Delivered in the House of Commons on Wednesday April 23, 1834*. London

Richard Ellis Chartered Surveyors 1984. *Structural Survey Report on 14 Queen Anne's Gate*

Robinson, J.M. 1979. *The Wyatts: An Architectural Dynasty*. Oxford

Roland, M.-J. 1800. *The Works (Never Before Published) of Jeanne-Marie Philipon Roland*. London

Roscoe, I. 2009. *A Biographical Dictionary of Sculptors in Britain 1660–1851*. New Haven and London

Scott, G.R. 1957. *The History of Cockfighting*. London

Smith, J.T. 1807. *Antiquities of Westminster*. London

— — — 1828. *Nollekens and His Times*, I. London

Society of Antiquaries 1815. *Vetusta monumenta quae ad Rerum Britanicarum memoriam conservandam Societas Antiquariorum Londini sumptu suo edenda curavit*, IV. London

Spender, J.A. 1927. *Life, Journalism and Politics*. London

Strachey, A. 1913. 'The Towneley Museum', *Country Life* (16 August), pp. 233–34

[— — —] 1914. 'A Dialogue of the Dead, c. 1785', *The Spectator*, 27 June, pp. 1081–82

Strachey, J.S.L. 1922. *The Adventure of Living: A Subjective Autobiography*. London

Taylor, J. 1832. *Records of My Life*. London

Thucydides 2014. *History* I. Oxford

Towneley, J. c.1804. Translation of d'Hancarville's notes on the house. Uncatalogued MS at the British Museum, Department of Greek and Roman Antiquities (not part of the Townley Papers)

Townley Papers. British Museum, Central Archive. TY 1–22

Townley, C. 1799. 'Account of Antiquities discovered at Ribchester, in a letter from Charles Townley … to the Rev. John Brand …', *Society of Antiquaries* (1815), 4, pp. 1–11

— — — 1804. 'Parlour Catalogue'. British Museum, Department of Greek and Roman Antiquities. Informally catalogued as 'GR2'.

— — — Letter to John Wilkes, BL Add. MS 30873, f. 25

— — — Letter to Charles Greville, BL Add. MS 40714, f. 237

Townley, C., Knight, R.P. 1809. *Specimens of Antient Sculpture*, I. London

Vaughan, G. 1988. *The Collecting of Classical Antiquities in England in the 18th Century: A study of Charles Townley (1737–1805) and his circle*. Unpublished PhD thesis, University of Oxford

— — — 1996. 'The Townley Zoffany: Reflections on Charles Townley and his friends', *Apollo*, 144, no. 417, pp. 32–35

Volney, C.F. 1791. *Les Ruines d'Empire*. Paris

Waagen, G. 1854. *Treasures of Art in Great Britain*. London

Walker, J. 1988. 'Maria Cosway: An Undervalued Artist', *Apollo*, 123

Walker, S. 2004. *The Portland Vase*. London

Watkin, D. 1996. *Sir John Soane: Enlightenment Thought and the Royal Academy Lectures*. Cambridge

Waywell, G.B. 1986. *The Lever and Hope Sculptures*. Berlin

Webster, M. 2011. *Johan Zoffany*. New Haven and London

Whitaker, T.D. 1876. *A History of the Original Parish of Whalley*. London

Whitley, W.T. 1928. *Art in England, 1800–1820*. London

Williams, C. 1933. *Sophie in London, 1786, being the diary of Sophie v. la Roche*. London

Williamson, G.C. 1905. *Richard Cosway, R.A.* London

Wilson, N., ed. 2013. *Encyclopedia of Ancient Greece*. Abingdon

LIST OF ILLUSTRATIONS

Plain text refers to page number and appears first;
italic refers to illustrations

Dr Max Bryant completed his PhD in Architectural History at the University of Cambridge in 2016 (supervised by Dr Frank Salmon), and is currently a Whitney Fellow at The Metropolitan Museum of Art in New York.

For their help, the author wishes to thank Jan Ankarcrona, Daniel Anderson, Dirk Booms, Julius Bryant, Richard Butler, Celeste Farge, Aisha Farr, Stephen Lloyd, Hazel Logie, Frank Salmon, Charles Saumarez Smith and Mike Townend. Any errors are the author's own.

ISBN 978 1 911300 32 8

British Library Catalogue in Publishing Data

A CIP record of this publication is available from the British Library

Produced by Paul Holberton Publishing
89 Borough High St, London SE1 1NL
WWW.PAULHOLBERTON.COM

Designed by Laura Parker

Printed by e-Graphic Spa, Verona

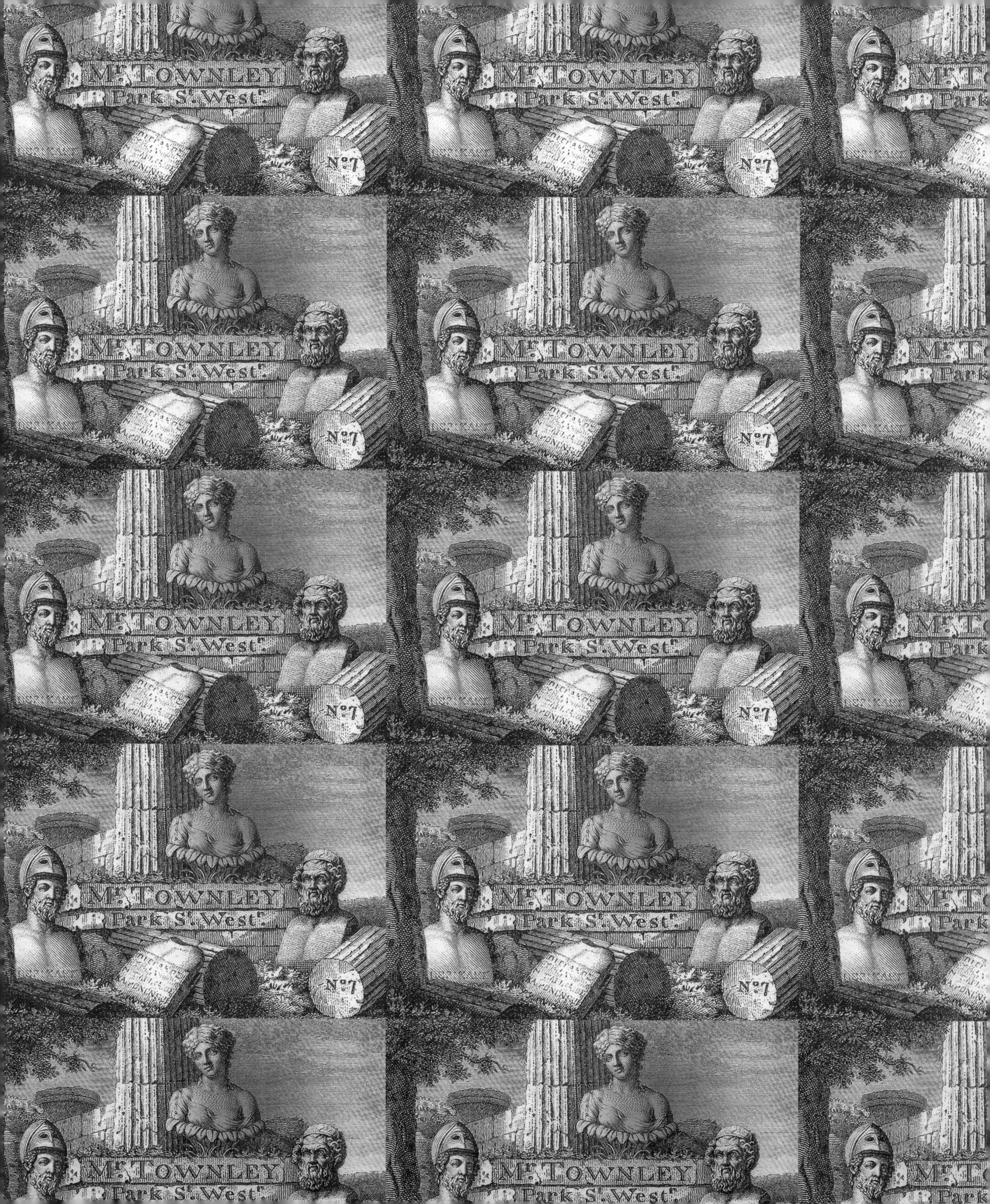
Mr TOWNLEY
Park St West.
No 7